Praise for
Saving for Retirement (Without Living Like a Pauper or Winning the Lottery),
First Edition

"A cover-to-cover must-read for everyone 16 to 60 who wants to live the American Dream. The earlier we choosetosave®, the sooner we can stop saving, and the later we start saving the more we need to know in order to catch up. What you need to know; where you can find the answers; how you can take action. It is all here."

> **—Dallas Salisbury**, CEO, Employee Benefit Research Institute and American Savings Education Council (www.choosetosave.org)

"Bookstores are full of tomes advising people how to save for retirement, yet millions of people are still hopelessly confused about what they should do. Gail MarksJarvis breaks it down into simple steps that anyone can do to ensure a more comfortable retirement. Read this book and prosper!"

> **—Liz Pulliam Weston**, MSN Money Personal Finance Columnist and Best-selling Author of *Your Credit Score*

"This book offers a sensible, sophisticated approach for tackling the daunting challenge of saving for retirement. The good news? You can retire—without living on canned food or buying lottery tickets—if you follow Gail's realistic strategies for saving, investing, and ultimately spending money in retirement."

> **—Susan Tompor**, *Detroit Free Press*

"You can wallpaper a warehouse with all of the awful investment advice offered up every year in newspapers, magazines, and books. One of the most difficult tasks is to separate the get-rich-quick hype from the truly worthwhile knowledge that will make you wealthy over time. I'm thrilled to say that Gail MarksJarvis has cut through the claptrap of investment cacophony and provided not only a solid plan for retirement saving, but a realistic, common-sense approach to personal finance in general. This is a triumph."

> **—John F. Wasik**, Reuters Personal Finance Columnist and Author of *The Cul-de-Sac Syndrome*, *The Merchant of Power*, and *The Audacity of Help*

Saving for Retirement (Without Living Like a Pauper or Winning the Lottery)

Updated and Revised

Saving for Retirement (Without Living Like a Pauper or Winning the Lottery)

Updated and Revised

Gail MarksJarvis

FT Press
FINANCIAL TIMES

An Imprint of PEARSON EDUCATION

Upper Saddle River, NJ • New York • London
San Francisco • Toronto • Sydney • Tokyo • Singapore
Hong Kong • Cape Town • Madrid • Paris • Milan
Munich • Amsterdam

Vice President, Publisher: Tim Moore
Associate Publisher and Director of Marketing: Amy Neidlinger
Executive Editor: Jim Boyd
Editorial Assistant: Pamela Boland
Operations Specialist: Jodi Kemper
Marketing Manager: Megan Graue
Cover Designer: Chuti Prasertsith
Managing Editor: Kristy Hart
Project Editor: Jovana San Nicolas-Shirley
Copy Editor: Krista Hansing Editorial Services, Inc.
Proofreader: Sarah Kearns
Senior Indexer: Cheryl Lenser
Senior Compositor: Gloria Schurick
Manufacturing Buyer: Dan Uhrig

© 2013 by Pearson Education, Inc.
Publishing as FT Press
Upper Saddle River, New Jersey 07458

FT Press offers excellent discounts on this book when ordered in quantity for bulk purchases or special sales. For more information, please contact U.S. Corporate and Government Sales, 1-800-382-3419, corpsales@pearsontechgroup.com. For sales outside the U.S., please contact International Sales at international@pearsoned.com.

Company and product names mentioned herein are the trademarks or registered trademarks of their respective owners.

Printed in the United States of America

First Printing: August 2012

ISBN-10: 0-13-296303-5
ISBN-13: 978-0-13-296303-9

Pearson Education LTD.
Pearson Education Australia PTY, Limited.
Pearson Education Singapore, Pte. Ltd.
Pearson Education Asia, Ltd.
Pearson Education Canada, Ltd.
Pearson Educación de Mexico, S.A. de C.V.
Pearson Education—Japan
Pearson Education Malaysia, Pte. Ltd.

The Library of Congress cataloging-in-publication data is on file.

To my adoring parents, Helen and Jerry,
and my delightful family,
Jim, Lauren, and Rebecca.

Contents

Acknowledgments

Over the past decade, thousands of readers have called me or sent e-mails asking questions about the financial issues they struggle to solve. They have pulled me deeply into their lives, sharing their hopes and sometimes tears about their future and the role of money in life's challenges. I have been struck by the common questions and misconceptions that arise as people try to do what's right with their money. And I thank my readers for providing this insight. Their frustrations, both in interpreting financial advice and in using it, have had a major impact on how I have written my columns and this book.

I am grateful to the many sources of information that have been available constantly to me during 20 years as a financial journalist, especially to The Leuthold Group, Ibbotson Associates, Morningstar, Lipper, and the Employee Benefits Research Institute. Their research has enhanced my columns and also this book. I also want to thank the CFA Institute for introducing me to provocative thinkers ranging from John Neff and John Bogle to Robert Arnott and Jeremy Grantham. And I want to thank Harry Markowitz for explaining to me how modern portfolio theory has been misunderstood and misapplied.

I must also thank money managers, financial planners, and certified public accountants who have spent hours with me explaining how they make decisions for clients. Because they have helped me understand both the science and art behind their work, it is possible for me to give you the principles you need to help yourself. Special thanks are due to Gary Greenberg, Paul Lewis, Marc Hadley, Matthew Hanson, and Beverly DeVeny. In particular, Gary Greenberg must receive extraordinary thanks. He has been a friend and mentor for more than a decade, critiquing my columns and reviewing my manuscript.

As I look back at more than a decade of personal finance writing, I must thank my former managing editor, Chris Worthington, for nudging me to start my first personal finance column in the *St. Paul Pioneer Press,* editor Sue Campbell for encouraging me to write a book, plus Michael Lev, *Chicago Tribune* associate managing editor, and Pete Reinwald, Chicago Tribune Money and Real Estate Editor, for their continuous support. I also feel great appreciation for the team at Pearson FT Press, who enthusiastically welcomed the idea of helping everyday Americans handle their money and who piloted this book to publication for a first and second edition. My thanks go to Executive Editor Jim Boyd, Development Editor Russ Hall, Project Editor Jovana Shirley, and Copy Editor Krista Hansing.

Finally, my family has been extraordinary. I would not be writing this book in the first place if it hadn't been for my dear father, Jerry Marks, who taught me to write and, along with my devoted mother, Helen Marks, laid the groundwork for seeking answers and using them to make the world a better place. No thanks are enough for my cherished husband, Jim, and daughters, Lauren and Rebecca. They have been my editors, coaches, and friends. All cheered me on and graciously gave me space as I committed more hours to this book than any of us anticipated. Finally, I must thank my late brother-in-law and statistician, Tom Jarvis, for touting the power of compounding as a 20-year-old, while most of his generation was "living for today."

About the Author

Gail MarksJarvis is an award-winning, nationally syndicated financial columnist for the *Chicago Tribune,* as well as a TV commentator, speaker, and author of the best-selling first edition of *Saving for Retirement (Without Living Like a Pauper or Winning the Lottery).*

Her columns on the financial markets, the economy, and personal finance strategy run in the *Chicago Tribune* and reach millions of readers in leading newspapers throughout the country. She has been recognized with more than a dozen journalism awards, including Best Financial Columnist from Northwestern University's Medill journalism school, a National Clarion Award for human rights reporting, and the 2012 Award of Excellence from the University of Minnesota School of Journalism and Mass Communication.

The first edition of *Saving for Retirement (Without Living Like a Pauper or Winning the Lottery)* received widespread national media praise. Oprah Winfrey placed it on her select list, MSN Money highlighted it as one of "Eight Great New Books About Money," and Kiplinger named it one of the "Great Money Books for Young Investors."

MarksJarvis delivers analysis and advice regularly on WGN-TV and radio, CLTV, and WTTW public television in Chicago. She has been a regular commentator for PBS's *Nightly Business Report* and on National Public Radio, and has appeared on CNBC, *PBS NewsHour, Fox Business, Talk of the Nation,* and the CBS *Early Show,* as well as on NBC, CBS and ABC affiliates throughout the country.

Formerly a reporter for public radio's *Marketplace* program and *USA Today,* MarksJarvis serves on the board of directors of the Society of American Business Editors and Writers, which sets ethical standards for business journalists. In speeches throughout the country, she simplifies the investing process so that regular Americans handle 401(k)s, IRAs, and 529 college plans successfully and without worry. Visit her on the Web at www.gailmarksjarvis.com and Facebook at gailmarksjarvis5.

Introduction

A brilliant college professor at wits' end about investing first planted the seed for this book a few years ago.

Despite his accomplishments in the social sciences at St. Thomas University in St. Paul, Minnesota, he didn't have a clue about how to invest his money. He was in his 40s, had been saving for retirement for years, and didn't like the look of his future.

"There will be no golden years for me," he told me when he called my newspaper office.

This man had diplomas on his office wall and accolades for research in his field. But like the great majority of Americans, he felt like a dunce when it came to his money.

Every time he read a headline about the unstable future of Social Security and Medicare, he imagined himself eating cat food in retirement. He had just read an article that said people would need $1 million to provide $40,000 a year for living expenses after they retire. "Getting there is hopeless!" he said.

Actually, he wasn't in the bad shape he imagined. He had amassed almost $200,000 the hard way—socking away large amounts from his paycheck into a savings account. It was a flawed approach. He was earning virtually no interest. If he kept that up, I told him, he would never get anywhere.

Fortunately, he had options, and they wouldn't be difficult. They're the same options available to everyone. If he just invested money in a smart mixture of mutual funds in an IRA investment account, fed his retirement plan at work on payday, and kept stashing money regularly into the appropriate stock and bond mutual funds, he'd still have time to transform his lethargic, go-nowhere savings into the $1 million he wanted. He could actually save less than he had been saving and still make it to $1 million by investing with a little finesse.

During my years as a personal finance columnist, I have received calls from thousands of people asking for help with investing. They are surprisingly alike—rich and poor, young and old, highly educated and less educated. Yet they are all wresting with the same basic confusion as the professor.

Overwhelmed with the responsibilities of building careers, putting food on the table, or taking kids to music lessons and soccer practices, they have little time or money to devote to investing.

And they feel inept. They put money into a savings account, and it never amounts to anything. They put money into a mutual fund, and it evaporates through some mysterious process known as the stock market. They try to listen to financial experts, but they hear a language that seems to come from a foreign country. They consider investing, but they get those school-day pangs of math phobia. So they procrastinate and ruminate or defer to friends, spouses, or even incompetent financial advisers who know little more than they do.

When they call me for help, they think they are unique. Whether they're millionaires checking on the stocks their brokers picked or 21-year-olds trying to make sense of their first 401(k) at work, they are sheepish. They confess their ignorance to me and think they should know more than they do about investing in general or some aspect of it.

They think that somehow—maybe through osmosis—they are supposed to know how to handle their money. In fact, the majority of Americans do not.

In a 2004 Harris Poll of Americans, 76 percent said they didn't think people could handle private investing accounts if the federal government offered them for Social Security money. Since the horrifying financial crisis and market crash of 2008–2009, polls have shown that many individuals are so traumatized that they have stopped putting money into retirement savings plans at work. Others are shooting themselves in the foot with knee-jerk investing and setting themselves up for more losses and a disaster in their retirement years.

It doesn't have to be this way. The concepts involved in investing are not difficult. But the insider language of the financial services industry has made investing seem difficult. And neither schools nor employers have done much to help Americans understand the few basics they need and can handle.

People feel paralyzed. Stock market news sounds like chatter. People let valuable years pass by without starting to save in 401(k) plans or IRAs. Others invest but repeatedly commit the same mistakes, choosing mutual funds that were wrong for them or letting the stock market wipe out a chunk of savings they worked so hard to build in the first place.

If people get beyond the mystery language the financial world tosses at them, the concepts are simple. The average person can make them work with less time than they devote to planning an annual vacation.

And if you're nervous about math, relax. You need nothing more than fourth-grade arithmetic. In fact, with the free Internet calculators that I help you find and use, you don't even need to do any math.

I hate gimmicky books. And this is not one. I'm not going to promise to make you a millionaire. But I am going to assure you that if you start investing as little as $20 a week early in life, use a few basic investing concepts, and follow the steps I lay out in this book, an ordinary American can accumulate $1 million for retirement without living like a pauper or winning the lottery. If you missed out early in life, knowing just a few techniques that financial planners use will help you catch up.

All the conversations I have had with people like you tell me that, when you finish this book, you want to be smart, right, and fast about using simple ways to invest money. This book is designed to give you exactly that. I've listened to the investing messes people get themselves into and the confusion that thwarts their good intentions, and I've written this book to spare you the grief and give you easy strategies that work.

Too many books, articles, and workplace 401(k) instructions start you in the middle of the investing process. So you never get it, no matter how hard you try.

It's comparable to telling people not to get hit by cars when crossing a street but failing to tell them that a red light means "stop" and a green light means "go."

Somewhere along the way, someone taught you to recognize the lights, so you know how to take care of yourself in traffic. Now you are going to know how to take care of yourself as an investor, too. And as you step off the curb, you should feel comfortable, not worried.

Whether you are 15 and trying to figure out where to invest summer job money or 55 and coming up short for retirement, this book will help you. In easy language, I'm going to tell you what financial planners know so that you can think like they do instead of feeling like a foolish outcast from a complex secret society. But I don't bog you down with theory and rules. I just explain the gibberish and tell you how to apply it so that you can make wise, fast investing decisions yourself.

This is not complicated. You will find it reassuring. You will carry solid investing concepts in your brain from now on so that they become common sense—like stopping at red lights and driving through green ones, with barely a second thought.

How to Use This Book

Here's how to navigate this book.

I've organized this book based on the way people seem to think—step-by-step through the investing process, with everything explained simply. I start with your basic questions about how much money you will need by the time you retire and why: Is it $50,000 or $1 million? Without that information, you can delude yourself or worry needlessly. I don't want you to do either. I want you to have the facts so that you can take control.

Chapter 2, "Know What You'll Need," should be eye-opening for you as you contemplate your future and how to get there through investing. If you are in your 20s, you can move through Chapter 2 quickly to get a flavor for where investing is supposed to carry you. Whatever you do, don't skip the section on compounding. It's vital. It tells you how to apply magic to your money so that nickels and dimes turn into hundreds and thousands.

If you are older, you might wish you'd known how to harness that magical power earlier, but go for it now while you can still turn hundreds into thousands. Also, if you are approaching 35 or are older, spend some time in Chapter 2 and run the easy calculators I suggest so that, in ten minutes, you will know whether you are headed to the retirement you want or need to invest smarter. If you are approaching 50, running these calculations is essential so that you can catch up for lost time.

In Chapters 3, "Savings on Steroids: Use a 401(k) and an IRA," and 4, "An IRA: Every American's Treasure Trove," I start giving you the investing strategies you need to begin making a major difference with your money. I don't want you to suffer like the professor, pulling painful amounts of money out of your paycheck and getting nowhere.

If you've wondered what to do about a 401(k) or 403(b) at work, I answer every question you've ever had so that you harness the power of these money-making gizmos and transform pocket change into thousands. I do the same with IRAs, another tremendous money grower.

If you've maxed out all of these, I'll tell you what to do next. And if you have only a little money and are trying to figure out whether you should fund college for the kids or your retirement fund first, advice is on the way.

Then it's on to the stock market because you must invest in stocks and bonds and know how to do it right. If you've never invested a cent, you will find it fascinating to understand how stocks move up and down, and why, and what mutual fund managers do to try to make your money grow. If you've been investing for a while and mutual funds seem to act in mysterious ways, eating your money instead of growing it, I put an end to that.

I know that some people feel betrayed by Wall Street and misled by investment professionals. Too many empty assurances and stock market cheerleaders misled people in the financial crisis. Too many short-sighted financial advisers lulled individuals into thinking that stocks were safer than they are. I am not a stock market cheerleader.

Instead, in Chapter 6, "Why the Stock Market Isn't a Roulette Wheel," I unveil the Jekyll-and-Hyde nature of the stock market. Then in subsequent chapters, I show you how to survive and thrive no matter how cruel the stock market becomes.

In Chapters 8, "Making Sense of Wacky Mutual Fund Names," and 9, "Know Your Mutual Fund Manager's Job," I decipher the wacky names you see on mutual funds so you know what to pick and why. You can read over Chapter 9 quickly at first, but you'll want to come back to it whenever you have a mutual fund choice to make for a 401(k) or another retirement fund. For IRAs, some specific fund names in Chapters 9 and 13, "Index Funds: Get What You Pay For," will help.

Ultimately, I teach you to mix and match the right funds so that they do no harm and give your money a good jolt. Chapters 10, "The Only Way That Works: Asset Allocation," and 11, "Do This," keep you from running in front of oncoming traffic. Chapter 11 is like a paint-by-number chapter for mutual funds, or a cookbook with easy-to-follow recipes. It helps keep you from using too much of one ingredient and not enough of another.

When you arrive at Chapters 13 and 14, "Simple Does It: No-Brainer Investing with Target-Date Funds," you will be ready to take some shortcuts with your money. You might wonder why I didn't start there. People destroy thousands of dollars by using shortcuts in the wrong way because they didn't understand the stock market or mutual funds at the outset. With shortcuts, you can make money easily, but only if you don't commit the mistakes the earlier chapters help you avoid.

This book is all about making money and keeping the money you make. So learn the logic and basics of investing first, and then head to the shortcuts if you want.

Finally, Chapter 15, "Do You Need a Financial Adviser?" helps you find reliable advice if you think you need it. Some people go to advisers as a first step, an easy way out. That would be fine if all financial consultants were capable and interested in people like you. Unfortunately, too many aren't. They can't put food on their own tables if they spend time telling you how to invest a couple of thousand dollars in a retirement fund at work.

So get informed about both investing and picking qualified advisers. Then if you seek help, you will be the type of client that good financial planners say they like best: informed, smart, not a coward, and not a daredevil.

Jump right in—no more thrashing about in the dark, no more second-guessing. You are about to become a competent, confident investor.

1

START INVESTING EARLY OR START NOW

What a confusing mess.

Whether you are 25 or 45, you are probably getting this message from hearing political bickering over Social Security, chatter at work, or conversations with friends or relatives: You need to figure out how to save more and invest right for retirement so you don't end up living a dreary life in a broken-down hovel when you are 70.

Yet responding is daunting. The recession of 2008 might have destroyed a good chunk of your savings and left you insecure about your future and investing. You probably have a job that takes too much of your time, family and friends vying for your attention, a need to have a little fun and more sleep, loans to pay, and a paycheck that is already stretched to the limit. In short, you are like most Americans: stressed out about time and money.

So maybe you look for a quick fix: Perhaps you turn to a friend, coworker, neighbor, or spouse, thinking that person must understand the mystery behind the befuddling process of investing better than you. Maybe you defer to that person, sticking your money where he or she says to put it or second-guessing yourself.

But you could end up like Lorraine, the 72-year-old woman who called me for a way out of her job at a Minneapolis dry cleaner a few years ago. Despite failing health, she couldn't quit because she had turned to a coworker for advice on her $120,000 in savings. She had done exactly what he suggested and put the full $120,000 into a mutual fund that had made him a lot of money. Unfortunately, like most Americans, he knew little about investing. The mutual fund he recommended turned out to be a disaster. Lorraine lost all but $55,000 in a few months, and if she had responded to her aching back and knees and retired at that point, she wouldn't have had enough to cover rent, food, and medicine each month. She could count on only about $1,000 a month from Social Security and not even $400 a month from her savings.

At 72, Lorraine's mistake was a devastating one that would keep her toiling at the dry-cleaning business for years longer. But people of all ages commit similar errors when they follow their friends and coworkers—or even worse procrastinate.

If you have been procrastinating, you are the norm, not the exception. Over the years, I have heard from thousands of people like you. You might be afraid of making a mistake with your money. You probably promise yourself that when you have more time or more money, you will figure out the 401(k) retirement plan at work or sort out all the TV blather and hype about IRAs, mutual funds, and the stock market.

But if you follow the usual pattern, the extra money never materializes. If you are like today's average college graduate, you start life sickened by the $25,000 in college loans overshadowing your future. You are figuring out your job, or hoping to find the right one. You tell yourself that you'll have plenty of time for retirement saving later and that making sense of the confusing 401(k) plan at work can wait another day.

Then come car payments. And time passes. There's still no money left just before payday, and you are so busy you can hardly think. Next, your first home and mortgage payments arrive, maybe along with kids. Soon you are buying Adidas and PlayStations, helping with homework, and rushing from work to parent–teacher conferences at school. And the kids' college years get closer and closer, with nothing stashed away to pay for any of it.

That's why you need to start saving small amounts for retirement now and, if you've already begun, to invest smarter now so that each penny counts. What you do matters. And saving early matters greatly: It saves you from the heavy lifting you will need to do if you wait. Here's the illustration often tossed about in training seminars for financial planners:

Imagine twins at age 21. One twin decides to start stashing away money. She opens a Roth IRA, a magical moneymaking tool I explain in Chapter 3, "Savings on Steroids: Use a 401(k) and an IRA."

She puts $3,000 into that Roth IRA retirement savings account at age 21, invests it in the stock market, and adds another $3,000 each year for the next five years. After age 26, she never puts any new money into that account. As the years go by, her money grows an average of 10 percent a year in the stock market. And when she retires at the end of her 65th year, she has more than $1 million, or roughly $1,048,000.

Now consider her sister, who decides at age 21 that she has plenty of time left to save. She waits to start until she is age 30. Then she invests $3,000 in the same mutual fund her sister has been using for years. Every single year until the day she retires, she diligently invests another $3,000.

Despite that determination, she never catches up to her sister. The twin who waited until she was 30 ends up with only about $987,000, about $61,000 less than the sister who became an investor at age 21. And to amass that smaller amount, the 30-year-old put aside a total of $108,000 of her own money, or $3,000 year after year. Contrast that to the sister who started at 21. She took only $18,000 out of her pocket during six years; then not another penny, and yet she ended up with more than $1 million.

Let's look at this another way: Assume that you want to have $1 million when you retire at the end of your 67th year. If you start investing at age 20, you will have to put only about $20 a week into a mutual fund to get there if you earn an average of 10 percent a year. In other words, you would invest roughly $1,050 a year and earn approximately what the stock market has historically provided investors.

But if you wait until you are age 25 to start, you'll need to invest about $33 a week, or roughly $1,700 a year, to get to $1 million. If you are 35 when you start, you will have to save about $87 a week, or approximately $4,500 a year. And if you are 45 and haven't saved a dime, you will have to stash away about $245 or $12,750 a year, to get to the same point at retirement that a 20-year-old does by investing only $20 a week. You can try this yourself on an Internet calculator like Millionaire Calculator, at www.timevalue. com/products/tcalc-financial-calculators/millionaire-calculator.aspx, or the Compounding Calculator, at www.moneychimp.com. (Keep in mind as you use various calculators that each rounds numbers and makes assumptions about timing; outcomes will vary somewhat. Seek a ballpark idea instead of expecting a precise number.)

The moral of this story: Start investing early because your early savings magically transform nickels and dimes into thousands of dollars. You might think you are making a sacrifice to save when you are young, but you are actually making life easier on yourself later.

On the other hand, if those early days have already passed you by, don't think saving is futile. Starting now still puts you way ahead of where you would be if you waited ten years or even a few more months. If you are 40 and start investing $50 a week sensibly now, you still could have about $300,000 when you retire. Is that a lot or a little? I'll help you put that into perspective in the next chapter.

The key is to start now because today's money will get you much further than next month's.

Feeling Incompetent

Let me assure you; if you doubt your capability to invest wisely, you are not alone. In a Harris poll of people who were investing in stocks, bonds, and mutual funds, only 2 percent said they felt like they knew everything they needed to know to make their investment decisions. Eighty-two percent wished their financial advisers would do more to educate them so they could make better investments.

If you were investing in a 401(k) or IRA at the beginning of 2000, you are probably still wondering where half of your hard-earned money went then, what you did wrong, and how to fix it so that it never happens again. If you regained most of your money after that miserable period and then got slapped again by the 2008 financial crisis, you might be wondering whether investing is a losers' game that you can't possibly win. The bruising blows of two of the worst stock market crashes in history probably eroded what little confidence you had.

This book removes the confusion and helps you put your good intentions into action that works. Saving merely $20 to $50 a week now can rather easily set you up for a $1 million retirement if you start when you're young, understand my simple lessons on the stock market and mutual funds, and use retirement accounts that give your money the best boost possible.

I don't thrust theory and tips at you and send you away to struggle with this later. I tell you where to go to get the best investment deals and how to buy what you need to buy. I provide models that you can easily copy. There's no "just trust me" to this book; you learn *why* you are doing what I'm telling you to do. That will give you the confidence to proceed through life even when the stock market seems scary. Anyone who has graduated from high school has the innate ability to grasp and do what I suggest.

Shared Ignorance

If Lorraine's story didn't make you cautious about trusting another person with your money, maybe this one will show you that you are part of a large club of people who are all in the dark about handling their money.

A couple years ago, I got a call from a 25-year-old who had just graduated from business school. He wanted to know the names of good index mutual funds and where to find them. In Chapter 13, "Index Funds: Get What You Pay For," I tell you more about these funds because they are an excellent, and easy, investment choice. But for now, I merely want you to focus on this 25-year-old business school graduate.

He'd learned in business school that an index fund was a smart way to invest. But that was it. He still had no idea how to put the concept to work. So he called me for advice.

"Where do I find the best index fund, and how much money do I need to get started?" he asked.

I ran his question in my column, along with tips for him, and it caused quite a stir among my readers. Because his question was so elementary, some of my readers were sure that either the question was a phony or the young man had attended a rotten university.

Neither was true. And I tell you the story now, as I told it then, for one reason: A person can be educated in business, run a business, be brilliant in math, and read the business pages in newspapers, and *still* lack practical tools for investing, such as where to find a good mutual fund.

So before you turn over your investing decisions to a friend or spouse, think twice about your own capabilities. As a columnist, I constantly hear from perfectly capable people with valid questions. Still, they believe they are unusually ignorant. They almost always start their calls to me with a confession: "I don't know what I'm doing." Many assume they lack some innate ability. But it just isn't true. The language of the financial world simply makes people *feel* incompetent, and the stock market unsettles people because it appears to work in mysterious ways.

Yet you should know that few people have an edge over you. A stunning number of multimillionaires and successful businessmen ask me to review their investments because they aren't sure whether their broker has led them astray.

Keep this in mind: The person you think is so advanced compared to you might simply *appear* more confident or more educated. He or she might simply be more willing to jump into the task of investing money. But you can do it, too—and maybe better than a financial adviser—if you merely follow the steps I lay out for you.

If you learned addition, subtraction, multiplication, and division in grade school, you have more math than you will probably need. And the Internet calculators I suggest will do the work for you. Eventually, you will be able to eye your 401(k) account or an IRA and quickly pick mutual funds with the ease you would in following a recipe. And you will feel comfortable that you won't live like a pauper now or when you retire.

Get Real

People are great at deluding themselves and telling themselves that everything will work out when it really won't.

A few years ago, Towers Perrin surveyed people within 10 years of retiring. Among those who had saved nothing, 58 percent not only were confident that they would have everything they needed in retirement, but expected to be able to take trips and buy luxuries, too. This delusional thinking gives new meaning to the term *American Dream.* We are a nation of optimists, but this takes it a bit too far.

Don't fool yourself. If you don't save, Social Security alone won't do it for you, even if the system lasts instead of crumbling the way some analysts are predicting. You won't be buying luxuries. You will be wondering how you will pay for electricity and heat your home or apartment. According to a survey of seniors done by AARP, half of retirees worry they won't be able to pay their utility bills in the next few months.

And it's no wonder. About half of seniors now depend on Social Security to cover at least 50 percent of their living expenses. And the average senior gets about $1,200 in Social Security a month.

So let's get real. Think of your lifestyle now and how you'd handle it if you were living on just $1,200 a month.

But let's take this a step further. Imagine that you are positioned like half of Americans who are 10 years away from retirement: You have $103,200 or less saved for retirement. (That's what the Congressional Research Service found in a study.) What would $103,200 give you? About $345 a month for living expenses. Add that to the average Social Security payment of $1,200, and you would have $1,545 to live on each month.

How does that sound?

Oh, and one more thing: People often think Medicare will cover all their health needs during retirement. But that's not true. The average retired couple has to pay about $330 a month for extra health insurance because Medicare pays only part of what people need, according to the Medicare Payment Advisory Commission. And then there are prescription drugs. Remember, older people aren't usually as fit as younger people.

Perhaps you've heard that a new Medicare program provides free drug coverage. But that's not true, either. It *helps* pay for drugs. Even with the new coverage, the ordinary retiree must spend about $790 a year for prescriptions, according to a Congressional Budget Office estimate.

So now look at a monthly income of about $1,150 after paying for medical insurance and medicine.

Could you handle it?

2

KNOW WHAT YOU'LL NEED

You might find yourself longing for your parents' or grandparents' generation.

When you go to the airport, the golf course, or restaurants, they are there en masse, looking tan, relaxed, and well dressed. They're enjoying retirement. Yet many of today's seniors didn't have to do nearly the thinking about retirement saving and investing that you must do while you are still working.

This hit me a couple years ago when I took my father to see a Bill Cosby performance in Minneapolis. We were in a huge theater, and the audience was a mass of gray and white hair. And I asked myself whether Cosby appealed only to seniors. I have no idea of the answer. But the tickets were about $150 a piece, and retirees filled the theater. The same happened when I took my father to a symphony concert. Clearly, a segment of the older generation has the financial ability to buy expensive tickets, and people under 65 were absent.

Now, don't get me wrong on this. I know that these two experiences are no measure of a complete generation. And as a personal finance columnist, I get plenty of calls from seniors who are having a tough time in retirement and worry about how they will pay for the rent or the heat. But there is a sizable segment of relatively well-off seniors who are doing better than past generations. A few years ago, I set out to find out why.

I wondered whether they'd been disciplined savers and clever investors.

The Retirement Difference: Pensions

I went to an AARP convention to try to understand how middle-class workers of the 1950s, 1960s, and 1970s had turned into retirees living the good life in the 2000s. After all, if they held the secret to a relaxing retirement, subsequent generations needed to hear it.

But in interview after interview, these seniors sounded a lot like today's working people. Some lived a little more modestly in smaller homes than today's families while raising children. They had often survived with two bedrooms, cramming multiple kids into a single bedroom. Many also said they'd had dumb luck: They had retired and sold their homes just as values happened to skyrocket amid heavy demand from baby boomers starting families. But beyond that, the story of their lives was a familiar one: They had essentially lived paycheck to paycheck, struggling to raise children and get them through college, just as parents do today. They hadn't had money to save. Most had been ignorant about investing. A few had turned investing into a hobby after they retired.

But one strong difference emerged: Even while struggling to raise their families, these seniors enjoyed a level of comfort that generations behind them do not have or shouldn't have if they think they are going to model their parents' lives.

Besides Social Security, their comfort was often based on one cozy little fact: They figured they could count on their employers to help them where Social Security left off. The key: After a lifetime of work, they were entitled to old-style pensions from their employers, the type of no-worry pensions that are becoming extinct. In addition, 66 percent of large companies gave employees health insurance for life.

The best pensions, along with Social Security, were designed to pay people about 70 percent of the income they had grown accustomed to living on during their last working years. Every month after a person retired, he or she would get a reliable check—a sure thing: money for rent, golf, or a trip.

Employers shouldered the entire responsibility to make sure the money grew enough and would be there when an employee reached age 65 and started to need the cash. The workers themselves didn't have to know a thing about investing money; the pros in the pension office did the heavy lifting for them.

With a deal like that, people didn't have to save much, if anything. They didn't need to know how to select a mutual fund. They didn't have to worry if money sat in an account and barely budged year after year. They didn't have to worry about years like 2008, when the stock market obliterated 37 percent of savings in a single year. They didn't have to wonder whether they needed to put aside 5 percent or 15 percent of each paycheck into a 401(k) or an IRA.

If they didn't save at all, they could still get through retirement quite comfortably. Their old employer would make it happen for them.

In the 1970s, almost half of all people working for a private employer looked forward to their employers helping them with that form of easy, dependable retirement money. Then 44 percent of workers with pensions were entitled to that no-brainer type: Their employer put away money for them, promised to manage it wisely, and guaranteed them that when they retired, they would receive a decent paycheck every month. Not all of them would get a hefty sum, but they would have some amount of dependable money besides Social Security.

Working men and women could concentrate on doing their jobs and raising their kids while their employer's pros managed their eventual retirement money. But these defined-benefit pensions got expensive for employers. They had to devote talent and money to making sure the investments were wise, and they had to fill the pension fund with enough money to cover the monthly paychecks that retirees expected. If you still have one of these delightful treasure chests, consider yourself one of the lucky few. Now only 17 percent of workers have them. Even those who do can no longer count on them, as demonstrated through United Airlines' recent bankruptcy or agreements with government workers in Rhode Island.

Today's Responsibilities Are Yours

Instead of offering the carefree pensions of the past, employers have shifted the responsibility to their employees. Half of Americans now have retirement savings plans at work with uninviting names such as 401(k), 403(b), or 457. By offering employees these savings plans, employers have taken themselves off the hook. They no longer have to invest money wisely for thousands of people. They guarantee employees nothing at the end of their working lives. The employees themselves now have to do the heavy lifting and make these retirement savings plans count.

Now, whether you have a 401(k), 403(b), 457, or none of those choices at work, the idea is the same: Your destiny clearly is in your own hands. If you use a 401(k) or an IRA well, you might end up on the golf course, at a concert, or in an airport at age 70. Skip it or choose the wrong mutual funds, and you had better like your own cooking instead of restaurant food, and television shows instead of a vacation.

About 50 million Americans have 401(k) accounts. Other workers struggle without any support at work. So now the masses of Americans—not their employers—have to figure out how to invest money so that it will grow enough to pay for the food, medicine, and entertainment they need and want during their retirement years. As part of their life's routine, they must remove enough money from every paycheck and deposit it into a 401(k) or 403(b) so that retirement doesn't creep up on an empty account.

Confusion Reigns

Most Americans don't have a clue about whether they are handling this responsibility wisely, and an uneasiness nags at them. In a Harris Interactive survey of women, 46 percent said they worried about ending up like bag ladies later in life. And relatively high incomes didn't help. Among women earning at least $100,000, 48 percent said they were afraid of becoming bag ladies. While many of these women felt sure of themselves in their jobs and other aspects of their lives, they were unsure of their ability to invest and plan for their financial futures.

The angst is not merely a women's issue. In 2012, only 14 percent of Americans were very confident they would ever have enough money to retire, according to the Employee Benefit Research Institute. And in a Harris poll of affluent Americans, 40 percent said they fear that even if they save diligently, they won't end up with the money they need for the future. People are worried about the future of Social Security and Medicare, and they question their ability to invest wisely.

Evidence of their financial failings abounds. Confused, about 30 percent of people with retirement plans at work are letting the opportunity to use them pass them by, even though their employers would give them thousands of dollars of free money—called a "match"—simply for participating. About 70 percent of Americans aren't investing 401(k) money correctly, so they are undermining their hard-earned savings, according to a review of 401(k) accounts by Financial Engines.

In addition, the average person using a 401(k) retirement savings plan is stashing away 6 percent of his or her pay, far below the maximum allowed and too flimsy to allow retirees to keep up the lifestyle they had grown used to living during their working years. (Retirement planning experts recommend investing 10 to 15 percent of pay—of course, that can include employer-matching money when it's available.)

Young people are missing the most crucial time in life to stash away small amounts and turn meager pocket change into a fortune. About 60 percent of Americans haven't figured out what they will need for retirement. And for the most part, their suspicions about their future are correct—they are falling far short of growing the nest egg they will need.

The Boston College Center for Retirement Research has calculated that Americans between ages 32 and 64 are so short on saving that they are on course to be $6.6 trillion behind what they will need for retirement. In other words, about 51 percent of people won't be able to live in retirement as well as they live now. The Employee Benefit Research Institute has calculated that 44 percent of baby boomers and Gen Xers are so far behind that they won't have the savings they need to cover basic living expenses., And when I say *basic,* I'm not talking about money for golf course greens fees and restaurants. Basic is food, medicine, lights, and a roof over your head.

What Do You Need?

You can meet those basic needs if, when you retire, your savings can give you about 50 percent of your preretirement pay for each year of retirement, according to the Center for Retirement Research at Boston College.

But with that 50 percent and Social Security, there will be little left for indulgences. It's a standard no-frills approach. And if you are like half of Americans, you have saved less than $36,000, according to the Congressional Research Service. That's hardly the level of savings you are going to turn into half your salary for every year until you reach 80, 90, or even 100.

Still, you have time to improve the outlook as long as you get serious now. If you are in your 20s or 30s, you can make it fairly easily without living like a pauper. Consider two spouses, both 35 years old and earning a total of $55,000 a year. The couple needs to accumulate about $700,000 to keep up their modest lifestyle in retirement. With $900,000, they should be comfortable, although that's still not luxury living.

I know that $700,000 and $900,000 look like overwhelming numbers. But they are less shocking when you consider how you get there. If the 35-year-old couple starts devoting about $390 a month to a retirement savings account such as a 401(k) and then follows up by continually investing 8.5 percent of each paycheck, they should be able to amass a livable nest egg of roughly $800,000.

I'm assuming that they get modest raises of 2.5 percent a year and their investments average gains of 8 percent a year. If they are lucky with the stock market and their investments average a 10 percent return per year, they should cross the $1 million threshold. If they get matching money from an employer and it boosts their savings over 8.5 percent of their pay, all the better.

But what do you personally need for your future to keep living the way you want—$100,000, $500,000, $1 million, $2 million?

Answers vary depending on the number of years until you retire, whether you will get a guaranteed old-style pension, how long you are likely to live, how much Social Security and Medicare you will get, how you invest, and the lifestyle you expect. I help you think through this in the rest of this chapter.

For now, keep this in mind: With $625,000 in savings, you could remove $25,000 to $31,250 during your first year of retirement for your living expenses. Then year after year, you could increase the amount slightly to cover rising costs from inflation, and you'd probably have enough in your nest egg to carry you through 30 years of retirement. With $1 million, you could provide $40,000 to $50,000 and be fairly confident that your nest egg would last for 30 years of retirement.

The key now: Don't close your eyes. Looking ahead prepares you for the future you want.

How Financial Planners Evaluate Your Needs

Sheryl Garrett is a financial planner in Shawnee Mission, Kansas, who started working with a couple in their late 40s a few years ago. They are a typical two-income, upper-middle-class couple. They came to her for advice because they were uneasy about their future. But they had no idea how vulnerable they actually were.

They'd put good intentions to save money on the back burner over and over while instead being generous with their children and charities. They'd put their kids through college and then helped them get their feet on the ground after graduating. Steve and Carol weren't spendthrifts. They were devoted parents who didn't want to say "no" when they saw that their children clearly needed help.

But the result was tough to bear: With 17 years to go before they planned to retire, they had $87,000 in retirement accounts. Yet they were used to living on $121,000 a year and had never contemplated a drastic cut in their lifestyle.

To be able to live as they had on $121,000 a year throughout retirement, Garrett calculated that they would need about $1.5 million. But they had only 17 years to get there. And the news about what that would take was shocking: If they truly wanted to have enough money to keep up with the lifestyle they'd known on $121,000, Garrett calculated that they would have to save $39,360 every year until retirement and invest it smarter than they had in the past.

For Steve, that meant taking more risks with mutual funds because he'd been overly conservative with bonds; he hadn't been giving his hard-earned savings an adequate chance to grow. For Carol, it meant being a lot more conservative than she'd been. One reason she'd saved so little for retirement was that she had been ignorantly swinging for the fences with dangerous mutual funds she thought were solid in the 1990s. She paid the price of being overly aggressive. In 2000–2001, the stock market had crashed and cut her hard-earned retirement savings in half.

The suspicion that they were blowing it as investors prompted Carol and Steve to seek out a financial planner. And often that impetus, or the search for the elusive *right* mutual funds, leads people to a financial planner's doorstep.

But like most trained financial planners, Garrett didn't start by trying to pick the right mutual funds. Instead, she started by trying to figure out what Steve and Carol would need at the end of their working years. Everything the couple had to do as investors would flow out of that one piece of information.

Garrett had to do a calculation for Steve and Carol.

Saving Enough?

This is where you should start, too—calculating what you will need for retirement.

This task might sound daunting. In talking with many people over the years, I have found that even the simple word *calculation* prompts some to start to sweat.

But there's no need for a bout of math phobia, thanks to the Internet. The Web is full of calculators that walk you step by step through the process of calculating what you will need for retirement—you don't have to do the math. The calculators simply tell you what information is required, and you put in the data from your own life. Some calculators are better than others. Several of my favorites are at www.choosetosave.org. Try the Ballpark Estimate on the right side of the home page, and then click Inter-active Ballpark. You can also try "Are You Saving Enough?", at www. kiplinger.com, for a simple overview and see CNN Money Retirement Planner, at http://cgi.money.cnn.com/tools/retirementplanner/retirementplanner.jsp, for a more comprehensive look at how all the moving parts of your money add up to provide the income you need for retirement.

You can find hundreds of other calculators on the Internet. I simply refer you to a few that are easy to understand and don't distort your view. I don't like calculators that leave Social Security and old-style pensions out of the calculation. If you qualify for a pension, that's real money that will help pick up where your savings leave off. Social Security should be considered, too. It's true that the future of Social Security is in question, but I don't advise ignoring it completely.

As you try various calculators, don't be upset when you see somewhat different numbers. All these have built-in assumptions and are designed to give you a glimpse of the future; they aren't precise down to the last dollar. Also, as the Web changes over time, some of the calculators I've mentioned might slip from view. If this happens, try www.gailmarksjarvis.com, and I'll keep you current.

But before you start your calculations, read the rest of this chapter. I help you gather all the pertinent information so that when you sit down to do the calculation, the process and its result will be simple and useful.

Doing the calculation I suggest takes about two minutes if you do the short "ballpark estimate" version at the Choose to Save site; it takes about ten minutes with the more thorough versions. When you finish, you will know whether you are on the right track or whether you need to make adjustments. The rest of this book tells you how to optimize those adjustments instead of flailing around like most Americans do.

Don't Let Fear Sidetrack You

Don't skip this step because you are afraid of the results. Carol and Steve found out that they needed to save more than $35,000, a year, which, of course, was a terrifying proposition—impossible to fulfill. But now that they have done a reality check, they are starting to think about what they can still control: If their health holds out, they plan to work a few more years beyond age 65.

If they work to age 70, they will get more Social Security and will need less of their own savings to cover living expenses. But don't make the mistake of assuming that Social Security payments will carry you through retirement. Americans get an average of $1,200 a month, hardly a cushy lifestyle. The amount depends on your income. At the minimum wage level, Social Security replaces about 60 percent of a person's earnings. Average wage earners get about 42 percent of their monthly pay, and people earning more than $100,000 can expect only about 26 percent. Carol and Steve figured that together they'd get about $3,320 a month in today's dollars. You can figure this out for yourself at www.socialsecurity.gov/retire2/. Try a fast calculation at www.ssa.gov/OACT/quickcalc.

By deciding to work longer, Carol and Steve did more than increase their Social Security. They gave themselves three more years of saving in earnest. They started looking for sources of cash to save and invest. With their children grown, they thought about moving to a smaller home with lower mortgage payments and devoting the entire savings to retirement accounts. They are cutting back their lifestyles a bit without living like paupers. Just skipping Starbucks on the way to work provides about $780 a year. Skipping one meal out a week saves about $2,600 a year, and with the kids grown, they can slash their life insurance.

Carol and Steve are determined now to save with gusto during the next 17 years. Instead of putting away what's left at the end of the year, they start with a disciplined approach: putting away a high percentage of each paycheck from the start. Wishful thinking is gone; realism and action have taken over. Instead of guessing, Carol and Steve have calculated the impact of more years of working . They have decided that, instead of having 100 percent of what they had while working, they will settle for 70 percent; they'll cut what they need to save to about $16,320 a year. They no longer have butterflies as they wonder whether they will survive.

You, too, can experiment on an Internet calculator with the effect of more working years. When using the ballpark estimate at www.choosetosave.org, see what would happen if you worked until age 70 instead of age 67 or held a part-time job after retiring. Consider how you would end up if you decided to replace only 70 percent of your salary instead of 100 percent. You can try the calculation with a lower replacement rate—maybe 60 percent. But keep in mind that if you go much below 70 percent, you aren't likely to live as you do now.

Don't Save Too Much

On the other hand, maybe you are saving too much. If so, you should know that, too.

Some financial planners would advise me not to say this. They would argue that, given the uncertainties of inflation and a strong probability that people with good genes will live into their late 90s, there is no such thing as saving too much. They would also urge anyone who is young to save at a high level in case an unforeseen setback—a job loss, a family emergency, a tax increase, or a brutal stock market cycle—sneaks up on them later and undermines their ability to save adequately.

I agree with this thinking.

But you might be like Lisa, a journalist I've known for years. Journalists, of course, tend to follow news carefully. And Lisa had visions of living like a bag lady in her old age every time she read an article about the Social Security system's eventual demise. She was in her 30s, a diligent saver, and because she felt so out of control about the future, she gave up on a lot of small indulgences she would have liked.

When I had Lisa do a calculation, she found that she was saving much more than she had to save. She was able to relax a little—be less hard on herself and spend a little more.

Think of your calculation like going to the doctor. You might dread the bad news, but you will get the diagnosis and prognosis. You will be then able to take action and repair the damage or improve your financial health for the long run. The doctor can prescribe medicine that will heal you or put you on course for a healthier life.

Your finances work the same: If you know the prognosis, you can put your money on a prescription, so to speak. In this case, that prescription comes down to how much you save and whether you are wasting money on taxes and your investments; you need to know which ones you need and how much of each. Perhaps you are relying too much on a savings account or the wrong types of mutual funds. Perhaps you need different mutual funds or a different type of IRA. Perhaps you need to cut back on certain mutual funds.

Understanding your investments is the next step after calculating what you will need for retirement. I explain everything you need to know about selecting mutual funds in Chapters 7–13: what mutual funds are, how they work, where to get the best ones, and how you can use them so they help you rather than hold you back. In short, mutual funds will no longer be things with confusing names that move in baffling ways. They will no longer be the things that turn bad every time you think you've selected a winner.

But first: the calculation.

Doing a Retirement Calculation Like a Pro

All competent financial planners start in the same place: They ask you for some information so they can put it into a calculator for you. They ask about your current income, dreams, and aspirations. They want to know whether you are likely to stay in your job or move to another that would pay more or less, and they ask when you want to retire. They then tally your likely expenses in retirement and compare them to today's.

The idea isn't to get friendly with you. The idea is to calculate the amount of money you will need so that it's enough for the lifestyle you want now and throughout all your years of retirement.

I know it's difficult when you are young to anticipate what you might want in 30 years or more. And if you don't know, don't worry about it. Remember, the aim of this process isn't to tell you with 100 percent certainty that you will have a certain amount of money or need a certain amount of money when you retire. It's to get close, to give you a ballpark understanding of whether you are currently on course or wildly off course.

As you go through life—especially if you change jobs or make changes such as marrying, divorcing, or having a baby—it's a good idea to go back to the Internet and run another calculation. Life circumstances change your financial needs and wants dramatically.

Imagine Your Life at 65 and 75

For now, try to think about what you want your life to be like when you are 65 or 75—not in detail, of course. But ask yourself questions like these: Will I be comfortable sitting at home, watching TV or reading, or cooking my own food? Or will I want to indulge myself with restaurant food, trips, or expensive hobbies? Will my mortgage be paid off, or will I still be making monthly payments on it, on a car, and on credit cards? How often will I buy a new car? Is it realistic to think that I will sell my house and retire where housing is drastically cheaper, or is my retirement destination just as costly as where I live now? Even if you plan to stay around the house, puttering in the yard might cost a lot.

A few years ago, I interviewed Rita and Richard, recent St. Paul retirees who had moved south and were shocked at what they were spending during retirement. Richard had spent his life working for a nonprofit organization, and Rita had taught home economics; they had never been extravagant. But in retirement, Rita took up a hobby of planting wildflowers, while Richard golfed three times a week. And they took a couple trips a year to visit their children in other cities. With those simple pleasures, they were spending more in retirement than they had while working.

A financial planner told them they'd need to cut back or they would exhaust their savings at age 85. Since they were healthy and their parents had lived long, they knew that running out of money in their 80s would be a problem. A rule of thumb is to never remove more than 4 to 5 percent of your retirement savings a year, if you want it to last.

So when you do your calculation, keep this in mind. The calculator will ask you whether, during your retirement years, you will want your savings to replace all or part of your old salary. It will ask you, do you want to replace 70 percent, 100 percent, or some other amount? Whatever you say reflects the lifestyle you will accept. Rita and Richard thought they could live on 70 percent of what they were making. But the life they wanted meant more than 100 percent.

You might not know what percentage to use for yourself. But this might help. Remember the old-style pensions I described earlier? The best of those pensions are based on a premise: Along with Social Security, the aim is to provide retirees with 60 to 70 percent of the income that they enjoyed while working. That 70 percent is also a rule of thumb with financial planners. The thinking is that if you amass enough savings during your working years to fund an annual income that is 70 percent of your last salary, you will be okay. Many planners prefer clients to get 85 percent or 100 percent, if they can afford it, primarily because rising healthcare costs are an expensive wildcard and because people spend more than they think on fun.

But experiment with numbers. On the calculators I've suggested, a couple computer clicks can give you a picture of what it means to replace 70 percent or 100 percent.

Again, I must emphasize that no exact number exists for you. Instead, you are starting to think about a target you want to aim at for retirement. When you decide on the percentage of your old salary that you want, you move on to see what you will have to do to meet that number. If getting to 85 percent requires you to live too much like a pauper now, maybe you will accept 70 percent or 60 percent later. Just remember that when you say 70 percent for retirement, it shouldn't be wishful thinking. With 70 percent, you will be able to provide necessities, but if you imagine trips and luxuries, then get real. The math just does not work.

If you want more than to just get by, this might also help you think about your future: Generally, when people retire, their needs change as they age. At first, they like to have fun. Rita and Richard, for example, were so busy with gardening and golf in their late 60s that they wanted to go to a restaurant for dinner once in awhile. And Richard couldn't stand Denny's, so it cost them a little more than fast-food or "family restaurant" prices.

But as people move toward their 80s, they become less active. They spend less on entertainment. At the same time, medical costs can pick up. Most Americans don't realize that Medicare doesn't cover all their medical costs. But Medicare covers only part, and retirees today buy supplemental insurance that can cost about $150 to $250 a month per person, or $300 or $500 per couple. Cost fluctuates by area of the country. For people who retire before age 65, $1,000 a month for medical insurance isn't unusual, so think that through carefully before you retire early.

Health Costs Are a Black Hole

Despite help from Medicare, people have to dip into their own pockets to pay for doctors, hospitals, and medicine. Medicare pays only a portion of retirement health care costs. A Social Security Administration report estimated the median out-of-pocket cost for retirees at $2,740 in 2005, and the cost has grown 64 percent since 1997. About a quarter of retirees are spending a third of their income on health care. By 2030, people will be spending an estimated 67 percent of their Social Security income, on average, for medical costs Medicare doesn't cover.

If your employer offers healthcare for retirees, don't count on it. Only 11 percent do, and 85 percent of those offering it say they are looking for ways to reduce the benefit or cut it completely, according to the Employee Benefits Research Institute.

Plan to pay for health insurance yourself. What might that expense run? Costs have been rising about 7 to 10 percent a year. The Employee Benefits Research Institute has calculated that a man who lives into his late 80s or early 90s could need about $195,000 for health and drug coverage, and it's

$221,000 for a woman. For a couple, that's over $400,000—a shocking number. Keep in mind that almost half of women are living to age 90 now, so that means even higher expenses for medical care.

Guessing healthcare costs is difficult at a time when the Medicare system is financially troubled and all healthcare costs have been rising at an extraordinary clip. Many financial planners deal with it by not trying to guess. They simply have their clients build up a nest egg, prior to retiring that will be large enough to cover 100 percent of the last working year's salary for at least 30 years.

This was part of Garrett's calculation when she came up with the $1.5 million that Steve and Carol would need. She assumed that Steve and Carol would live to 100 because both their parents were healthy.

When Will You Retire?

For years, about 80 percent of baby boomers have been telling AARP pollsters that they plan to work during retirement. Most enjoy working and want to continue. Yet some know that they will *have* to work because they won't have enough money saved. About 33 percent have estimated that they will need to work so they can pay for necessities.

With the recession of 2008–2009, the need to work longer has intensified. One in six people within about ten years of retirement age lost jobs, and many dipped into their retirement savings to put food on the table and pay mortgages. Those that left meager savings intact, lost a chunk as the stock market took a toll. Now 67 percent realize they are far behind with their savings, and many are betting on working well past age 65. In an Employee Benefit Research Institute study, 26 percent told researchers they think they will have to work until at least 70.

In a way, this is an encouraging conclusion. A body of medical research shows that people who work, either for pay or as a volunteer, after retirement are happier and healthier. The two seem to be interlinked.

However, planning to work to age 70 is naïve and filled with risk. Instead of working longer, half of current retirees report that they had to retire earlier than expected because of health problems, disability, or layoffs. The 2008 recession dramatized the risk. While young workers lost jobs more frequently than people over 50, the people in their 20s and 30s were rehired relatively quickly. Among people 51 to 60, however, the Urban Institute found half still trying to find work more than six months after getting laid off. Those lucky enough to find jobs accepted a 23 percent pay cut on average. Only a third of people 62 and over were able to get jobs within 12 months of getting laid off. When people hit age 62, they were giving up in frustration and settling on collecting Social Security early.

On the face of it, that might seem like a decent plan. But retiring early slashes your Social Security. If you wait until age 66 or 67 to start collecting Social Security, your benefits increase 25 percent.

So thinking that you will work during retirement is well and good. But now, during your working years, you must be realistic about this, too. What happens if you resolve now to skip saving and just plan to work? You might or might not be able to make that happen. If your health holds out, working might be fine. Yet, be realistic about age and health.

In an AARP survey of retirees, great differences emerged between young retirees and older ones (people over 65). When asked how healthy they felt, 54.5 percent of the younger group said they felt very good. But only 38 percent of the older group did. Think about this: If you don't feel very good, are you going to want to work at 70 because you are running out of retirement savings? Also, even if you are in top shape, is your employer going to let you keep working? Although there's been a lot of chatter about keeping baby boomers in the workplace longer, research shows that few employers are set up to do it, and age discrimination is abundant.

Nursing Homes

Here's one last reality check: According to a study by *The New England Journal of Medicine,* 43 percent of people over 65 will spend at least some time in a nursing home. It might not be a permanent move: They might be there to recover from an injury or a disease—at a cost of about $200 a day— and then go back home to fend for themselves.

Health insurance doesn't pay for these stays, and Medicare covers only the first 100 days in a nursing home. This expense can be a huge drain on your savings. Financial Planning News reports a few examples of maximum time periods and costs under Medicare:

Cardiac condition	16 months and $75,800
Stroke	21 months and $99,500
Alzheimer's disease	96 months and $455,000

Most people can't save enough to cover all this. Long-term care insurance might be the answer, but it's controversial because of costs and the stability of insurance companies offering it. Often low-income people can get help with the costs based on financial need, and some financial planners think that affluent clients might be better off accumulating their own savings instead. Think through this matter carefully as you approach your retirement years. Phyllis Shelton's book, *Long-Term Care: Your Financial Planning Guide* (LTCi Publishing, 2008), may help.

How Long Will You Live?

Next, think about how long you are likely to live. I am stunned by the number of retired people who call me worried about running out of money. When they retired, they envisioned their 70s, not their 80s or 90s. They lived it up early in retirement, but when they're still healthy in their mid-80s, their life's savings are about to run dry.

Retiring without contemplating how long you might live is like taking a trip across the desert. If it's going to take you a day, you might need a gallon of water. If it's going to be a week, you had better have several gallons.

Of course, you never know exactly how long you will live. And some people tell me they would rather not think about when they will die. Instead, they would simply like to live each day so that it counts, spending their money while they have it. I wish they could talk to some of the 80-year-olds who have called me over the years. They would like to live each day so it counts, too. Yet one had a meals-on-wheels dinner delivered to her house each day, and she made it last all day, eating a little for lunch, a little for dinner, and sometimes a drop of leftovers for the next day's breakfast. To save on energy costs, she kept the food warm on a radiator instead of putting it in the refrigerator and reheating it at night.

Although you don't know with certainty how long you will live, consider how long your parents have lived and then adapt that for your lifestyle and the advances of modern medicine. Life expectancy continues to increase. When Social Security began, if you made it to age 65, you were expected to live 13 more years. Now if you make it to 65, the Society of Actuaries estimates that half of men will live to 85 and half of women to 88.

Financial planners advising healthy clients with parents who lived well beyond 65 tend to have individuals plan to accumulate enough savings for a lifetime that extends to age 95 or 100. When you look at averages, you must ask yourself if you seem to fit the average. Your genetics and lifestyle might position you to live well above or below the average.

Even money can be a factor in your longevity. Some studies show a possible connection between having enough money and living a healthier, happier life. That doesn't mean you have to be rich to be happy. In fact, academic studies have dispelled the notion that being rich makes people happy. But in one study, men with large pensions lived longer than men with small pensions.

For help in calculating your own life expectancy, try the calculator at www.livingto100.com. Again, however, this is simply an educated guess to help you focus on how much money you might need as you do your calculation.

Women Live Longer, Need More Money

Women have to be particularly cognizant of their longevity. Typically, they live longer than men, have smaller or no pensions, and receive smaller Social Security checks. Consequently, according to the Administration on Aging, they are twice as likely as men to live their retirement in poverty. And half of the elderly widows now living in poverty were not poor before their husbands died.

If she reaches age 65, a woman has a 44 percent chance of living to age 90—and about a quarter of women will live to age 95, compared to only about 16.5 percent of men. Women tend to marry men older than they are, so many married women will be widows for 15 to 20 years before they die. Often widowhood means less money because women exhaust the household's savings caring for dying husbands.

Women frequently end up in a squeeze during retirement because they never envisioned living 30 or 40 years and simply didn't accumulate enough of a nest egg for such a lifespan. Those who have relied on husbands to do the investing for them can be vulnerable prey for unscrupulous financial consultants. Over the years, many widows have called me in tears because they trusted brokers who did not have their best interests in mind.

This is why all women—married and unmarried—should learn the basics about investing that I have explained in this book. And if they are counting on a husband to handle the money, they should discuss investing together and go to brokers or other financial consultants together.

In addition, women should know that financial companies, such as brokerage firms, are studying women extensively because they currently make up about 47 percent of investors and have growing wealth. That research shows that women, as a group, are less confident than men about investing but tend to have better results because they study stocks and mutual funds more thoroughly and are slow to pull the trigger.

Many finance books are written specifically for women, and brokers put on seminars just for women. I view many as gimmicky because they create the impression that investing is different for men and women. It's not. When a stock or mutual fund goes up or down, it doesn't know whether you are a man or a woman.

The only factor that makes women unique is greater longevity. That makes it essential that women run the retirement calculation I have suggested. They must assume that they will need more savings than men. And if they are married, women need to realize that, at some point, either because of a divorce or the husband's death, they probably will need to be responsible for handling money.

If you are a woman reading this book, you are taking that seriously. If you are a man, don't leave your partner in the dark.

Dig Out These Records

All the thinking I have encouraged you to do so far relates to thinking ahead about lifestyle and health. Now, to do the calculation right, you need some information about your finances.

When you retire, your money will come from the following sources: Social Security; any old-style pension you might be lucky enough to get from an employer; your own savings from IRAs, 401(k) plans, or other accounts; and perhaps an inheritance.

If you are counting on an inheritance, be practical about what you expect. A few years ago, researchers were predicting a windfall for baby boomers, but that hasn't been happening. With the help of advanced medicine, parents are living longer and spending down their savings. Recent research by AARP has found the median inheritance to be about $30,000.

Here's how to get the figures you need to put into the calculator at a site such as www.choosetosave.org.

How Much Security Is Social Security?

When you near your birthday each year, you get a letter from the Social Security administration. It tells you how much your monthly paycheck should be each month of retirement if you retire at age 62, at 70, or at the typical retirement age (now ranging from 66 to 67, depending on your birth date). People born between 1943 and 1954 must wait until age 66 to retire if they want full benefits. People born in 1960 or later must wait until age 67.

The amount of Social Security you will receive is based on the salaries you have been receiving throughout your working years. This is one reason women tend to get smaller Social Security checks. They often disrupt their salary history by taking time from work to care for children and family members. They also work in larger numbers in careers that provide lower pay.

If you can't find that mailing from the Social Security Administration, you can get the information from 800-772-1213, www.socialsecurity.gov/retire2/, or www.ssa.gov/OACT/quickcalc. To calculate future benefits, at the Social Security site, click Calculate Your Benefits.

You might wonder what figure to use, given all the hand-wringing over the future of the Social Security system. In other words, Social Security is projected to run short of money within the next few years—should you count on Social Security? And if you do count on Social Security, should you figure that you will get everything you've been promised?

I don't have a crystal ball on this one. Nor can I predict what Congress might do to reinforce the system or to decrease benefits. I can tell you that, over the past few years, I have interviewed players from every end of this debate—academia, interest groups, the Bush administration, the Obama administration, and Congress. At least for the baby boomer generation, no one can see Social Security disappearing completely. The reason is simple: The boomers are a gigantic generation; 77 million people make up a powerful voting block.

So politics alone suggest some kind of continuation of Social Security. On the other hand, second-guessing politics is no easy matter. If you are in your 20s, your generation is large, too—about 84 million. Size should provide some clout. Still, the politics are a moving target. My suggestion? Do what some financial planners do: Use what we currently know about the system. In other words, in about 10 years, the Social Security system is expected to face financial problems, and by 2037, enough money will remain to pay retirees only 75 to 78 percent of what's been promised to them. So when you see what you are expected to get in Social Security, remove about 25 percent of it for each month. When you look into your future and use an Internet calculator to estimate what you will need for retirement, run the calculation three times: once with full Social Security benefits, once with no benefits, and once with 25 percent less than you've been promised. Then you will see best- and worst-case scenarios, and you can plan your saving around them.

This will be easy to do with the Ballpark Estimate calculator at www.choosetosave.org. It provides a link to your Social Security calculator so you don't have to hunt for the Social Security site.

Olden Days with Old-Style Pensions

If your employer will pay you a pension when you retire, you are one of the lucky few. Consider yourself fortunate if you hear the words *defined benefit plan* at your workplace: It means that a guaranteed check routinely will arrive at your home while you are retired. But don't expect it to take care of your every need.

If you haven't spent your full work life with one employer, your pension probably isn't going to come close to being the only source of money you will need besides Social Security. Usually you have to work for 30 years to get the full pension, although you are likely to get a sizable chunk if you have been there for 20 to 25 years.

If you have worked at a company less than five years, you probably aren't entitled to any guaranteed pension. But typically after five years, you will get a modest sum when you retire, even if you left that employer years ago. Of course, this assumes that your employer was offering such a benefit on the day you quit your job.

It's worthwhile to check with past employers to see whether you eventually will be entitled to a guaranteed monthly paycheck from them. And if you currently work for an employer that offers an old-style pension, you can figure out what it will mean to you in your future.

The amount of time you work for the company and your age at retirement are key to the formula your employer uses to calculate your benefits. Some companies let you start collecting a pension at age 55, but others say 62 or 65. If you start collecting it at 55, it will be sliced to a smaller amount than if you wait until 62 or 65.

To understand how your retirement age and years of service at the company impact the amount you are due, turn to a document at work called a summary plan description. You are entitled to see it. Unfortunately, you will probably find it overwhelming, filled with a mass of gibberish. But charts might help you understand what you might get.

The easy way out is to go to your company's benefits or human resources office and ask the appropriate staffer to calculate the amount of your pension for you. This is good to know at any age. When you figure this into your calculation, you will considerably ease your burden about saving.

If you have worked a calculator offered by a mutual fund company, bank, or brokerage firm, they sometimes don't ask you to factor a guaranteed pension, or even Social Security, into your calculation. The result is terribly distorted. It looks as though you must save and invest thousands—sometimes hundreds of thousands—more than you must.

Here's a simple example to illustrate the concept. Say you worked at a place for a decade and then left; someday you will be able to get a guaranteed pension of $1,000 a month. That's big money when you look at it in its entirety. Over 30 years of retirement, it's $360,000. So if you also have accumulated $600,000 in a 401(k) retirement savings plan or IRAs and add the $360,000 in pension money, the sum is close to $1 million.

You will have multiple sources of income in this retirement scenario. Without a regular paycheck anymore, you cobble together your income. The first year, you pay yourself $24,000 from your retirement savings accounts, your pension delivers another $12,000, and let's say Social Security provides $20,000. Your total income is $56,000.

The combination may allow you to breathe easier. It's certainly more comforting than considering a mere $24,000 a year from the money you personally amassed. But don't relax too much. Inflation has recently been below the 3 percent average, but it is always a factor in eroding your buying power for the future. Consequently, counting too much on a pension could be a mistake. Pensions often don't increase over time, and $1,000 20 years from now will buy much less than it does today.

The money you have saved and invested on your own will be critical because, unlike the pension, you can invest it and keep it growing. In a fairly conservative investment mixture of stocks and bonds, you might earn a 6 percent return a year. That will allow you to draw out an annual income that will help you keep pace with inflation.

Some pensions have cost-of-living enhancements or raises, so $1,000 could get slightly larger each year. This is unusual, so figure that yours doesn't increase unless you know otherwise. Also don't assume that you have a pension coming to you from an employer unless you check on it. After all, in the example I provided, having a pension gives you a total of almost $1 million for retirement. Without the $360,000 from the pension, you might need to do more saving before you finish working.

And if you work for a company on shaky ground, keep this in mind if you're counting on a pension: There is a backup if a company collapses and can't pay its pensions. But that's not a full guarantee. The group that is intended to protect your pension is the Pension Benefit Guaranty Corporation, but it has stated that the demands on it are so great that it isn't positioned to cover all the potential failures. Even under current conditions, there's a limit to how far the PBGC will help: It guarantees only up to about $56,000 a year. If you retire early, the guarantee is reduced.

401(k), 403(b), 457, and Profit Sharing

In the next chapter, I explain how to use these fabulous money-growing machines at work. So don't worry now if you are still a bit perplexed by them.

For purposes of your calculation, you need some basic information: Start by finding out how much money you have in a 401(k) or the other similar plan you have at work—these plans have names like 403(b), 457, or deferred compensation. Perhaps your employer also is putting aside money for you in something called a profit-sharing plan.

Whatever these plans are called, check on what's in them or what's called the "current balance." You might find this online through a 401(k) Web site that your employer offers, or you might have received a statement at the end of the month or end year that tells you this. If you don't have it, stop in or call your benefits office or human resources contact at work. If you don't know who this is, go to the person who gives you your health insurance information. Tell them you want to find out how much money you have in your 401(k), 403(b), or other retirement savings plan.

Also, ask (if you don't know) how much money you are setting aside in one of these plans from each paycheck. This is good to know under any circumstance. Internet calculators ask how much money you put into your retirement plan each month.

As you search for your 401(k) information, you might discover an unpleasant surprise. You might think you are participating—making money for retirement. But, in fact, you might never have signed up and, consequently, do not have a penny to your name.

Benefits firm Hewitt Associates did a nationwide survey of employees not contributing to their 401(k) plans and found that people often erroneously assume that they are getting the benefit of a 401(k) plan at work when they aren't. About 29 percent of people thought they were contributing to a 401(k) plan when they were not. In other words, they thought they were building up money for retirement, but nothing was happening.

You don't want to find this out when you are a few years from retiring. You want to find it out now, while there is still time to call in the doctor and take your medicine for your financial future.

If you have a profit-sharing plan, the information will be fuzzier because precise amounts vary and might come only at the end of a year. Perhaps you can get an estimate from your benefits office.

IRAs and Other Savings Accounts

Again, you don't need to understand individual retirement accounts, or IRAs, if you don't have one. I explain everything you need to know about them in Chapter 3, "Savings on Steroids: Use a 401(k) and an IRA"; Chapter 4, "An IRA: Every American's Treasure Trove"; and Chapter 5, "IRA Decisions: How to Start and Where to Go."

For now, to do your retirement calculation, you need to know whether you have an IRA. If you do, find your last statement, which probably comes in the mail shortly after the end of each month. Find out what you have in the account. Look for words such as *total account value.* If you aren't sure where to look on the statement to find that number, call the telephone number on the statement, ask what your total account value is, and ask where you can find it on the statement for the future.

You need to know something else about your habits or practices. Do you put money into the account every month, every week, or once a year when you do your taxes? If you aren't sure and can't find it on your statement, think about where you went to open the account. Was it a bank, a brokerage firm, or a mutual fund company? Call a central telephone number for the institution and ask to speak to a representative about your IRA. Say that you aren't sure when you last put money into the account. Ask when you did it and what the amount of money was. Ask about previous contributions, too. You will need your Social Security number to access the information.

With this, you will know how much money you put into the account each month or each year. That's a specific number you need for the calculation.

The Big Guess Numbers

All calculators request two numbers, and you might not have the slightest idea what number to use. The first number is inflation, or the average rate at which the prices of everything you buy go up each year. Inflation can vary, but I'd use at least 2.5 percent, and maybe 3 percent. Inflation has been unusually low the last few years as the economy has struggled to recover from the 2008 recession, but 3 percent is the longer-term average.

The other number you will be asked is your rate of return. What does it mean? It's what you are going to earn on your money. Typically, when people are asked to plug in this number, it's pure fantasy to them. They have no idea what makes sense. During the 1990s, it would not have been crazy to plug in 18 percent for stock market investments. For the year 2005, it was only 5 percent in the stock market. In 2011, it was 2.1 percent and in 2008—a horrible year—people lost 37 percent of their money in the stock market. So which "return" do you pick? I suggest none of these numbers. One year in the stock market is irrelevant because it moves up and down. If a financial planner was doing the calculation, he or she might select 10 percent for your stock market investments such as stock mutual funds. That's because 9.8 percent has been the average annual rate of return in the stock market since the end of 1925, according to respected research firm Morningstar.

For the near-term future, however, Wall Street strategists think growth in the stock market will be slower than it has been—maybe a 4 to 8 percent return a year. If you are young, you are investing for many, many years, so some financial planners would tell you to assume 7 to 8 percent to be relatively conservative or 10 percent to follow the historical average of the stock market.

You will feel more comfortable with this item in the calculation after I explain the stock market and mutual funds in later chapters.

For now, I have to draw a distinction among the various rates of return you might use. If you are investing only in CDs or bonds, you can't assume that you will earn 8 or 10 percent on your money. Historically, the return on U.S. government bonds has averaged 5.7 percent a year, according to Morningstar. If that's where your money is, use about 5 percent. If you have all your money in a savings account, you are getting nowhere; you aren't earning much at all—maybe 1 percent.

When you are doing your calculation, try different rates of return to see the dramatic difference it will make in your nest egg. For example, if you have saved $40,000 and will keep it invested for 20 more years, you will have $154,787 if it grows 7 percent a year. But if you get just 1 more percent of growth, for 8 percent, you will have $186,438 (see Table 2.1 for more examples).

In the chapters ahead, I describe how to combine stocks and bonds so that you enhance your returns without taking undo risks. A person who puts half of her money in stocks and half in bonds might use history to project a possible average annual return of approximately 7 or 8 percent.

Table 2.1
How a $10,000 Investment Grows over Time with Various Rates of Return

Years of Investing	5% Return	6% Return	7% Return	8% Return	9% Return	10% Return
10	$16,289	$17,908	$19,672	$21,589	$23,674	$25,937
20	$26,533	$32,071	$38,697	$46,610	$56,044	$67,275
30	$43,219	$57,435	$76,123	$100,627	$132,677	$174,494
40	$70,400	$102,857	$149,745	$217,245	$314,094	$452,593
50	$114,674	$184,202	$294,570	$469,016	$743,575	$1,173,909

The Easy Calculation

If you feel comfortable with a little math and want to quickly get a glimpse of your future, you can skip the details I have suggested and simply eyeball your money. To estimate what you are likely to have for retirement, you can figure when your current savings will double. This is called the rule of 72.

Here's how it works: You divide the number 72 by your expected rate of return on your investments. So let's say that you decide you are likely to earn 7 percent on your money annually. Seven goes into 72 about ten times. Thus, your money will double in about ten years.

What does that mean? Imagine that you have saved $40,000 and have 20 years to go until retirement. With this eyeball method, you could estimate that, in ten years, you will double your money and have approximately $80,000. Then in another ten years, or the full time until you retire, you will have about $160,000.

The trouble with this easy method is that you don't know what you are aiming at. You have a sense of what you are accumulating, but it doesn't help you know what you will need. The Internet calculators I've suggested will help you see the entire picture—what you need and the progress you are making to get there.

Still, if you're a paper-and-pencil person, not a computer person, Charles Schwab financial planning researchers offer this simple calculation: If you divide your total savings at retirement by 25, you will see what you can remove for annual living expenses retirement each year. For example, if you have $1 million, you can remove $40,000 the first year—that's 4 percent of your nest egg. (Among financial planners, 4 percent is a rule of thumb. They have calculated that, generally, people can remove 4 to 5 percent of their savings the first year they retire and then tweak the sum slightly for inflation each year after that. Removing more spending money than that, however, is risky. It puts people in jeopardy of running out of money too early in retirement. Living within the 4 percent rule is supposed to make money last 30 years. I provide more detail on this concept later in this chapter under "Using Your Calculation: The Advanced Lesson.")

You can do the quick calculation in reverse, too. Say you want to be able to take $50,000 out of your retirement accounts during the first year of retirement. To see if that's possible, multiply 25 by $50,000. You find that you will need a total of $1,250,000 in your retirement accounts. So if you are on course to accumulate $1,250,000, you will likely have what you need.

You might be feeling demoralized at this point. Perhaps you are looking at the meager $50,000 that $1.25 million in savings provides. But stop and think for a minute. The $50,000 comes from your savings. That's only a portion of your retirement money. Let's look at this holistically.

Maybe at retirement you want to have an income of $90,000. Is it possible? You check on the Social Security you will be getting and find that it's $25,000. You also know you can add another $15,000 from a part-time job or possibly an old-style pension.

Your first year of retirement, using a $1,250,000 nest egg, looks like this:

Money from savings	$50,000
Money from Social Security	$25,000
Money from job or pension	$15,000
Total spending	$90,000

The next year, of course, the cost of living will rise—maybe about 2.5 percent a year. You will be able to increase your withdrawals from your nest egg slightly each year to cover this modest inflation as long as your investments continue to grow about 6 percent a year. If you have 60 percent of your money invested in stocks and 40 percent in bonds, that should give you the 6 percent growth you need. But investments are always a wildcard; they could do better or worse than you expect. That's why financial planners don't want you to withdraw more than about 4 to 5 percent from your nest egg each year.

As you will learn in Chapter 6, "Why the Stock Market Isn't a Roulette Wheel," you can never guess when you will encounter a bad cycle in the stock market. And if it hits you early in retirement, it could slash your savings. As you will read in that chapter, many retirees had to go back to work after the stock market crashes in 2000 and 2008. Those who were depending exclusively on stocks lost about half their retirement savings.

Common advice from financial planners is to start retirement by removing only 4 to 5 percent of savings. Then if you hit a benevolent cycle and your retirement savings multiply at a sharp rate, you can withdraw a little more as time goes on.

Two Easy Rules of Thumb

If you only want to eyeball your savings and see quickly how you are doing, you can apply another simple rule of thumb: For every $100,000 you have in savings, you can remove $5,000 a year for retirement, or 5 percent of your nest egg. With this method, if you think you will need $20,000 a year plus Social Security, you'll need $400,000 on the day you retire. When you consider your annual income in retirement, keep in mind that you will be paying taxes. Consequently, not every drop of savings is yours free and clear. Also, I need to remind you again that prices go up as years pass, so as you eye your savings, realize that $20,000 in 20 years will buy less than $20,000 buys today. If you doubt this, think about what your first car—or your parents' first car—cost, compared to cars today.

Calculating living expenses for the future is difficult, but the retirement income calculator at www.dinkytown.com does the job for you by building in inflation and taxes. Use it if you want a sense of what your savings will actually buy at the point when you retire.

If you want to skip all these calculations, you can fall back on another simple rule of thumb that will at least move you close to where you will need to be when you retire: Save at least 10 percent of your salary, making contributions to your investments from every paycheck, throughout your working years. It's not foolproof, and many financial planners recommend 15 percent because of longevity considerations. But if you are in your early 20s, 10 percent should put you on the road to where you need to go. If you are in your 30s and didn't make the 10 percent threshold in your 20s, you can generally catch up by saving 15 percent of your salary. If you are in your 40s and skipped investing during your 20s and 30s, you have some serious catching up to do. Consider investing 25 percent of your salary.

But if you can't save that much, do what you can; you will be making more progress than you think. Run a quick Internet calculator, such as the ballpark estimate at www.choosetosave.org, while you still have time to make amends and mold the future you'd like.

How Do You Turn $25 a Week into $1 Million?

How does a person accumulate $1 million simply by investing $20 to $25 a week? It's through the magic of compounding. That's a math term, but you don't have to be a math pro to make it work for you. You saw the power in the earlier numbers.

Here's how it works: After you put aside money for retirement, it keeps growing even if you don't add anything else to it. And the longer it stays there, the more magic it works. It's like Rumpelstiltskin spinning straw into gold, only it's not a fairytale. It really works.

Consider a simple example. Let's say that, at age 25, you are working at your first job and you open an IRA at the end of the year. You put $2,000 into it, and you invest it in a stock mutual fund. (I explain what an IRA is and how to handle it in Chapters 3 and 4.)

For now, I just want you to notice how savings add up to huge amounts without requiring you to dig deeply into your pocket year after year. The magic of compounding is at work. Let's say that, by the end of the first year, you have earned 10 percent on your original money. Your $2,000 is now $2,200. But from that point on, you can't afford to save any more; you just keep the money invested in the stock market, and year after year, you earn money on the original $2,000 you invested plus whatever the stock market gives you. So let's assume that, year after year, you average a 10 percent return on your money in a stock mutual fund.

After the first year, you have $2,200—your original $2,000 plus the $200 you earned on the $2,000. You leave it invested for a year and earn money on $2,200. It consequently becomes $2,420 by the end of the year. You start the next year with $2,420, and by the end of that year, it has become $2,662. The next year, you start with $2,662 invested, and it becomes $2,928. Now it's the fifth year. You start with $2,928, and by the end of the year, you have $3,221.

It starts getting really exciting now. Remember, you never added any new money from your pocket. After five years, your original $2,000 turned into $3,221 simply because you left it invested. Now watch the power of compounding. The same process that I described keeps happening year after year, so by the end of 10 years, you have $5,187; by the end of 20, you have $13,455; at the end of 30, you have $34,899; and after 40 years, you have $90,519.

That's right. You took $2,000 out of your pocket at age 25, invested it in stocks through a mutual fund, and ended up with $90,519.

But now let's assume that you are 25 and have $2,000 invested. You decide that you are going to keep adding $2,000 in new money to your investments each year. Then, at the end of 40 years, you will be a millionaire. Try the Compounding calculator at www.moneychimp.com to see how it works. After 40 years of investing $2,000 a year, you end up with about $1,064,000.

If $2,000 is too demanding on your pay, you could start investing $20 a week at age 25, or just $1,040 a year. Through the same miraculous power of compounding, that simple investing habit over a lifetime will provide you with about $507,000 when you are 65, assuming that you average a 10 percent return on your money annually. Start increasing the amount you save weekly as soon as you get raises, and you can make it to $1 million or more.

Using Your Calculation: The Advanced Lesson

If you run your calculation now, you will have a ballpark idea about what you are likely to need for the type of retirement you want and what you should save to make it happen.

But keep in mind that none of these calculations is a guarantee. If two or three years after you retire, the stock market goes through what's called a bear market—a scary downturn of at least 20 percent—you could use up your savings quicker than your calculations show. And despite your best efforts, you might have to cut back on your lifestyle.

On the other hand, if you happen to retire at a point when the economy is solid, inflation is controlled, and the stock market is climbing nicely, your savings could mushroom and you could end up with more than you will ever need.

To illustrate the uncertain impact of your investments on your retirement, the Vanguard Retirement Center provides this scenario: Say that you are 65 years old, you have saved $500,000, and you plan to take $25,000 out that year and another 5 percent for each year of retirement. That, of course, is within the range that's considered prudent. During both the first and second years of your retirement, you have some bad luck. The stock market goes into a bad cycle, and your investments lose 10 percent of their value each year—not an unusual occurrence, if you look at history. The third year, the stock market remains troubled, and your investments lose another 5 percent. You have still been removing the 5 percent you need each year from your nest egg. Those withdrawals, plus the nasty market, have left you with only about

$318,300 in your nest egg. And even though the stock market climbs nicely after that and you earn 7.5 percent on your investments for each of the next 20 years, you will run out of money in the 19th year, when you are 84.

Now assume a different scenario: You retire at 65, and the stock market is very kind to you. For every year during the next 19 years, you earn a 7.5 percent return on your money. When you are 84, you have more than $663,060 left.

This happened purely because you avoided a big loss early in retirement. In this scenario, you can better handle a loss in the stock market. Vanguard suggests that, after going through 28 years of retirement, you then lose 5 percent in the stock market and 10 percent during each of the next two years. You die at age 95 and have more than $351,000 left to pass along to your children or favorite charity (see Figure 2.1 for an illustration of how a bad stock market early in retirement hurts worse than one later).

Figure 2.1

You can't predict cycles: Timing is everything in retirement.

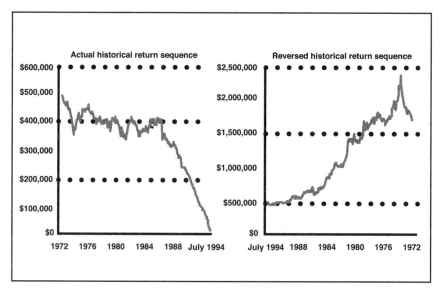

A person retiring in 1973 with $500,000 would have run out of money within 22 years because of the stock market crash in 1973 and 1974 (left), whereas a person retiring in 1994 would have had the good luck of a strong market at the outset, and his $500,000 would have expanded over 22 years (right).

Source: Ibbotson Associates, a Morningstar, Inc., company

Does this uncertainty make you nervous? Do you feel like I just had you run your saving calculation for nothing? You didn't run it for nothing. It was a good starting point. It gave you a target and helped you think about your future. And if you went to a financial planner, he or she would do just the type of calculation I've had you do and would send you on your way with an investment plan, and you'd feel nice and secure.

But the best financial planners don't do that. They realize that the averages typically used in retirement calculations are flawed. They are based on history. When you go to retire, an average alone is not a guarantee. For example, it's true that, historically, the stock market has gone up an average of about 10 percent a year. Yet you must also realize that some years it falls 20 or 30 percent. In 2008, stocks fell 37 percent and kept falling. At the end of the plunge in 2009, people had lost about 57 percent. If you happen to hit one of those dreadful times at the beginning of your retirement, you might run out of savings while you'd like to still be enjoying life.

To plan for unusually bad times, financial planners run what are called Monte Carlo simulations to test how different combinations of stocks and bonds might hold up during a horrible period in the stock market. They use powerful computer programs to analyze a slew of historical events, jumble them up, and then predict what might happen to your retirement savings. These simulations can show you whether you are 50 percent likely to run out of money before you retire or whether you have plenty of money and are 80 percent or 100 percent secure.

This is the type of simulation Charles Schwab researchers ran to come up with the strategy I outlined in the previous pages, of removing only 4 to 5 percent of your savings during the first year of retirement and then adjusting that only slightly higher for inflation each following year.

The Schwab approach was designed to give you a 90 percent certainty that you won't run out of money during 30 years of retirement. But maybe you don't need 90 percent certainty. Maybe you'd be comfortable at 80 percent or 70 percent. Thanks to the Internet, you can run one of these calculations yourself in about a minute's time. Again, you don't need to know any math or be a computer whiz. The complex data is all behind the scenes. Go to the Retirement Income calculator offered by T. Rowe Price, at www3. troweprice.com/ric/RIC.

Still, be aware of what this means. The 57 percent crash of 2008–2009 was an unusual event that doesn't show up clearly when doing one of these calculations. The crash is in the mix, but blurred by long periods of better times. So you could be 90 percent sure that you had plenty of money for retirement, and a crash this severe early in retirement could leave you among the 10 percent who would be hit too hard to make the money last. If that is disconcerting, there is a way to survive when retired. If you hit one of these shocking events, you try for a few years not to pull as much spending money out of savings as you had planned. You will see later in Chapter 11, "Do This," how you can recover.

Meanwhile, to try the Retirement Income calculator and stress-test your savings, you put in information such as your age and when you plan to retire and for how long. I need to explain a couple items so that you enter the right data.

When the calculator asks for your retirement assets, that's the money you have accumulated for retirement. When it asks for your portfolio, it is asking about the combination of stocks, bonds, and cash you will have. (After you have read Chapter 11, you will understand more about this.) If you want to try the calculation now, select the portfolio that's identified as 60/30/10. That means you'll invest 60 percent of your money in stocks, 30 percent in bonds, and 10 percent in cash. That's a classic, or moderate, investment approach.

When you are asked to simulate success, you are being asked to choose how much certainty you want about your savings. Do you want enough money to be 100 percent sure you won't run out? Or will you settle for a 70 to 80 percent chance, which is still fairly reliable? If you drop down to 50 percent, that won't give you much confidence.

Work the calculation and see how you come out. It will tell you how much chance you have of making your retirement savings last, no matter what surprises the stock market might deal you.

Now that you know where you need to head, I tell you how to get there by making wise investments.

3

SAVINGS ON STEROIDS: USE A 401(K) AND AN IRA

If you are like a lot of people, when you hear the word *saving,* the image of some sort of miser shoots into your head. Maybe you envision a pale, humorless guy hunched over a table, painstakingly ticking off numbers on a detailed budget with a pointy pencil—or maybe a penny-pinching parent or relative admonishing you to give up something fun.

You might want to shout, "I'm young, leave me alone! Saving for retirement is for old people—I have plenty of time for that stuffy behavior later in life."

As I have written about saving for retirement over the years, people with that miser image in mind have repeatedly said to me, "If I don't enjoy my youth while I'm young, when will I?" That might explain why Aon Hewitt Consulting Services found that only 54 percent of people in their 20s use 401(k) retirement savings plans when they are offered at work.

But no matter what your age, I'm not urging you to deprive yourself. You might take a more modest vacation than you intend, but you can still take a vacation. You might keep a car longer than you'd prefer, but you will still get around. You might settle for a closet with plenty of shoes instead of one stuffed with them. Maybe you will watch a movie at home with friends instead of going out. You might brew your own coffee in the morning and fill up a mug for the road instead of dropping $3 each day at Starbucks.

If you are 22 and in your first job, all you need to do is come up with $20 a week and add more when you get raises; you should eventually build up $1 million. Make it just $15 a week throughout your working years, and you could still accumulate around $500,000. Or if you are 35 and saving for the first time, you can invest $50 a week and get close to $500,000. Add another $20 a week, and you should approach $700,000. Yet people often don't try investing small amounts because they don't understand the power they have over $10 or $20 a week. When the Employee Benefits Research Institute asked Americans of all ages and all income levels a few years ago whether they could afford to save $20 more a week, most said "Yes." They just didn't think it would do any good.

Of course, $20 does a tremendous amount of good. But you can turn nickels and dimes into hundreds of thousands of dollars only if you are smart about investing it. What's unfortunate is that too often people get the hard part down (the act of saving, or yanking money from their pocket and setting it aside for another day). Then, they get the easy part wrong (the act of sticking their small savings in the right place so that investing transforms a pittance into thousands). This is a shame—and absolutely unnecessary.

You have a couple simple strategies available to you. And if you have an elementary school education, you can master them with little effort. I'm talking about two tools that work almost like alchemy, turning pocket change into a pot of gold over time. One is an IRA, a savings account designed specifically for growing money into a retirement nest egg. (You usually have to set up an IRA away from where you work.) The other might be right under your nose where you work. It might be called a 401(k), a 403(b), a 457, or some other equally uninviting name. (They get their names from tax laws.) All are retirement savings plans, and I explain step by step how to handle them a little later.

First, I want to get past the off-putting names, or perhaps the incessant nagging from someone who has made you want to ignore them. These tools might sound as unfriendly as the miser. But they are powerful money-making machines. Choosing whether to use them is like choosing between driving a car and walking to a destination that's 10 miles away. You might well be able to walk 10 miles, but you'd be silly to try to do it if you are in a hurry to make an appointment in half an hour. If you drive a car instead, the trip takes a few minutes.

Likewise, you can build up retirement savings either the hard way, through devices such as savings accounts at banks, or the easy way, through IRAs and 401(k) plans. Too many people make life hard on themselves because they don't choose the easy investing way.

The Hard Way

If you don't use a 401(k) or an IRA, it's like walking a long distance, and you might never get to your destination because it will take extraordinary, laborious, unfulfilling effort. You will have to deprive yourself either during your savings years or after you retire. But if you use the two simple tools I'm advocating, it will be the opposite. You will feel the difference very quickly between the futile efforts you've been making and the smarter approach.

It will be like driving a car. You will speed toward your destination with very little effort if you start early enough. You won't have to live like a pauper while saving or during retirement.

Here's an example: Let's say you are 35 years old. You have been pulling hard-earned cash out of your paycheck for the past 15 years and diligently saving it in the bank. You have $30,000 and 32 years to go before you retire. When that day comes, you know you will need at least $500,000 to keep up your modest lifestyle. But times have turned rough, and you aren't in a position to save additional money for retirement. The key for you will be to let your existing $30,000 grow effectively.

If you leave that money in a savings account in a bank, what will you have on the day you retire at age 67? Maybe about $46,000— not enough to get you through more than a handful of retirement years.

Now let's look at that same original $30,000 one more time. This time, let's assume that you've been smart. Instead of using a savings account, you have put it all either in your 401(k) or 403(b) savings plan at work or in an IRA, and, invested the money wisely in a mutual fund that contains stocks and bonds. And let's say that you earn an average of 8 percent a year for the next 32 years.

By using either the 401(k) plan at work or an IRA away from work, your $30,000 should become about $385,000 by the time you retire when 67—not the puny $46,000 that would have resulted in a savings account.

So, you see, amassing money doesn't have to be about deprivation. It has to do with being smart about where you stick the money.

What's the Difference?

Why is there such a dramatic difference in what $30,000 can become in a 401(k) or IRA versus a savings account?

Let's start with the 401(k) because it gives you three huge advantages over a savings account: stock market investments, enormous tax savings, and potentially thousands of dollars in free money from your employer.

When you have a savings accounts at a bank, you will never make much money. You might earn about 2 percent a year, if you are lucky. But in 401(k) plans, people can invest in mutual funds that select stocks and bonds. I explain these in Chapter 7, "What's a Mutual Fund?." For now, I just want you to know that, historically, money in the stock market has grown 9.8 percent a year, on average. If you blend stocks with bonds in what's known as a balanced fund, the average gain over many years has been about 8 percent, according to Morningstar's Ibbotson division. That's not a specific guarantee for the future, but if history repeats and you are using good mutual funds in your 401(k), you could make 8 percent a year, on average, instead of the 2 percent in your bank account. That's a tremendous difference over many years of investing.

That's not all. Employers often give you free money when you participate in the 401(k) plans they offer you at work. They give you what's called "a match" or "matching money." For you, it's like getting a raise every year— maybe $1,000 or more simply as a reward for participating in the company 401(k). What could be better? It's free money, and it's a reward for doing what's already good for your future.

Employers don't do this out of the kindness of their hearts. They need a lot of participants in their 401(k) plans so that they can handle all the paperwork and administrative tasks economically. They also provide matching money because, under federal rules, they have to get people of all income levels to be involved in their retirement savings plans. If lower-income people shrug off the 401(k), employers have to cut back on the benefits they give management. Of course, employers don't want to do this because they won't be able to recruit sharp people. Talented managers are well aware of the value of a 401(k) plan, and they want to get everything they possibly can from it.

But don't think of the company match as some kind of plot with weird strings attached. You aren't being unfairly manipulated. What you see your employer offering is real and good. Don't be like half of workers 20 to 29 who ignore the 401(k) they are offered. Take a lesson from the savvy managers at your firm. They are using their 401(k) benefits to the hilt, and you should, too.

Get the Match

Getting free money from your employer is a great deal that you'd be crazy to pass up. Imagine if your boss came to you and said, "We'd like to give you another $1,000 a year for working with us, and you don't have to work one extra hour or take on any more responsibility to get it." Would you even consider telling the boss you weren't interested in the money? I doubt it.

Say you make $50,000 a year at your job, and you can qualify for $1,500 that year in matching money under your plan (3 percent of your pay). If you were 35, did what you needed to qualify for the full match each year, received 3 percent raises a year, and earned an 8 percent return on your money in your 401(k), you would end up with about $237,300 at retirement simply from the free matching money alone—not from any money you personally set aside from a paycheck. Now, that's a deal!

That should be a huge motivator, a sure thing. It's certainly better than betting on the lottery. Still, according to a survey by the Consumer Federation of America, 21 percent of Americans think the "most practical" way to accumulate a few thousand dollars is to win the lottery. Only 26 percent think they can save $200,000.

You did it simply with your employer match. And with your own money plus the free matches, you ended up with a grand total of $712,000—an even better deal!

The Power of Warding Off Taxes

Perhaps the top advantage of them all is that a 401(k) keeps the tax man away from your money year in and year out. You don't pay taxes on the money you put into a 401(k), and you don't pay taxes on the money that builds up in your 401(k) account over the years. Eventually, you pay taxes after you retire and start spending the money you saved. But the impact of delaying taxes is tremendous. I'm not talking chump change—it's potentially hundreds of thousands of dollars.

Avoiding taxes legally is one of the smartest tactics at your disposal to spin tiny savings into gold. Every wealthy person with a financial adviser uses this trick to the fullest. This is how they turn a small fortune into a cushy lifestyle, luxury vacations, and trust funds for their kids. But you don't need an adviser to make your way through the same terrain.

One of the common man's most delicious tax breaks is served to employees at work each day on a platter. It comes through the company 401(k) plan.

When you see a 401(k) plan, it is like posting a "Keep Off" sign on your money to ward off the IRS. And it should beckon you—it says to you, "Put your money here, and Uncle Sam won't touch it." Years can go by, and your original $30,000 can become $50,000. And Uncle Sam won't make you share any of that $20,000 gain with the government. More years can go by, and your original $30,000 can become $500,000. And Uncle Sam still keeps his hands off.

In fact, the way it's possible to amass that $500,000 is by holding Uncle Sam at bay. If each year he was showing up at your doorstep and making you share some of the money you had gained with him, you would end up with nowhere near half a million dollars.

If you put all your money into a savings account, none of it is protected from taxes. Uncle Sam shows up every year at tax time and says, "Give me some of that interest money you have made." You have no choice but to pay because you put the money where it's open season for the government.

Let me show you the contrast in real dollars. Let's go back to that original $30,000 sitting in a savings account in the bank. Look at what taxes do to it if you are in the 25 percent tax bracket. Remember that, if you kept that money in a savings account until you were 67, you would have roughly $46,000. If you had been able to keep the IRS at bay, it would have been better—still nothing to rave about, but better. Instead of $46,000, you would have had about $57,000 when you retired.

So let's leave the bank savings account and look at another equally vulnerable approach to saving.

Mutual Funds Get Taxed

Let's assume that you jumped ahead in this book and learned that mutual funds can do a lot more for your future than a savings account. But let's say that you skipped this chapter about the tax advantages of a 401(k) plan. So you ignore the 401(k) plan at work and also an IRA. You go straight to a mutual fund company and plunk your $30,000 into a solid fund that invests in stocks, and you don't protect it from taxes.

Year after year, you earn good money in that mutual fund—let's say the same 8 percent annually you would have made in your 401(k). But outside your 401(k) or IRA, there is a dramatic difference. Uncle Sam shows up every year for his take and makes you fork over part of the money you made on your mutual funds. The result: On retirement day, you have roughly $171,000, not the $385,000 you would have had if you had simply invested the same $30,000 in your 401(k) plan at work. (I assumed a 25 percent federal tax rate and took a couple liberties with this example.) With an actual 401(k), you would not have been able to invest $30,000 in a single year, but rather could have done it over two years. But I wanted you to see the comparison with the earlier savings account example in which a person invested $30,000 and ended up with only $46,000 at retirement. Meanwhile, if you want to see the impact of your tax rate on savings, try the calculator I used: "How will taxes and inflation affect my savings," at http://calculators.aol.com/ tools/aol/ savings06/tool.fcs.

So amassing money isn't just about digging deeper into your pocket and depriving yourself so much that you feel like a pauper. It's simply about being smart about where you put the money. It's knowing one simple fact: If you aren't paying taxes on your savings year in and year out, the money can grow vigorously. It's like putting your money on steroids. It's the only way to turn $20 a week into a sum close to $1 million. And Uncle Sam wants you to do it so that some day you aren't a destitute old person and a burden on society.

Of course, when you are retired, you will have to pay some taxes on money you remove from your 401(k) for living expenses. By that time, if you have invested well in the ways I describe in this book, you will have amassed a tidy sum and will be able to afford to pay the tax. Also, because you won't be working then, the tax rate you pay might be smaller than what you pay now.

An IRA Instead?

But what if you don't have a 401(k) at work? Only about half of Americans do. You still have another option that is just as good at keeping the IRS at bay so that you can turn meager savings into a retirement treasure chest.

It's an IRA, an individual retirement account. Using one takes a slightly greater effort than using a 401(k) because you usually can't take care of the paperwork right at work. But it's not difficult to do, as you see in Chapter 5, "IRA Decisions: How to Start and Where to Go."

For now I just want you to understand that if you had that very same $30,000 in an IRA and used the very same mutual funds as in a 401(k), the result would be identical after 32 years: At retirement, you would have about $385,000 because Uncle Sam would have had a hands-off policy for your money during the full 32 years you needed to grow it.

Why not just use an IRA and skip a 401(k)? Nothing is wrong with that approach from a tax perspective. But for three reasons, you shouldn't turn your back on your 401(k) at work: The first two I have already provided. If you don't use your 401(k), you essentially tell your employer that you don't want the free money offered to you, and that's just plain stupid. Also, your 401(k) is easy and convenient; it's at your fingertips every day you go to work. Ten minutes spent filling out the paperwork sets the groundwork for making thousands—maybe hundreds of thousands—of dollars.

But there are limits to how much money you are allowed to stash away for retirement without Uncle Sam raiding your account. Based on federal rules, a typical 401(k) lets you put away up to $17,000 a year ($22,500 if you are 50 or older). But you can put only $5,000 into an IRA (or $6,000 if you are 50 or older).

More about those limits later, but now I want you to understand that, in the best of all worlds, you would not choose between a 401(k) and an IRA. You would use both—your 401(k), if you have one, and an IRA. This is especially important if you are approaching retirement and have saved very little. In that case, stashing away just $5,000—or even $6,000—a year probably won't be enough. By putting as much money as possible in both your 401(k) and an IRA, you can make up for some of the lost years. And Uncle Sam will help you by keeping his hands off while you save.

How to Use Your 401(k) or 403(b)

Before we start, make sure you are really using a 401(k), a 403(b), or a similar retirement savings plan offered by your employer. That probably sounds like a ridiculous statement, but it's not.

A few years ago, benefits consultant Hewitt Associates surveyed employees at large companies about their 401(k) plans. What the researchers found was disturbing: A full 29 percent of people who weren't participating in their company 401(k) plans thought they were.

Somehow someone got some wires crossed—maybe because many employees find 401(k) plans so confusing, and maybe because employers often fail to give their staff understandable information. Regardless, for these workers, a disaster was in the making.

If these people thought they were building retirement money for their futures, they would face a rude awakening on retirement day. They were on their way to having nothing because they weren't putting a penny into the 401(k) plan, and their employer wasn't doing it, either.

Don't assume that you are participating in your 401(k) plan at work simply because you have heard that your company offers the plan. To participate, you usually must take action. In many companies, you have to notify your employer that you want to participate. You do this by signing a form or saying "Yes" on your company's intranet site. The company likely calls this "enrolling." When you do it, you are telling your employer to remove some money from your paycheck each payday and to keep the money for you in the 401(k) plan.

Notice that I said you *usually* have to take action by enrolling in your 401(k). Since a new law passed recently, many companies are beginning to sign up employees for the 401(k) plan without asking for their permission. This is called automatic enrollment, and if your employer does it, the approach is good. The idea is to get more people to take part in this critical preparation for retirement instead of waiting while people procrastinate.

Just make sure that either you or your employer has signed you up. Don't guess. You don't want to miss out on this.

After you have enrolled in your 401(k), every time you get a paycheck, a little money will be removed—as much or as little as you want. But don't feel trapped on this. Even if your employer automatically removes money from your paycheck and deposits it in your 401(k) account without asking for your permission, you are the boss. You can change your mind at any time about the amount. You can even stop contributing anything, if you want, and you can increase what you save. You can make changes constantly.

Changing Your Mind

If you tell your employer to remove $20 from each paycheck, that's what your employer will do. On each payday, instead of putting the $20 into your paycheck, your employer will put it into a 401(k) account with your name on it—like a bank account, only with all the advantages I just described.

A month later, if you decide that $20 is too much, but you think you can afford to give up $10 from your paycheck, you tell your employer to drop your old request and start putting $10 into your 401(k) account on payday. It's simple to do. You contact the person or office at your company that handles benefits such as health insurance and either fill out a form or visit the Internet site provided by your employer. It takes less than a minute to do.

If you put aside $10 for several months and you are able to pay your bills and have some fun, you might decide that you can afford to put more into the 401(k). Then you just tell your employer that you want to make a change.

You could raise the amount to $15 per paycheck if you wanted and go higher over time—especially when you get raises.

Whatever feels comfortable to you is fine. Making changes is perfectly acceptable—your employer expects them. At many jobs, you can change the size of your contributions every day, if you want, although they won't show up until the next paycheck.

If you suddenly get strapped for cash and decide that you need every penny from your paycheck, you can go back to your employer's benefits office and say that you want to stop contributing to the 401(k) plan for a while. Even if you want some more fun money for a few months, you can go back to your employer and stop contributing. No one will ask you why you made a change; they simply do what you request.

Meanwhile, any money that you already contributed stays in an account with your name on it. Your employer acts just like a bank and holds on to the money for you for as long as you want.

As months and years pass, the money in your account keeps earning interest, or what is called a return. As the years go by, your return makes the pot of cash grow larger. When you retire and no longer get a paycheck from a job, you pay yourself out of that pot of money you were kind enough to provide for your own future.

Getting Started

To get started for the first time in your company's 401(k), you simply need to call or visit the person or office at work that handles benefits. If you don't know where to go, think about the last time you received information on health insurance. It probably originated at the same place that handles the 401(k), or at least someone in that office can point you to the right person. You can also ask your boss or coworkers. It's not a dumb question.

When you contact the benefits staff, say that you want to start contributing to the 401(k) plan. You'll get a short form to fill out or learn where to find it online. On that form, you state the percentage of your salary that you want to put away for retirement each time you get a paycheck.

You don't have to figure out a dollar amount. All you need to state is the percentage of your income you will put aside. Some people just pick an amount that feels comfortable—somewhere between 1 percent and 15 percent, or maybe even more. But if you want to know what a percentage will mean to you in the dollars you will take home with each paycheck, an Internet calculator can give you the full picture in a few minutes.

Large employers often offer you dandy calculators over the Internet to figure out what to do with 401(k) plans. If yours doesn't, simply go to www. paycheckcity.com and use the 401(k) Planner calculator or see "How Do 401(k) Salary Deductions Affect My Take-Home Pay?" at http://calculators. aol.com/tools/aol/paycheck01/tool.fcs. You can play with different percentages to see what feels right to you.

For example, if you are making $35,000 a year and you get paid every two weeks, the calculator shows that if you have your employer put 5 percent of your pay into the 401(k) plan, your take-home pay will be reduced $59.50 every time you get a paycheck. That means each week you will have only $29.75 less to spend than you normally would. And if you are in your early 20s and keep it up, that small weekly sacrifice could eventually turn into $1 million—and almost certainly will become that if you add part of each raise in the future.

While you are at the calculator, give yourself a chance to see what would happen if you devote just a little more of your pay to the future. Redo the calculation to show what 10 percent would do to your take-home pay. In the example of making $35,000 a year, giving up 10 percent would mean $119 less in spending money every two weeks. That's $59.50 a week. But the larger amount greatly increases the chances of building up a comfortable nest egg, especially for a person who never saved anything during his or her 20s.

A rule of thumb states that if you put 10 percent of your pay into a retirement account, starting with your first job, you will have what you need later in life. Some financial planners feel more comfortable with 15 percent because healthcare costs are growing so much and could drain savings fast for a retiree.

There are limits, however. If you have a 401(k) in 2012, you can put as much as $17,000 into it for the year and get the full tax benefits. If you are 50 or older, you can add another $5,500, for a total of $22,500.

The limits change from year to year based on inflation and tax policies. So look for alterations in 401(k) and IRA limits each year and adjust your contributions to the times. Table 3.1 provides the limits for 2012.

Table 3.1

Annual Limits for Retirement Accounts

Retirement Savings Plan	Eligible Individuals Contribute Up to	Employer Contributions
Traditional Tax Deductible IRA	$5,000 ($6,000 if 50 years old or older)	None
Roth IRA	$5,000 ($6,000 if 50 years old or older)	None
401(k), 403(b) 457	$17,000 ($22,500 if 50 or older)	Employer match varies; often is 3% of pay
SIMPLE IRA	$11,500 ($14,000 if 50 or older)	2% or 3% of employee's pay. Deductible as a business expense.
SEP-IRA	0	Up to 25% of participant's compensation or $50,000, whichever is less. Deductible as a business
Individual (Solo) 401(k)	$17,000 ($22,500 if 50 or older)	The lesser of up to 25% of pay or up to $50,000. The dollar amount must be reduced by any employee deferrals made to the plan.
		The combined employer & employee contributions can't exceed $50,000. ($55,500 if 50 or older.)
		Deductible as a business expense.
Profit Sharing	0	Up to $50,000, but not more than 25% of pay

*2012 limits. Check www.IRS.gov for annual inflation adjustments, rule changes, and your circumstance

More Tax Help Than You Imagined

If you did the take-home pay calculation I suggested in the preceding section, you might be a little perplexed at this point.

You might see that when you contribute 5 percent of $35,000 to your 401(k), you give up $59.50 in take-home pay. But you are actually putting $72.92 into the plan for your retirement.

How can that be? You might assume that your reduction in take-home pay would be exactly the same number as your contribution to the 401(k) plan. But you have just uncovered one of the truly delightful parts of using a

401(k) plan. I told you previously that Uncle Sam doesn't touch the money you make within the plan. But it gets even better than that.

The government is so worried that you won't save enough for retirement that it gives you a tax break right up front every time you put a penny into the 401(k) plan. This, too, should come as delicious news for you, especially if you are worried that your 401(k) contributions will immediately slash your ability to pay your bills. What it means is this: You aren't really sacrificing nearly as much today to save for your future. Because Uncle Sam immediately cuts your taxes on anything you put into your 401(k), you are still keeping more take-home pay than you would have imagined.

If you earn $35,000, the government reduces taxes on your paycheck by $13.42 cents. If you contribute the same $72.92 to your 401(k) on every payday, you will save $13.42 on taxes each time. For the year, that's about $348 in tax savings—not bad at all. It makes saving for retirement cheaper than you think.

Here's a quick way to envision your tax savings: If you are in the 25 percent tax bracket, every $1,000 you put into your 401(k) cuts your federal taxes by $250 that year. So you aren't really doing without $1,000 of your pay. You are simply doing without $750 because Uncle Sam is letting you keep a larger chunk of the money you have earned.

So when you use your 401(k), it's like buying a better future for yourself by using a 25 percent discount. You aren't stashing away your money at full price. Instead, it's as though you are making use of a 25 percent off coupon. That lets you acquire a better future without living like a pauper.

Take Baby Steps

Increasingly, employers are not asking their employees whether they want to participate in the 401(k) plan at work. Instead, these employers automatically put employees into it. As I said previously, don't assume that you are in or out of your company's 401(k) plan without asking your benefits office.

Yet if your company has an "automatic plan," your employer might be removing 3 percent of your pay—or some other amount—and putting it into an account for you every time you get a paycheck.

If that is the case, you are fortunate. You are taking a step in the right direction. Don't simply turn your back on your 401(k) and consider the deed done, however. You still must think about what you will need for retirement, and 3 percent of your pay isn't going to do it for you.

Consider moving your contribution up to 5 percent or 10 percent of your pay. If you have never saved for retirement and are in your 30s, 40s, or 50s, this is especially critical. Go to your benefits staff, request a form, and simply change the percentage of pay they will take from each paycheck. If you want to know what this will do to your paycheck, try the calculators I mentioned: See www.paycheckcity.com and use the 401(k) Planner calculator, or go to "How Do 401(k) Salary Deductions Affect My Take-Home Pay?" at http://calculators.aol.com/tools/aol/paycheck01/tool.fcs. If you don't have a computer, you can use one free in a public library.

If you don't think you can afford to put 5 or 10 percent of your pay into the 401(k), experiment with a lesser amount—knowing that you can increase it later. If you can't decide what you can spare from your paycheck, don't wait to figure it out. Indecision is your enemy. You could lose valuable months and years procrastinating.

Jump in now, and promise yourself to think about it again later. Write it on the calendar so that you actually do it.

Can You Spare a Dime?

If you are terrified about getting by if you save some money in the 401(k), start with a low number—even 1 percent. If you want to prove to yourself that you can survive without a little money, try an exercise: Every day, empty spare change from your pockets or purse and put it in a jar next to the sink. At the end of the week, add up the amount. That's the money you lived without during the week. Did you survive without it?

You probably did just fine. So make use of that revelation. Go to your benefits office immediately and start having your employer remove that amount from your paycheck. I have been suggesting this to people for years in my columns and have asked people to let me know if saving that amount of money each week was ever too much. I have never heard anyone say it was impossible to get by, and a lot of people have said it was just the assurance they needed to get started.

If you start out in your 401(k) with a very small contribution, ask yourself in a few weeks how you are doing. Are you paying your bills and putting food on the table? Are you still having a little fun in life? Put a date on a calendar so that you don't forget to ask the questions. If you are doing just fine, go back to your benefits office and increase the amount—maybe go to 5 percent. Don't wait, because days will turn into months, and months into the lost power of compounding—thousands of dollars.

If you are already at 5 percent, go to 7 percent. Also promise yourself that when you get a raise, you will put half of it into the 401(k) plan. Don't wait for the first paycheck reflecting the raise. Get a 401(k) form as soon as you hear that the raise is coming, and increase the percent so that you deploy some of your raise to your retirement future from day 1.

That's often the most painless way of increasing retirement savings because people don't miss money they never were used to having.

Finding Cash

Over the years, numerous people have contacted me to tell me where they found money to save—painless ways that don't require them to live like a pauper or cut out the things they love.

Here are some of their suggestions:

- Dump one cell phone in a two-cell-phone family. Save about $480.

- Dump caller ID on the land-line phone into your home. Save about $90.

- Use calling cards instead of a long-distance carrier. Save about $100.

- Get rid of the second phone line into your house. Save about $275.

- Shop for groceries with coupons, or shop at a cheaper store. Save about $780.

- Carry higher deductibles on home and auto insurance. Save $300.

- Eliminate one coffee-shop coffee or one alcoholic beverage a day. Save $730.

- Stop smoking. Save about $1,450.

- Cut out two restaurant meals a month. Save about $350.

- Use the library instead of buying books. Save $180.

- Cancel cable TV. Save $600.

- Order prescriptions through the mail. Your insurance company likely charges a lower copayment than a drug store.

Also beware of missing credit card payments. Often you are hit with a $29 charge, and your interest rate can rise if your payments are late. In addition, be aware of the money you waste when you carry a credit card balance from month to month. The money you are paying in interest could have gone toward savings. To get rid of credit card debt, pay some amount above the minimum, and get techniques from reading Liz Pulliam Weston's book *Deal with Your Debt* (Prentice Hall, 2005).

If you have raised children and they are now on their own, you might find additional savings simply by cutting back life insurance. For more saving ideas, see financial planner Sue Stevens' list "101 Ways to Cut Expenses," at www.morningstar.com.

Then try to look for small savings in your own lifestyle. For the next two weeks, carry a pocket notebook. Every time you buy something—whether it's a treat from the candy machine, a magazine, or whatever—mark down the item and price.

At the end of two weeks, look over the list and put a check mark by the items you wouldn't really have missed. Tally it up. The dollar amount is what you could save. Let's say it's just $5 a week. If you invested that amount week after week for about 40 years and earned a 10 percent return, you'd have more than $138,000. Try it yourself with the Quick Savings Calculator in the personal finance section of the Money CNN Web site: http://cgi.money.cnn.com/tools.

Qualifying for the Match

Although I told you to start out by contributing only 1 percent, if that is the only way you can feel comfortable, there is a better way if you can swing it. Put enough of your own paycheck into the 401(k) each payday to qualify for every penny of matching money your employer provides.

It's impossible for me to tell you how much you need to put aside to get all the free money your employer is willing to give you. That's because different companies use different formulas. You can ask your benefits office what you must do to qualify for the maximum matching money your employer provides.

Look at why it matters. Assume that you are 25 and are making $35,000. You get a very common match from your employer: 50 cents on every dollar you contribute, up to 6 percent of your salary. So at age 25, you decide to put in the full 6 percent of your salary, or $2,100. And your employer provides the full match, $1,050.

Every year for the next 40 years, you contribute 6 percent of your salary so that you get the largest match possible from your employer. The result: With that matching money, your contributions, and an 8 percent return annually in your 401(k), you'll have about $1.2 million when you retire. And your employer's matching money was not chump change in the outcome. If your employer hadn't been giving you any match and you had been socking away the same 6 percent year after year, you would have had only about $809,000 at retirement.

As you decide what to put into your 401(k) plan, know what you must do to get the maximum matching money from your employer. If you contemplate passing up some of that money, picture your boss standing in front of you with outstretched hands brimming with $400,000 in cash. He says to you, "I'd like you to have this." As a $1,000 bill falls from the pile and floats to the ground, do you say, "That's very nice of you, sir, but I think I'll pass"?

Instead, try calculating the impact of your employer's match using the 401(k) Calculator at www.bloomberg.com/personal-finance/calculators/401k/. Incidentally, besides a starting salary of $35,000, I figured in raises of 3 percent a year for each of the 25-year-old's 40 years of work.

Procrastination—Not Money—Hurts

So now you have a decision to make: Just how much money will you put into your 401(k)? Don't back-burner that decision—if you do, all the research into 401(k) behavior shows that you will put off the decision for months and maybe years. You will get busy working at your job, carrying out the garbage, or driving the kids to music lessons and soccer games, and you'll forget about it. Instead, go to your benefits office right now while you are thinking about it; if you start with a small contribution, mark on a calendar when you will make yourself consider increasing your 401(k) contribution.

Don't think of this as a sacrifice, or you might not get started. Instead, look at it as helping yourself. You are making an investment in your future, not depriving yourself. Think of the kindness you are showing yourself by starting now. Consider that a 20-year-old can become a millionaire by retirement simply by investing about $20 a week. Yet a 35-year-old who wants to be a millionaire, and has done nothing about it, has to give up a lot more per paycheck to get there—about $87 a week. For a 50-year-old, it's about $450 a week.

So no matter what your age, move into action now. Tell yourself that if you get into gear now, you will remove the chance that you will deprive yourself later.

If you are like 36 percent of people who don't participate in their 401(k) plans, you might be saying to yourself, "I just can't spare a dime." But the evidence shows that you can. Hewitt Associates studied thousands of 401(k) plans and found that inertia, not money, seems to be the biggest deterrent to saving.

The consultants looked at what people do when they have to sign up for 401(k) plans and how that differs from the few companies that don't require people to sign up. In about 10 percent of companies, people aren't required to sign up for the 401(k). Their employer simply enrolls them automatically and starts removing a little money from their paycheck.

Now, here's the interesting part. In companies that put people into the plan automatically, workers have to go to the benefits office and fill out a form if they don't want to be in the 401(k) plan. In other words, it's the opposite process of the usual. The action step is to fill out a form saying "No" rather than filling out a form saying "Yes." In that case, guess what happens?

Very few people bother to say "No." Hewitt found that only about 10 percent of people decide to opt out of the 401(k) plan when their employer put them into it automatically. So somehow they get by financially with a tiny contribution coming out of their paycheck each month for retirement.

What's the explanation for this huge discrepancy? Why do only 10 percent say they can't put money away for retirement versus the 36 percent who don't when it's up to them to make a decision? Hewitt's answer: procrastination, not money, is why most people skip the 401(k).

Most of us can give up a little of what we have earned to provide for our future. In fact, Fidelity investments has calculated that a 25-year-old who earns $35,000 and gets a 1.5 percent raise over the cost of inflation each year will make $1.9 million over a lifetime.

So don't let valuable years go by for you. If your employer doesn't enroll you automatically in the 401(k) plan, go fill out your form now.

And if you think you are already using your 401(k) plan, ask the benefits staff to confirm it. Ask for a statement that shows how much money you are putting into the plan and where it's going. You might get overloaded with material at this point. You will probably see a befuddling mix of gobbledygook. But don't worry about that now. By the time you finish reading the chapters on mutual funds and investing, this stuff will never be vexing to you again. You will look at today's mess of 401(k) choices with the same familiarity you look at the list of flour, salt, and sugar in a recipe.

For now, I just want to encourage you to start putting money into the 401(k) if you haven't already done so.

Leaving Your Job

If you change jobs, all the 401(k) money you accumulated at your old job continues to belong to you. You have some options: You can either take the money with you or leave it in the 401(k) plan at your old job.

If you take it with you, do not spend it, because you will pay dearly for that mistake. Uncle Sam will show up and charge you a 10 percent penalty, plus taxes. In addition, you will cut off your future by losing the power of compounding to make your money grow huge.

If you leave your job, do one of three things: Leave your money in your old 401(k), ask your employer to transfer it to the 401(k) at your new job, or open an IRA (as I describe in Chapter 5) and have your old employer transfer your old 401(k) money directly into the IRA.

Make sure you follow the rules, using an official transfer, or "rollover." Only that will insulate you from getting slapped with a shocking tax bill.

Leaving your money in your old 401(k) is the easiest approach. If you don't like your investment choices there, moving it to an IRA will give you all the choices you could want. Uncle Sam will continue to keep his hands off your money so it can grow.

Emergency Bailout

If you have a 401(k) and run into an emergency—or just need cash—you can borrow money from yourself in your 401(k). I want you to know this because it should enhance your level of comfort, knowing that if you are in financial trouble, you have options.

But I also want to tell you not to raid your 401(k) if you can possibly help it. If you do, there are stringent rules. You generally can borrow money at any time, but you also must repay the money with interest within five years, or Uncle Sam will tax you hard—not just the taxes you'd normally owe, but a penalty, too.

Meanwhile, borrowing works in reverse on the power of compounding. You could slash thousands of dollars from your future. So, resist friends who tell you that your 401(k) is an easy source of cash for something you *want* rather than *need*. If they are dipping into their 401(k) plans, they are undermining all the hard years of saving they have put into it.

If you have a home and want to borrow for a home improvement, a home equity loan is usually a smarter approach. If you are sending children to college, dipping into your 401(k) could reduce financial aid grants, or free money offered by colleges.

Students and parents can borrow money for college through federal loans available in college financial aid offices. These are better options than robbing your future by tapping a 401(k). Remember, after graduation your child has a lifetime to pay off college loans, but the time is drawing near for your retirement. And if you run short of money in your 70s because you drained your 401(k) to pay for your child's college, no bank will give you a loan to buy groceries and medicine.

4

AN IRA: EVERY AMERICAN'S TREASURE TROVE

If you have earned any money working this year, you can open an IRA or a Roth IRA. And you should.

If you haven't worked for pay but have a spouse who has, you can still open an IRA or a Roth IRA. And you should.

In fact, even if you are in elementary school and mow lawns, wash cars, baby-sit, or do anything else for pay, you can open an IRA or a Roth IRA. And if you do, you will be setting yourself up to become a millionaire.

That's because IRAs, particularly Roth IRAs, are powerful money-making machines. And the earlier in life you start one of these miraculous individual retirement accounts, the wealthier you will be.

Nothing makes the point more clearly than an illustration often used in seminars to educate financial planners: Jack Surgent, a certified public accountant in Devon, Pennsylvania, who trains planners, explains how one of his clients is turning a child into a multimillionaire. It all started when the child got her first IRA when she was only about two years old. Here's what's happened.

Surgent's client is a businessman who used photos of his toddler in business promotional materials. Then he paid the child $3,000 for being a model and put the entire paycheck into a Roth IRA for her.

It was perfectly legal. Although the toddler didn't know it, she was doing work for pay. That's the criteria that must apply when opening an IRA or a Roth IRA, a close relative of a regular IRA.

Look at the impact of this creative strategy: Surgent notes that if the parent repeats the same process of paying his child $3,000 a year for modeling for each of the next three years and puts the money each time into the Roth IRA, the child will be a millionaire when she retires in 60 years. Actually, it's a lot better than a millionaire. It's not far fetched to anticipate $4.2 million if she averages a 10 percent return per year.

And here's the shocking part: The child will use only a total of $12,000 of her own pay—just $3,000 a year for four years—to amass that fortune. If she never adds another penny of new money to her Roth IRA after she is 5 years old, she is likely to accumulate her $4.2 million fortune.

So if finances get tight later in life or she gets busy sending her own kids to summer camp and college as she ages, she won't have to worry about saving for retirement.

Keep in mind there are no bizarre get-rich-quick investment strategies or hot stock tips involved here. Surgent isn't suggesting anything other than a simple investment in a stock mutual fund that invests in the entire stock market. I explain how to make such an investment in Chapter 13, "Index Funds: Get What You Pay For." But if that investment simply earns 8 percent on average a year, the toddler model will go into retirement with about $1.4 million.

How can this be? How can you turn $12,000 into $1.4 million without any slick tricks whatsoever?

It happens for two reasons: First, the child is so young that she has years upon years to earn interest on that $12,000, using the magic of compounding described in Chapter 2, "Know What You'll Need." Second, an IRA—whether a traditional IRA or a Roth IRA—doesn't get taxed at all while the money sits in the account, growing bigger and bigger over the years.

I explain the difference between a traditional IRA and a Roth IRA in the next chapter. For now, just think of the two IRAs as brothers—similar in many ways, but with a few unique characteristics when it comes to profoundly helpful tax savings. Both shield your tiny savings from taxes so that you accumulate hundreds of thousands of dollars—or, after many years, even millions. So when I refer to IRAs, I am referring to what either a Roth IRA or a traditional IRA will do for you. And a little later, I explain the fine points and help you select one.

Now, I want you to understand that, similar to the 401(k) I described in the preceding chapter, an IRA (whether a traditional IRA or a Roth IRA) has a "Keep Out" sign on it meant specifically for the IRS. Uncle Sam stays away from the interest (or "return") you earn during all the years of saving and investing. The toddler's money can turn into $50,000, and the IRS won't touch a penny of the earnings. It can become $500,000, and the "Keep Out" sign will keep turning the IRS away. It can even turn into $5 million, and at tax time each year, the government still won't show up and ask for anything.

In fact, if you use a traditional IRA correctly, the only time Uncle Sam shows up with an outstretched hand is when you retire and start taking some money out of the account. Then you pay taxes just like you would on a pay-check. But you pay taxes only on the amount you take out of the account per year. The money in the account can still keep growing, untouched by Uncle Sam. That's valuable.

Consider an example. Imagine that you save throughout your entire life in a traditional IRA and have $500,000 in it when you retire at age 65. You aren't getting a paycheck from a job anymore, so you plan to start using your IRA to give yourself a paycheck for living expenses and fun. You take $20,000 out of the IRA for the year and pay taxes on it, just like you would on a regular paycheck. Meanwhile, the $480,000 left within the IRA is still growing, nicely protected from taxes.

Roth IRAs are even better than this. Uncle Sam stays away forever, even after you've retired. But more about that later.

The key is this: With any IRA, you get a fabulous deal that you cannot get with a savings account or a mutual fund that isn't protected in an IRA or a 401(k). Remember, Uncle Sam anoints both IRAs and 401(k) plans with tax protection. If you save your money anywhere else, Uncle Sam shows up every year at tax time and requires that you give him some of the money you earned. Then you're basically throwing away the easy money.

How much? Say you are in the 25 percent tax bracket, you have $10,000 invested for retirement, and you earn 8 percent a year on the money for 35 years. If the money is protected in an IRA, you'd amass about $148,000. If you invested the same money in an account that Uncle Sam can access, you'd end up with only about $77,000.

As of this writing, Congress is worried about the lack of saving by Americans and is considering other inducements that will help you save without paying taxes. In the future, you might encounter more tax-protected types of accounts that will work as well as today's IRAs or 401(k) plans. No matter what the government ends up calling these future accounts—whether it's a traditional IRA, a Roth IRA, a 401(k), or a newly designed account with a name like Lifetime Super Duper IRA—these accounts will be valuable to you for one key reason: You can build up savings without paying taxes. That's potentially worth hundreds of thousands of dollars to you. If you bypass any of these accounts and depend instead on those without tax savings, you will shortchange yourself thousands of dollars.

Let's go back to the lucky 2-year-old who put her $12,000 in modeling money into a Roth IRA before she could even read. If her father had put that money into an account that would have been taxed every year, she would have ended up at retirement with only about $1 million instead of the $4.2 million.

The message is irrefutable: Save money in a traditional IRA, a Roth IRA, a 401(k), or a combination of them because they are protected from taxes. If you are young enough, you might even be able to turn $20 a week into $1 million. Certainly, saving this way is the easiest route to building up retirement money without living like a pauper when young or old.

More on the Magical Power of Compounding

While you have the rich toddler on your mind, I want to return briefly to the miraculous principle of compounding I explained in Chapter 2. Watching compounding turn $12,000 into $4.2 million should be a constant motivator from this day forth. Hopefully, it will entice you at any age to put whatever cash you can possibly spare to work in an IRA, to make compounding work for you. Starting now gives you a jump on the future.

Ignore compounding, and you will have to live more like a pauper late in your savings years or during retirement than if you had simply started saving—or saved more—a few years earlier.

Let's look beyond the toddler. Imagine a 16-year-old with a job and a benevolent grandparent. If she puts $2,000 a year into a Roth IRA, does the same thing for the next six years, and never deposits another penny of new money, the 16-year-old will have $1.1 million at age 65 if it grows by 10 percent a year on average. That's $1.1 million for what? Just $2,000 for each of seven years, or a total of only $14,000 out of pocket.

Compare that to a person who doesn't start a first IRA until age 32. That person can contribute $2,000 every single year until retirement and won't come near the $1.1 million. Even if she earns the same 10 percent a year as the younger saver, she will have less than $500,000. She took a total of $66,000 out of pocket to end up with about $600,000 less at retirement than the 16-year-old with a helpful grandparent.

Now let's look at it a little differently. Let's say you're like most people, and your father wasn't working with a financial adviser clever enough to put you on the road to becoming a millionaire when you were a toddler. And Granny wasn't capable of throwing $2,000 your way when you were a teenager.

Instead, you open your first IRA when you are 25 years old. Your paycheck is much too small to allow you to put the maximum of $5,000 into an IRA. But you decide to dig deep and come up with $3,000. You open your first IRA, and every year for the rest of your working life, you put another $3,000 into the IRA. And let's assume that you average a 9 percent return on the money each year, a more modest expectation than I used for the 16-year-old.

When you retire at age 65, you will have about $1.1 million. And what did it take to get there? Only $3,000 a year, or $250 a month. In other words, to have $1.1 million, you had to take a total of only $120,000 out of your pocket for the full 40 years. Not bad! Compounding did most of the heavy lifting for you, and because the money was in an IRA, Uncle Sam kept his hands off, too. Consequently, you didn't have to sacrifice and live like a pauper when you were young—and you won't have to when retired, either.

Let's say you didn't start at 25 because rent was killing you. Ten years pass, and you are 35. You are now suffocating from house payments and haven't stashed away a penny for retirement. But the news stories about the demise of Social Security are starting to make you worry. So you kick into action and put $3,000 into your first IRA. You've got the commitment in place now, so for every year until retirement, you put $3,000 into an IRA.

But the 10 years you lost between your 25th and 35th birthdays were very valuable. Instead of having the $1.1 million that you would have had if you had started stashing away $3,000 a year at age 25, your $3,000 a year in savings will end up at less than $500,000, even if your investments make the very same return as we assumed for the 25-year-old: 9 percent a year.

You can fix this, of course, but it will cost you. If you want to amass $1 million, you have to save about $6,730 a year every year until retirement instead of $3,000. So for the next 30 years, you remove almost $202,000 from your pocket, put it into your IRA, and average a 9 percent return annually on your investments. You won't get to the $1.1 million that the

25-year-old amassed by giving up a mere $120,000 over her working years to build a future, but you still accumulate a nice sum without causing yourself great pain.

But now let's look at the painful way of saving for retirement. Perhaps the house payments and the wear and tear on the paycheck from everything from rising energy costs to soccer equipment for the kids have made saving seem impossible for the past 20 years. You are 45 now, with nothing saved for retirement. Soon the kids will be starting college, and you gulp at the $100,000 four-year-college price tag. But you tell yourself that saving for retirement is now or never.

So you come up with $3,000, open an IRA, and do the same thing year after year until you retire at 65. Like the 25-year-old, you are making a 9 percent annual return on your money. But the outcome is nowhere near $1.1 million. Instead, on retirement day, you will have accumulated only about $167,000.

If you decide at age 45 that you still want to shoot for $1 million, you might still be able to do it. You might not have to live like a pauper, but you will definitely have to dig deep into your pocket and make some sacrifices. To get to $1 million in 20 years, if you earn a 9 percent return on your investments, you will have to stash away about $17,900 a year. That's a total of about $358,600 out of pocket for 20 years. Compounding is still doing the heavy lifting for you, but with only 20 years before you retire, even magic has its limits.

5

IRA Decisions:
How to Start and
Where to Go

Just about any American with a TV set has heard the term *IRA* because brokerage firms and mutual fund companies tout the savings devices in their ads. That's not surprising. Besides the fact that IRAs (individual retirement accounts) are invaluable for individuals saving for retirement, they are about a $5 trillion business for financial services companies.

One out of every four retirement dollars is in an IRA, according to the Investment Company Industry, the mutual fund industry's trade group. About 40 percent of U.S. households have an IRA—we're talking about 46 million households.

Despite a familiarity with the term *IRA*, most Americans aren't sure what to do with them, which may be why most households still aren't taking part.

Over the years, I've received numerous calls from people like Jessica, who called me one day because her grandmother had sent her one of my columns urging people to open IRAs. Life had been a struggle for Jessica's grandmother. Her husband had died years earlier, and she was living only on Social Security. She had no pension and no savings.

Obviously, Jessica's grandmother hoped for a better life for her granddaughter, so Jessica listened when her grandmother suggested that she start an IRA. Immediately, Jessica appreciated the logic.

Jessica was 23—years away from retiring—but she told me she didn't want to end up like her 76-year-old grandmother, "sitting in a La-Z-Boy in front of a TV without the money to do anything else." Jessica knew she would need savings for a better life. Yet she couldn't imagine finding enough cash to open an IRA. My column said people could put $5,000 into an IRA. On an income of $25,000, Jessica said coming up with $5,000 was about as plausible as "looking in the mirror and seeing Paris Hilton."

She had made a common mistake. You don't need $5,000 to open an IRA. In fact, you don't even need $2,000, a frequent misconception that dates back to the early days of IRAs. Then people were allowed to put up to $2,000 in an IRA each year. But $2,000 was the *maximum* yearly contribution allowed by the government, never a minimum.

Recently, the maximum level has been $5,000 a year for people under 50 and $6,000 for people 50 and older. But there is no minimum whatsoever, and there never has been.

Tiny amounts of money are perfectly acceptable. The U.S. government, which sets the rules for IRAs, wouldn't object if you opened an IRA with just a few pennies. Financial institutions, however, might not want to bother with such a small amount because it would be a bookkeeping nightmare for them. Some mutual fund companies, such as Vanguard, want you to come through the door with $3,000.

Still, depositing a lot of money is not necessary. Some fine mutual fund companies let individuals open IRAs with as little as $50 if the person promises to put an additional $50 into the IRA every month. I told Jessica that if she invested $50 every month—or less than $12 a week—for the next 43 years in a solid mutual fund that invested in the stock market, she would probably have close to $400,000 at retirement.

That, of course, would put her in a lot better condition than her grandmother, but not good enough. "Get started with $50 a month," I said, "and then as you get raises, add at least half of that amount to your IRA."

I would have told her to do the same thing with a 401(k), but she didn't have that choice at work. Consequently, opening an IRA was vital to her future because it was her only tax-efficient way to save for retirement.

If you are looking for a firm that will let you start an IRA with $50, consider T. Rowe Price. I recommended that Jessica open the IRA and invest the money in the T. Rowe Price Total Equity Market Index mutual fund, a simple investment in the full stock market. (I discuss this further in Chapter 13, "Index Funds: Get What You Pay For.")

First, I want you to be aware of other common misconceptions about IRAs so that misunderstandings don't keep you from making yourself wealthy the easy way. And I explain, as I did to Jessica, where to go and how to open an IRA.

Married, with No Job

When one spouse stays at home while the other works, they too often miss out on an IRA. That's not necessary. They assume—incorrectly—that the spouse who isn't working cannot open an IRA.

It's understandable that they might make this mistake, but it's especially unfortunate for women who stay home to raise children. Statistically, such women are likely to end up in poverty or experience tough times late in life because their sporadic work history leads to low Social Security payments. Also, family savings often get decimated caring for a sick husband, yet the wife goes on to outlive him by 17 or more years.

So whether a spouse is working or not, both married people should open an IRA and fill it to the max each year, if possible. As a rule, a person can't put more money into an IRA than he or she earns from a job or a business. But there is an exception for a person who is not working and has a spouse who is working. Both spouses can have IRAs, and they can each put $5,000 into the account. So for a couple, that's a total of $10,000 a year as long as one or both spouses have earned at least that amount.

If you are over 50, you can stash away even more: a total of $6,000 per person or $12,000 per couple. The federal government recently raised the limits for those over 50 because Congress is well aware that people are far behind with their retirement savings. Political leaders are hoping that if they give people a chance to catch up after their kids have finished college and moved away from home, parents will jump into action.

If you are among them, don't breathe a sigh of relief the day you see your child in a cap and gown, and figure that you can start spending the thousands that were landing in the bursar's office over the past four years. When you return home after the graduation ceremony, open an IRA or increase what's in your IRA. While you're at it, increase your 401(k) contributions, too.

If you forget, jump into action the day you get the graduation photos back. As you gaze proudly at the pictures of your child, think, "I'm now going to be proud of myself for taking control of my future." Then get thee to your neglected IRA.

Where Do I Go? What Do I Do?

You can open an IRA in many places: your bank, a company that creates and sells mutual funds, a financial planner, or a brokerage firm.

If you use a local bank or brokerage firm, walk into the office and say that you'd like to open an IRA. If you deal with a mutual fund company instead, contact the company by telephone through its toll-free number or visit the company's Web site. (I supply several names and contact information in later chapters, and you can find any name through a Google search on the Internet or through help in the business section at a public library.)

Whether you start by phone, on the Web, or through direct human contact, the process of opening an IRA is virtually the same everywhere. It's an easy, quick task, similar to opening a bank account. You tell the firm's agent that you'd like to open an IRA, and you get a short form to fill out. You provide basic information: name, address, Social Security number, and beneficiary (the person who you want to get the money if you die). Then you specify whether you want a traditional IRA or a Roth IRA—I walk you through this decision later in this chapter.

After completing the form, you write a check that goes into your IRA account—maybe as little as $25 or $50, maybe as much as $5,000. After that, you have an IRA. But you aren't done.

Opening your IRA is only the first step. At that point, your money is just sitting there, doing nothing. You were smart to open an IRA for yourself. But the money won't grow until you take the critical second step. You must decide how to invest the money you just put into the IRA account. You need to fill out a second form stating what investments you choose. Your choices could make the difference between ending up with little more than you originally deposited or having hundreds of thousands of dollars later in life.

If you haven't finished reading this book, making investing choices might make you nervous. Don't worry, though. In the chapters ahead, you will become as wise as many financial planners, and I give you specific mutual fund names to help you choose.

Meanwhile, as you open your first IRA, be assured that you don't have to decide right there on the spot how to invest your money. Request a list of mutual funds to consider, and take it home with you if you need time to think. As a temporary move, you can tell the person who opened your IRA that you'd like to park your money in what's called a money market fund, a relatively safe choice that's similar to a savings account but that generally pays a little more interest and isn't FDIC insured.

Don't leave the money that way for long. You won't make enough interest on it to harness the power of compounding and make your savings blossom. Instead, you need to select mutual funds, including some that invest in stocks. I tell you exactly how to do that in the chapters ahead.

Now, however, I just want you to be comfortable opening an IRA so that nothing stops you. You might feel most confident opening an IRA at a bank because you've been there before and can walk in and talk with a human being. If you need that security for your first step into an IRA, go for it. Yet I want you to understand other options that might seem a little less comfortable at first but are just as simple and, ultimately, could be much more lucrative.

Too often banks aren't the best place for an IRA because they tend to charge high fees. They may charge a $25 so-called "maintenance fee" each year just to keep your money in an account. Mutual funds offered by banks also might include extra fees, called loads. On the face of it, these fees might look like small numbers, but over time, they erode your savings by thousands. I explain this in detail in Chapter 12, "How to Pick Mutual Funds: Bargain Shop." For now, just understand that fees matter a lot.

Ask about fees, and try to open your IRA at a bank, broker, or mutual fund company that won't charge you a fee to open the account or assess an annual "maintenance fee." There's no need to pay such fees, because equally good institutions don't charge them.

If you want human contact, you can do it through a brokerage firm or financial planner, as well as a bank. Perhaps you've heard of firms such as Merrill Lynch or Charles Schwab. These are brokerage firms; they sell stocks, bonds, and mutual funds. But they differ greatly in the fees they charge.

Merrill Lynch, Morgan Stanley Smith Barney, and other so-called "full-service brokers" charge fairly high fees. In theory, the fees are supposed to be the broker's compensation for giving you advice. But keep in mind that their advice can be good or bad. Brokers are hired to sell, and too often that means they sell what enriches *them* the most, a topic I cover in Chapter 15, "Do You Need a Financial Adviser?"

Charles Schwab and other so-called "discount brokers," such as Scottrade, Fidelity, E-Trade, and TD Ameritrade, generally charge lower fees, which is why I prefer the discounters. Discount brokers abound—too numerous to list. (Search for "discount brokers" on the Internet and compare the fees they charge and the ease of contacting them.) When you go to a discount broker, you need to know what you want: If you still need a significant amount of guidance, you won't get it there.

My goal with this book is to give you the tools you need so that you don't require much advice and can consequently save tremendous amounts of money by keeping your fees low at a discount broker or "no-load" mutual fund company. Still, if you feel that you need a helping hand, in person, to get started, don't stew and let valuable time pass. Go to a broker at a bank or brokerage firm, or find a certified financial planner. In Chapter 15, I tell you how to find qualified advisers who will work *for* you, not *against* you.

On the other hand, if you have the comfort level with mutual funds that I hope you get from Chapters 7 through 13, you can go directly to a low-cost mutual fund company such as Vanguard, Fidelity, or T. Rowe Price. I provide many other examples in later chapters. You can also use fund "screeners" to help find funds. Try www.morningstar.com or, at www.money.msn.com, click on "Investing" and "Funds." Morningstar's Web site offers "favorites" and "gold-rated" funds to help you find long-standing quality mutual funds. If you search most screeners by "low minimum," you'll find funds that let you start investing with $250 or $500.

Can't I Wait Until I File My Taxes?

When I first told Jessica to open an IRA and deposit $50 into it every month, she was perplexed. She, like many people, assumed that she was allowed to open IRAs only once a year: at tax time, as part of the process of filling out a tax return.

Again, it's understandable that people would make this mistake. Often people open IRAs when they complete their tax return so that they can use a tax-deductible IRA to reduce their taxes that year. Brokerage firms also turn up the volume on advertising around tax time because they know accountants will be advising clients to cut taxes with IRAs.

Still, you don't need to wait for the end of the year—and you shouldn't. By investing earlier in the year, you start earning money on your investments immediately. The magic of compounding begins to turn pennies into dollars.

For the purposes of doing your taxes, it doesn't matter whether you have contributed to an IRA early in the year, every month, or once a year. You just tally up all your contributions for a year and write the total on your tax return so that you can reduce your taxes.

Under tax laws, people are allowed to open an IRA every year, and they can put up to $5,000 into an old or new IRA for each tax year. The deadline for contributing the money comes at tax time, April 15. That's simply the cut-off date. For example, if you sit down to do your 2013 taxes in April 2014, and you haven't contributed anything to an IRA for 2013, you have until April 15, 2014, to open an IRA for the 2013 tax year.

In Jessica's case, all those $50 deposits would add up to $600 for the year. Then while preparing her tax return, if she wanted to boost the amount a little, she could. If she had an extra $100, she could add that to her IRA. If she had an extra $2,000, she could add that. She could add any amount, as long as she didn't put more than $5,000 into the IRA that year. In future years, she will have to pay attention to new limits by the government. When inflation kicks up, the government increases the amount you can put into an IRA for the year. For example, in 2007, the limit was $4,000. Then with inflation higher, the limit jumped to $5,000 in 2008 and remained there for several years.

The flexibility to save small amounts throughout the year and then add more at tax time should give you the impetus to open an IRA now instead of waiting for a stash of money that might never materialize. You can go to a bank, mutual fund company, or brokerage firm; fill out the form to open the IRA; deposit whatever amount you want; and then figure out the amount you can instantly add every time you get paid. For Jessica, it was $50; for you, I hope it's even more.

Regardless, ask to be put on what's called an automatic system, in which the institution removes your $50, or any other amount, from your checking account on a specific schedule. It might be once a month or every payday. Then you will constantly be adding money to your investments.

The nice feature about using an automatic plan is that you don't have to trust yourself to come up with $5,000, or even $600, at tax time. You are making sure that the money starts going into your retirement account from the moment you have good intentions. Given human nature, this is the one approach that seems to work most often.

Of course, you also want to put compounding to work. When you have zero in your account until tax time, you go through a full year without earning a return on your money. As soon as you put your first dollar into the account, compounding flexes its muscle. So why would you wait?

If you don't think a few months matters, just remember that time is your best friend if you start early and works against you every day you wait. If you doubt it, remember the toddler who amassed $4 million on $12,000 in IRAs.

The Choice Between a Traditional IRA and a Roth IRA

Too many people suffer from IRA paralysis because they can't figure out whether to choose a traditional tax-deductible IRA or a Roth IRA. I don't want you to succumb. Behavioral studies suggest that you will then let months or years go by without ever deploying your first $1 into one of these money-making machines. Simply because you are mulling the choice of IRAs, you might cost yourself thousands of dollars in potential retirement money as you leave savings gathering dust in a savings account.

Consequently, if you see that you would qualify for either, and you find yourself in the throes of procrastination, take out a quarter. Call one side "Roth IRA" and the other side "traditional IRA." Then flip that quarter in the air, and whichever side turns up, go for it.

I say this because both IRAs are tremendous choices—huge tax savers and, consequently, a no-brainer for growing your money. On the other hand, understanding the variations is not difficult. In a nutshell, the choice comes down to this: In addition to years of tax breaks, do you want an extra serving of tax help at the time you contribute money to an IRA, or do you want to delay it until you are retired?

The Traditional Tax-Deductible IRA

Let's start with a traditional tax-deductible IRA because there was a time when only one IRA existed—the traditional IRA. When the first IRA was introduced several years ago, people were sold on them as a way to cut their taxes each year. And that's still the appeal today. You can open a traditional IRA, deposit money up to the government's limit for that year, and use that contribution to reduce the amount of taxes you owe Uncle Sam at tax time for that particular year.

Say you earn $20,000 a year at your job, and you decide to put $3,000 into a traditional IRA this year. Because you did this, you will reduce your income when you fill out your tax return for this year. In effect, you tell the government at tax time that you didn't really make $20,000. Instead, your income was only $17,000 because you removed $3,000 to start the IRA.

Since your income is no longer $20,000, the government taxes you on only $17,000. So instead of having to pay $1,355 in taxes, you pay only $905. By opening an IRA, you cut your tax bill by about $450. If you want to try this calculation, go to www.dinkytown.com and use the tax estimator.

To look at it another way, because you saved $450 in taxes that year, it cost you only $2,550 to open your IRA, not $3,000.

Getting the tax break in a single year is a good deal. Of course, if you contribute again the next year, you cut your income and taxes again. You can do this year after year—every time you make a contribution, you reduce your taxes at year-end.

But the benefit is so much more than that. Year after year, Uncle Sam also keeps his hands off everything that's invested in the tax-deductible IRA. If your $3,000 earns $100, you will have $3,100 in your IRA, and you won't get taxed on any of it. If, years later, it's grown to $50,000, you still won't need to pay taxes on it. Consequently, your savings—free of taxes—will grow with gusto, thanks to the power of compounding on a pot of money that never gets whittled away by taxes.

That original $3,000 should turn into about $49,000 tucked away in your IRA for 35 years—but if you hadn't held the tax man at bay, you would have accumulated only about $24,000. (I'm assuming that you are in the 25 percent tax bracket and earn 8 percent annually on your investments.)

Now, here's where that traditional IRA takes a turn you might not like. The gig comes to an end when you retire. That's when Uncle Sam's bill starts coming due. Remember, you have been saving throughout your working years in an IRA so that you could start giving yourself a paycheck each year of retirement. As you go into that period of your life, Uncle Sam starts showing up every time you pay yourself. You can't do anything about it. He taxes any money you remove from the IRA. Of course, if you don't need the cash early in retirement and you just leave it in the IRA, you won't owe any taxes on your savings.

But Uncle Sam wants to make sure he gets a piece of the action, so he won't let you duck him forever. When you turn 70½, he will require you to remove a portion of your IRA money every year, whether you need it or not. Then Uncle Sam will take his share of that money, taxing it just as he would a paycheck. Still, the money remaining in your IRA—no matter how large—continues to grow without getting taxed.

So that's how a traditional tax-deductible IRA worked when it was first introduced—and still works today. It starts with a tax break the year you contribute, it protects you from taxes throughout your savings years, and then in retirement, you start giving some of the money back to Uncle Sam and your state tax coffers, too.

The Roth IRA

All said, the traditional IRA is a great deal for saving. But a few years ago, along came something even better: the Roth IRA. I think of it as the new and improved IRA.

Now, assuming that you meet the income levels and other criteria explained throughout this chapter, you have a choice between a traditional tax-deductible IRA and a Roth IRA.

With a Roth IRA, you do not get an upfront tax break the year you open one or when you make a contribution. So if you were earning $20,000 and put $3,000 into a Roth IRA, you would not cut your taxes by $450 that year. You would miss out on the basic attraction of a traditional IRA—that easy opportunity to cut your taxes in a single year.

On the other hand, when your money is in a Roth IRA, you get the same goodies as with a traditional IRA. In other words, year after year, the pot of money grows and you pay no taxes on the money in the account. If $3,000 turns into $3,100, you pay no taxes. If it turns into $30,000, you still pay no taxes, and so on through the years.

Now comes the really terrific part. When you retire, you still pay no taxes. Here the Roth IRA starts to act very differently from a traditional IRA. It becomes the Superman of IRAs, delivering a stupendous deal.

Everything you've built up in the Roth IRA is yours, free and clear, forever. You will never owe taxes on any of it. You could have $1 million or $10 million at 65, 85, or any age. Every cent will be yours.

Uncle Sam won't make you take a penny out of your Roth IRA at age $70\frac{1}{2}$—or ever—because he has no claim on it. If you remove $1 million a year, it's all yours. If you remove $100 or $3 million, it's all yours. If it stays invested, it's all yours. Even if you die and it goes to your spouse, children, or any heir, they won't have to pay taxes on any of it, either.

Now, that's one magnificent deal! When you are retired and living on a fixed income, you won't have any control over whether your property taxes shoot up or whether your medical bills triple or quadruple, or whether car prices go through the roof and your old wreck breaks down. But you will have one sure thing: your Roth IRA. No matter what you have accumulated in it, every penny will be there for you, with no tax man dipping in each year for a cut.

I think that certainty alone makes the decision between a traditional IRA and a Roth IRA simple: Go with the Roth.

Some accountants have done elaborate calculations to help people decide whether they'd be better off with a traditional IRA or a Roth IRA. The simple rule of thumb is this: If you think you will be in a lower tax bracket when you retire than you are now, you should go with a traditional IRA and get your tax break up front instead of when you retire. You can use Internet calculators to see where you fall. Do a Google search for "which IRA is best" and try one of the many calculators.

But here's the catch with the calculations: They assume that current tax rates will stay intact and that you can anticipate what percentage of your income you will owe in taxes when you retire. I am persuaded by Ed Slott, a certified public accountant and IRA expert, that planning based on today's tax system will probably be folly. With a large federal budget deficit, Congress is likely to raise taxes at some point. Even if you anticipate low taxes during retirement, that might not be correct. Consequently, Slott tells everyone, regardless of income, to select a Roth IRA and insulate themselves from the possibility of high taxes during retirement.

His argument convinced me. Of course, some skeptics argue that the government could also renege on its promise to keep its hands off Roth IRA money years from now, but people familiar with the public policy process tell me that would be a broken promise with gigantic ramifications from unhappy voters.

So if you want a simple solution, don't flip a coin. Go with the Roth IRA, leave your money in it until you are at least 59½, and enjoy tax-free savings for all the days of your life.

In his book *Parlay Your IRA into a Family Fortune,* Slott calls Roth IRAs "The Ninth Wonder of the World." He told me once that he thought young people were foolish to be sucked into the small tax savings they can get up front from a tax-deductible IRA. Maybe they save $450 on taxes one year on their first $20,000-a-year job, but when they are retired and it's turned into $41,000, they could end up giving away 30 percent of that in taxes.

There's nothing better than no taxes after you are retired. And that's precisely the deal the Roth IRA offers you.

The Choice Between a 401(k) and a Roth IRA

In the best of all worlds, you would be so well paid and have such a commitment to keeping up your lifestyle when you retire that you would use both of these fabulous tools to the hilt. I'm not delusional, however. Less than 10 percent of people hit the $17,000 limit on their 401(k)s.

Most people can't, or won't, do more. On average, Americans put away 6 percent of their income in 401(k)s—enough to survive with a roof over their heads and food on the table, but not extras. Many could do more, which is why I wrote this book—to nudge you and help you through it in easy ways.

Remember, when the Employee Benefits Research Institute asked people of all income levels whether they could afford to put $20 more into a retirement account each month, the majority said "yes."

Still, many Americans cannot put $17,000 into the 401(k) and also maximize a Roth IRA, so inevitably that raises a question: Which one do you use?

Follow this simple process: First, don't leave money on the table if your employer is offering it. Contribute at least enough to your 401(k) to get every drop of matching money possible. The only exception is if your 401(k) plan is a mess, with an array of awful mutual funds and high fees, or if you believe that your employer might not be putting the money into the 401(k) as required by law. Fraud is unusual, so there's no need to fixate on this. You would get hints if your employer were defrauding you (money not showing up on time in your account, or incorrect and late statements from your account).

Assuming that your 401(k) is solid, you proceed to the next step after you have put enough money into your 401(k) to get matching money for the year. At that point, with your match intact, you could stop contributing temporarily to the 401(k) and start routing money into a Roth IRA. When you've met the $5,000 maximum contribution for the Roth, then you would return to the 401(k) and fill it to the hilt. In other words, if the limit in your 401(k) plan is $17,000, go for it. Some people skip this last step, thinking there's no benefit because their employer isn't matching the contributions. They are wrong: The goal is to build up a nice retirement stash with the help of the tax system. So that means putting as much as possible into both a 401(k) and an IRA.

The route I've laid out—using a 401(k), then a Roth IRA, and then back to the 401(k)—works only for a disciplined person who will, in fact, follow up by opening a Roth IRA and feeding it regularly. If you can't trust yourself to do that, fill the 401(k) to the brim before you do anything else because it's there at work. You can set it up once and simply make contributions without thinking about them. In addition, when you hear you are getting a raise, it's easy to tweak the 401(k) forms at work so that part of that raise goes immediately toward funding your future.

The most important consideration for you is to make sure you get the money into a tax-sheltered account such as an IRA or a 401(k) so that you don't spend it—and also so that it grows free of taxes.

If you have been kind to yourself by funding both a 401(k) and a Roth IRA, when you retire, you will have the best of all worlds. The Roth will provide a pot of money that won't be taxed no matter how long you live, and your 401(k) will be another reliable source of money—but one that will require you to pay taxes. Every time you withdraw 401(k) money during retirement, you will have to pay taxes on it just like a regular paycheck.

Pushing IRAs and 401(k)s to the Limit

After you have a fully funded Roth IRA, if you can put any additional money aside—and you should—devote it to your 401(k). The additional money won't earn you a greater match from your employer, but it will give you a break on your taxes and continue to let compounding do its magic for you while holding Uncle Sam at bay.

And for people who have incomes too high to open Roth IRAs, simply filling the 401(k) to the maximum is a no-brainer. If you are younger than 50, shoot for $17,000; if you're older than 50, go to $22,500.

Rules You Must Live By

One of the reasons IRAs are so confusing for people is that Congress keeps changing the rules. Today's rules may change later, so before you open an IRA, make sure that your age, income, job benefits, and other factors still permit you to take the actions you want. You can read all the current rules in IRS Publication 590 at www.irs.gov/publications/p590/index.html, or see the simple version at www.rothira.com.

The following lists the main rules you must follow—rules that will either give you the right to proceed or hold you back on one or both IRAs. I am using 2012 limits to explain how the rules work, but keep in mind that the numbers you see in the examples will change in future years as the government adjusts them for inflation.

Can You Get a Tax Deduction from a Traditional IRA?

Not everyone can get a tax deduction by opening a traditional IRA. It depends on your income and whether you have a pension, profit-sharing plan, 401(k), or other retirement savings plan at work.

Most employers don't offer pensions. And half don't offer a 401(k), 403(b), or similar retirement savings plan. So if you work for one of these companies, you are free to open a traditional IRA and deduct it from your taxes. The reason is simple: You are on your own to provide for your retirement, so the government gives you an incentive to help yourself.

But if you have the benefit of some type of pension or retirement savings plan at work, the government is less interested in helping you. Your income level counts then. You can't deduct a contribution to a traditional IRA for 2012 if you are single and your income is over $68,000. And if your income is somewhere between $58,000 and $68,000, you can contribute, but you don't get a deduction for the *full* amount typically allowed for an IRA contribution ($5,000 in 2012). If you are married, this gets a little more complicated. If a couple's combined income is over $112,000, and they each have either pensions or retirement savings plans at work, they cannot deduct traditional IRAs from their income. And at $92,000, they have to start cutting back on what they can deduct. But if one spouse has a pension or retirement plan at work and the other doesn't, the spouse without the plan doesn't have to worry about the cutoff of $92,000 to $112,000; he or she can open an IRA and deduct the full amount if the couple's income is no greater than $173,000. If it's higher than that, the spouse might still qualify for a reduced deduction. But when a couple's modified adjusted gross income is over $183,000, no deduction is allowed.

What a maze of numbers! I wish I could make it easier, but Uncle Sam requires that you live within the rules.

To make things more complicated, these income levels aren't actually what your salary is. Instead, they relate to income levels after certain deductions occur and are called modified adjusted gross income. That means your salary is probably higher than the cutoffs, so you might have more leeway to use an IRA than you think. Tax-preparation software such as Turbo Tax can tell you where you stand so you don't have to wonder about your income level qualifying. Of course, an accountant or www.irs.gov Publication 590 can also help. The government also changes income limits from year to year, so check on them each year.

Is Your Income Too High for a Roth IRA?

One reason I like Roth IRAs is that the rules are so simple. Instead of running through a maze of do's and don'ts about qualifying, you have just one simple question to answer: Is my income within the limits? Few people have to worry about this because the maximum income is fairly high for Roth IRAs. So if you've been thinking about opening a traditional IRA and you have a workplace pension plan that will interfere with a deduction, turn to a Roth IRA. Remember, if you have a pension, 401(k), or other retirement plan at work, you are free to open a Roth IRA—and you should.

Given 2012 limits on contributions, you could put up to $5,000 into a Roth IRA for the year if you are single and have a modified adjusted gross income less than $110,000. Between $110,000 and $125,000, you would have to ratchet back the amount you put into a Roth, but you could still make a contribution of some amount. If you're married, you would start ratcheting back a full contribution when your income crossed the $173,000 threshold. Yet you could still contribute some amount to a Roth, as long as your income stayed within the maximum $183,000. Under current tax laws, the limits are supposed to be adjusted annually based on inflation, so as the years go by, search the IRS Web site to see how far you can go with each year's contributions.

There's also a formula behind how these so-called phase-outs work to limit contributions after a person's income crosses from the low end of the range (such as $110,000 for a single person) and approaches the high end ($125,000). You can find it at www.irs.gov. But I'll give you a quick understanding here. It has to do with where your income stands between the complete phase-out point and the start of the phase-out. Say, for example, that you are married and file your taxes jointly with your spouse. Together the two of you have a modified adjusted gross income of $178,000. That's half of the way up to the $183,000 cutoff for a Roth. Your limit on what you can put into your Roth IRA is then cut by a half. Instead of putting $5,000 into one that year, you can consider $2,500.

How Much Can You Contribute?

The answer: only as much as you earn from a job.

For example, if you are in junior high and you have been mowing lawns this year and will make $75 for the year, you can put the entire $75 into an IRA. But if you've been putting gifts from relatives into a savings account for years and have $5,000 in it, you can't pull the $5,000 out of the account and open an IRA with it. You are limited to the $75 you earned from working.

But let's say you earn something more than $5,000. Then you have to stay within the $5,000 limit. For example, you make $20,000 at your job and don't need any of it to live on because someone in your family is bankrolling you. Perhaps you'd like to put the full $20,000 into an IRA. But you can't.

Watch these limits, though. Congress is always changing them, and inflation adjustments are made from time to time.

Do You Meet Age Requirements?

A couple of ages are key: $70\frac{1}{2}$ and $59\frac{1}{2}$. But just to drive you nuts, the ages don't apply in the same way to traditional IRAs and Roth IRAs.

After age $70\frac{1}{2}$, you can no longer contribute to a regular IRA, and you must start taking money out at that point. But $70\frac{1}{2}$ doesn't apply in any way to a Roth IRA. As long as you have any income from working—even income as small as working as an election judge once a year—you can make a new contribution to a Roth IRA, no matter what your age.

Then there's the issue of removing money from an IRA. Typically, anyone can start removing money from a Roth IRA after age $59\frac{1}{2}$. But there's another rule tagged onto the $59\frac{1}{2}$ age. The money must also have been in the Roth for five years before the earnings on it are removed.

So if you put money into a Roth IRA at age 50 and want to remove it at age $59\frac{1}{2}$, that will be fine. But if you open a Roth IRA at 58, you have to wait until you are 63 to remove anything beyond your original contribution.

Last-Minute Regrets:
I Want My Money Back

I hate to tell you the following because I don't want you to use it. But I also know that this could make you a lot more relaxed about putting money into an IRA or Roth IRA. So here goes.

If you find that you can't live without the money you put into your IRA or you have second thoughts about the amount you deposited, you can change your mind under several common circumstances.

If you need the money to pay for college for yourself, your child, or a spouse, feel free to dip into the account. It doesn't matter what your age is. You won't have to pay the typical 10 percent penalty the IRS charges if you take money out of an IRA before you are $59\frac{1}{2}$. You just have to pay taxes on the money you have removed.

The same holds true if you are buying your first home and need the cash. You can take $10,000 out of the account. Married people can get their hands on a total of $20,000 if they each have their own IRA. And if you lose your job and need to buy health insurance, you can tap your IRA penalty free, too.

People with Roth IRAs have even more flexibility. Besides the right to take money out of an IRA for college, homes, and health insurance, they can yank any of the original money they deposited and use it for anything at any time.

Say you are 35, and you put $4,000 into a Roth IRA a week ago. A friend finds a great fare over the Internet to Europe. You could remove the entire $4,000. You wouldn't have to pay a penalty or pay taxes because, unlike a traditional IRA, you never got a tax break up front with the Roth IRA. You put the $4,000 in your Roth after paying taxes on it. So it's yours, free for the taking at any time.

If, however, you had the $4,000 in your account for a few months and it had grown to $4,100, you would not be able to remove the $100 for your European vacation. That's because you didn't pay taxes on the $100, and your deal with Uncle Sam is the following: Leave all earnings from your Roth in your account until you are at least 59½. As a result, if you removed the $100, you would have to pay both a 10 percent penalty on it and income taxes.

So relax about missing your money in an IRA, especially a Roth IRA. It's more accessible than you might have thought.

Special Help for Low-Income People

If your income is low and you don't think you can scrounge up anything to put into a retirement account, don't give up.

I have a deal for you, a gift from the federal government. It's free money—maybe as much as $1,000 if you put $2,000 into an IRA. Lesser amounts are also okay, but if, for example, you come up with $500 for an IRA, the government won't give you $1,000. Maybe you will qualify for only $100 in free money. Depending on your income (after certain deductions) and the amount of money you put into an IRA, the government might give you 50 percent, 20 percent, or 10 percent of the money you have deposited.

Anytime you can get free money, it's worth pursuing, especially when it's for a good cause—your future. This free money comes to you via the "saver's credit." You ask for it when you prepare your tax return at the end of a year. The government wants you to save for retirement, so the IRS gives you a refund if you contribute to either an IRA or your 401(k), 403(b), or other retirement plan at work.

Of course, that depends on your income. If you're single, your income has to be less than $28,750 . If you're married, it must be less than $57,500. (Check as the years go by, in case the government raises the limits.) Also keep in mind that you need to be working, not a full-time student.

Often young people qualify when they start their first jobs because their incomes are low. Sometimes they can borrow from a parent or relative, fund an IRA, and get money from the government so that their financial commitment is pretty small.

Even if your income is slightly higher than the limits I just gave, you might be able to squeeze into this deal. Remember, earlier in this chapter, I explained that when you put money into an IRA or 401(k), you cut your income. So conceivably, a single person could have an income around $30,000 and contribute $3,000 to a traditional IRA so that his or her income would be less than the $28,750 cut-off. Then this person could get a $300 saver's credit refund.

Anyone who can't come up with cash out of their pocket to fund an IRA might also try this technique: Complete your tax return a couple months before the April 15 deadline and report on the return that you are opening an IRA.

Perhaps your plan is to put $1,000 into the IRA. You would report a $1,000 IRA on your tax return. But you wouldn't put any money into the account then. Instead, you would wait until the government processed your return, gave you the saver's credit, and sent you a refund. After the refund arrived, you could use it to fund the IRA. Just be clear on this: You will face a penalty if you don't actually put the money into the IRA by that year's April 15 tax deadline. So don't forget or change your mind midstream.

For more information on the saver's credit, get IRS Publication 590 and Form 8880.

Even if you don't qualify for a saver's credit, paying your taxes early is a good way to come up with cash for an IRA. If you are entitled to any refund, don't spend it. As soon as the check arrives, put it into the IRA. This way, you will never miss the money and it will turn into thousands.

Help for Affluent People

What if you make too much money for a Roth IRA? If your income is too high for a Roth IRA, you still can keep Uncle Sam at bay so that your retirement savings will blossom. Just open a taxable IRA, called a non-deductible IRA.

At first, this might seem worthless because you don't get a tax break at the outset, and you don't set yourself up immediately to get the beauty of tax-free money when you retire. You do, however, get to keep Uncle Sam from taxing any money you earn in that IRA while it stays invested over the years.

Better yet, through a relatively new law, you have options that people at your income level never had until 2010. Since then, people have been allowed to convert a taxable IRA into a Roth IRA, no matter what their income.

If you do this, you will have to pay taxes on the money in the IRA when you convert it to a Roth IRA. Yet if you are quick on your feet, you might not have a tax liability at all. The strategy: Simply open a taxable IRA and immediately convert it to a Roth IRA before you have any earnings to tax. I know that this sounds strange. The logical person would say: Why go through an extra step of opening one type of IRA and then converting it to the type I want? The answer: The tax code isn't always logical. It is full of rules implemented at different times, and this one is an example. Use it to your advantage.

Once you have converted a taxable IRA to a Roth, you will have all the advantages I previously described. Your money will grow in it continually without being taxed, and when you retire, every penny will be yours. If it's worth $20,000, $2 million, or even more, Uncle Sam will never touch a cent in the account or anything you remove during retirement.

You have another alternative, too. Some employers are offering what is called a Roth 401(k) alongside your regular 401(k) at work. If your employer offers it, there are no income requirements for using the Roth option. So even if you make too much money to open a Roth IRA now, you can use a Roth 401(k) at work. And if you do, all the money you make in it over the years will be yours, free and clear, when you retire. Uncle Sam won't touch a penny ever. That's very different from a regular 401(k). When you remove money from the typical 401(k) for retirement, you must pay taxes on the money you withdraw.

So if you have a Roth 401(k) at work, this is an attractive choice, as long as you can live without the immediate tax break you get with a regular 401(k). You can put up to $17,000 for the 2012 tax year into a Roth 401(k), or $22,500 if you are over 50. But be aware that, before making those contributions, you pay your taxes on that income in full. Your tax break comes during your retirement years, not the year you make your contributions.

Many employers do not give employees a Roth 401(k) option. If your workplace does, and you'd like a tax break on contributions now but also are enticed by tax-free income for retirement, you have a solution. Simply route half of your 401(k) contributions to the tax-deductible part of the 401(k) and use the other half for the Roth 401(k) option.

What Comes First: College or Retirement Saving?

In the best of all worlds, parents would save for their children's college education in addition to retirement. College is expensive—currently about $100,000 for four years of tuition, room, and board at a public university, and about $200,000 at many private colleges. Prices have been rising about 8 percent a year, and few parents can save enough for the full package. If you have limited resources and must choose between funding your retirement and funding college, emphasize funding your 401(k) and IRA instead of the college account.

There are good reasons why: If you are 75 and spent a good chunk of your savings on your children's education, plus you can't work and have depleted your retirement savings, you can't go to a bank and take out a loan for food, utilities, and medicine.

But for college, students can get relatively large federal student loans to pay part of the cost. Obviously, loans can help make up for what you can't handle.

Of course, that could leave your children with debts as they begin their working years. The average college student with loans leaves college with about $25,000 in student loan debt, which is a hefty sum. It's understandable to want to save your children from such a fate, and you should, if you can. But keep in mind that college graduates have at least 10 years after school to pay off federal Stafford and Perkins loans. And during their working years, they generally will be in a better position to handle that burden than you will be to handle the life of a 75-year-old without savings.

Beyond that fact of life, there are other reasons to place retirement saving first and college saving second. If you have retirement saving well under control by the time the children start college, you can cut back on saving somewhat while they are in college and use a larger portion of your paycheck to pay for tuition during those few years.

Also, most students need some financial aid. But based on the quirky college aid formula used to grant aid, families with large college saving funds can erode their opportunities for sizable aid packages. Typically, colleges do not reduce aid based on well-endowed 401(k) plans or IRAs. So while I encourage people to save as much as possible for college, making retirement saving the priority can make college more affordable for middle-class families.

Don't take financial aid for granted, however, especially if your income is well over $100,000. Then you might find financial aid in short supply, and you will need all the savings you can accumulate. You can check now to see how likely your family is to qualify for financial aid.

Try the Expected Family Contribution (EFC) Calculator, at www.finaid.org, and use both the "federal" methodology for public colleges and the "institutional" methodology for private colleges. Middle-income families can sometimes find private colleges more affordable because endowments allow the schools to provide more generous aid packages than public colleges can offer.

If You Operate a Small Business

Often small-business people get buried in the ongoing stress of running their businesses and feeding their families. They promise themselves to think about retirement saving *soon*—but soon can come decades later.

Since planning for retirement too frequently comes late in life, available alternatives need to be used to the max. Putting $5,000 or $6,000 a year into a Roth IRA will help. Opening a Roth IRA for a spouse, too, is even better. But you need to go further.

Consider the following options, but keep in mind that, for a business, the decisions are more complex than for an individual. You must consider not only your income, but matters such as how many employees you have, what you might be able to contribute in good years and bad years, and the ease of handling a business retirement savings plan.

Talk to a certified public accountant to understand what matches your business and personal needs best. (Details are available in IRS Publication 3998, at www.irs.gov, and from the American Institute of Certified Public Accountants, at www.aicpa.org. Search for "IRAs and 401(k)s: How to Pick the Best Plan.")

Here's some basic information to get you started.

Individual 401(k) or Solo 401(k)

If you are a sole proprietor and long for the days when you worked for someone else and had a 401(k) at work, long no more. You can treat yourself to the very same thing.

Tax laws have been allowing self-employed people since 2001 to create what are called individual 401(k) plans, solo 401(k) plans, or single-participant 401(k) plans. These can include a Roth 401(k) feature so that you can save money and know that it will be yours, free and clear of taxes, when you retire.

The administrative fees can be a deterrent for an independent business person once assets exceed $250,000, but the benefits can be tremendous. With a solo 401(k), a sole proprietor can shelter huge amounts of money from taxes. That, of course, lets the person who ignored saving for years quickly build up a nest egg.

Self-employed people can save more than with most alternatives because they have two ways of stashing away money without paying taxes on it. As an employer, the individual can contribute up to 25 percent of his or her compensation, provided that it doesn't exceed $50,000. In addition, as an employee of his or her own company, the individual can contribute $17,000, or $22,500 if he or she is at least 50 years old.

So a 50-year-old sole proprietor earning $100,000 in a business could contribute $22,500 as an employee and $18,587 in profit sharing from the business in a single year, or a total of $41,087. Try the calculator at www.calcxml.com. Under consumer calculators choose "I'm self-employed, how much can I contribute to a retirement plan."

Because of the large sums of money, the plans are attracting a wide range of financial companies. Among those offering them are Fidelity Investments, T. Rowe Price, and Charles Schwab. Make sure you compare costs, because they can seriously eat away at the potential for your money to grow. Pay attention to the calendar, too. To make a contribution this year, you must set up the plan by December 31.

Also revisit the maximum contribution limits I have provided; the government adjusts them on the basis of inflation.

SEP-IRA Simplified Employee Pension Plan

If you can't afford to stash away a lot of money and want an easy-to-handle plan that won't require annual filings, special IRAs for businesses might be just the ticket.

With a SEP-IRA, or Simplified Employee Pension, you can contribute up to 25 percent of your business's net income, as long as you don't exceed the $50,000 limit. A sole proprietor making $100,000 could contribute $18,587 to this retirement account.

In lean years for your business, there is no requirement to make any contribution whatsoever. But if you have employees (even part-time employees), you must make contributions for them, too.

You don't have to do much advance thinking to contribute to a SEP. If you are approaching an April 15 tax filing deadline and you realize that you'd like to shelter income, you can respond at the last minute.

Having a SEP is similar to having a traditional IRA, except that you can contribute a lot more and shelter it from taxes. To get started, simply contact a mutual fund company, brokerage firm, bank, or other financial institution.

SIMPLE IRA (Savings Incentive Match Plan for Employees)

The name of this IRA tells all. It truly is simple to open, is inexpensive, and doesn't burden busy business owners with IRS reporting requirements.

Unlike with the other plans, however, business owners have to pay attention to the calendar. You must open a SIMPLE IRA by October of the year you want to contribute. (Use IRS Form 5304-SIMPLE or Form 5305-SIMPLE. Financial institutions will process most of the paperwork for you.)

And if you have employees who have earned at least $5,000 a year, you must allow them to contribute to a SIMPLE plan and provide matching funds between 1 and 3 percent of compensation.

Although this IRA is indeed simple, the drawback is the limit on contributions. You cannot shelter as much income from the IRS. This year, the limit on contributions is $11,500, although you can go to $14,000 if you are over 50.

For the 50-year-old sole proprietor making $100,000, it would be possible with the matching funds to save $16,788 in the Simple IRA for the year.

The Next Step

Now that you are stashing away good sums of money into IRAs and 401(k)s, the next step is to make sure your savings harness their full growth potential. That means investing well. The next few chapters enable you to do it.

6

WHY THE STOCK MARKET ISN'T A ROULETTE WHEEL

Before I help you invest your money, I have to talk about a casino billboard I saw over a busy Minneapolis freeway. It was aimed straight for the ordinary American's underbelly, with giant words asking passing motorists, "Does your 401(k) need some more Ks?"

The obvious solution posed by the billboard, of course, was to stop worrying about your meager little retirement fund and instead head for the casino, win, and then fill that 401(k) to the brim. No fuss, no muss—voilà, instant retirement!

Too bad it doesn't work.

As much as we savor the fantasy of instant riches, we know that if we spend $1 at the casino, we might get $1 worth of fun and maybe even a few bucks, but no Ks for the retirement account. The trouble is that we aren't sure what the alternative might be to build up those Ks by the time we need them.

For most Americans, investing in stocks, bonds, or mutual funds is a treacherous experience that doesn't make sense and doesn't feel much different than tossing some coins into a slot machine or choosing between red and black on the roulette wheel.

At work, employees are given a bizarre-sounding list of mutual funds for their 401(k), and somehow each person is supposed to make sense of the gobbledygook descriptions. Sometimes the employer brings in an investment expert who yaks for an hour in a foreign language and shows a befuddled audience some pie charts. At the end, the strange mutual fund words are just as confusing. So perplexed workers eye their list of mutual funds the way they would a roulette wheel and select one or a few. Then they spin the wheel and hope luck is on their side.

Too often black turns up when they cast their lot with red. So they lose money and decide to spin again. They ask people who know as little as they do how to win. And when they follow the leader and choose black for the next spin, the stars have realigned, and the investor loses yet again. Only this time, retirement is months closer than the last time Lady Luck failed to pay their 401(k) a visit.

The entire process seems like a mystery fraught with danger. And so some people joke helplessly that their 401(k) has turned into a 201(k)—in other words, cut in half. And then they naively move on to repeat the same mistakes with their retirement funds that decimated them in the past.

It doesn't have to be this way.

Investing is very different from gambling. And the stakes are high. Blowing $100 at a casino is entertainment. But if a 25-year-old blows $100 in his retirement account, he will be sacrificing about $4,500 by the time he retires. That's right, just a $100 flop is likely to cost $4,500 about 40 years later because of the power of compounding.

And it gets a lot worse if the individual inadvertently makes a habit of blowing $100 each year. If a 25-year-old destroys just $100 a year every year through ill-informed gambling moves in a retirement account, that's potentially a loss of $53,000 from his nest egg. Again, the power of compounding magnifies the impact of a $100 annual mistake repeated for 40 years.

So eyeing your list of 401(k) funds and then throwing up your hands in frustration and deciding to just spin the roulette wheel is idiotic. If I told you today that it wouldn't hurt you to throw $4,500 or $53,000 into the trash over the next 40 years, you'd look at me like I was crazy.

If you really invest money instead of gambling with your IRA or 401(k), you will be doing yourself a huge favor. You will give yourself a chance to make every $100 work for you instead of having to dig deeper into your pocket for another $100 to make up for the messes you have already caused.

If you have been investing in your retirement account for some time and have no idea why the money just sits there gathering dust or evaporates shortly after you've poured your cash into the account, you owe it to yourself to understand the harm you are causing yourself so that you can easily fix it.

You don't have to know math. You don't have to know how to pick a stock. You don't have to understand the Federal Reserve's tinkering with interest rates. And you don't have to understand the chatter on TV investing shows. But you must know one important fundamental point that is yanking at your money at all times when it's in stock mutual funds in your 401(k) or IRA: The stock market, and pieces of the stock market, move in cycles.

Taking Control of Cycles

Those cycles are what have been bashing your savings. And they can be cruel if you don't understand them. They are why your mutual funds shock you and hurt you. They are why the mutual funds you might have loved in the 1990s turned into the mutual funds you hated in the 2000s. They are why your winners turn into losers and why, long after you have dumped a loser in disgust, it suddenly looks like a keeper again. It could be why you figure luck is rarely on your side when it comes to investing.

Cycles are inevitable. You cannot stop them, but you can tame their impact on your money. I'm not going to get technical on you now. But I want you to know that cycles will hurt you much less if you come to expect them the same way you expect the seasons of the year to change. Just as I can assure you that the leaves on trees will change as summer gives way to autumn and then winter, I can guarantee you that, no matter what is happening to your money in stock mutual funds now, it, too, is destined to morph as it goes into a new part of a cycle. If you have a winning fund, it will turn into a loser. If you have a loser, it will at least become more of a winner later. The perplexing question for you will be, how much later?

Often it takes so long for cycles to change that people figure it will never happen. When life is good and you are making money, it seems like it will continue forever. When conditions are awful, and you are losing money, you figure all is lost forever. That's where people make mistakes and lose money ignorantly in the changing cycles.

And it's not merely about stocks or mutual funds. Cycles take every conceivable investment on a ride. It happened in the early 2000s in the U.S. housing market. People assumed that homes would always be dependable investments. They were soaring in value, and people figured they could never lose on a home. They might have lost money in their 401(k) in mutual funds, but they assumed homes were different—solid, tangible, a no-brainer way to make money, much safer than the stock market.

That very thinking powered the glorious winning part of the housing cycle into a horrible downturn in the cycle that ruined lives. Millions of Americans lost the American dream and the biggest investment of their life to foreclosure.

At first, no one could imagine a downside in the cycle. People were blinded by the gains everyone was making on homes. There was a euphoria in the air and an urgency to buy homes. Regular people were buying them and selling them for thousands more in a short period of time. TV was full of shows about fixing homes, flipping homes, and getting rich in the process.

Americans bought homes at exorbitant prices, figuring they'd better move fast because homes would continually move up in price. They stretched to buy homes they couldn't afford, thinking their home would be an investment that would always appreciate in value.

Then the crash came, and suddenly homes weren't selling, mortgage payments were due, and people couldn't afford to make payments they owed their banks. And because their homes had lost a third or more of their value, people couldn't even sell them for enough money to pay back the bank. Homes had gone from being no-brainer investments to being agonizing traps.

Instead of wanting to buy homes, the mentality changed. Millions wanted to be renters. After experiencing the downturn in a cycle, many came to the conclusion that a home would be a dangerous investment.

Someday, as memories of the housing crisis fade, the cycle will turn again and people will push financially to buy homes once more. There will probably come a time when people will figure again that prices will always go up. But the plunge has left millions wary, and the downside of a cycle always does.

The lesson should not be that homes are losers rather than winners. Instead, it should be that people must be alert to cycles and be cautious about depending too much on a single investment—especially when there's a mania around it and people assume that it's a no-brainer money maker. It doesn't matter whether the investment is a home, gold, stocks, or bonds. Cycles always apply. An overdose at the wrong time can be poison, and a taste early in a cycle can be delicious.

In stock market cycles, the stock market as a whole, or certain types of stocks or mutual funds, might look boring or even downright scary at the point in the cycle when people have lost interest or fled from the investments.

Then, after some time has passed, the once-ugly investments start looking better and better. They become increasingly popular with investors, eventually seeming like the hottest, smartest investment anyone could buy. This is usually when ordinary investors pile in, thinking the hot investments are a no-brainer that will make people rich forever.

But with more time, the entire group of hot stocks cools off—maybe because business conditions change or maybe because smart investors decide the stocks became so expensive that they are no longer a good deal. The shrewd pros look for a better investment—something cheaper, with more chance to take off in the next phase of the cycle. They sell the once-hot investments, and suddenly the ordinary guy is holding on to a stock mutual fund wondering what in the world happened to it. His beautiful investment of yesterday has turned into an ugly money loser and is turning uglier with each passing day, seemingly for no good reason.

About 40 different varieties of mutual funds exist, and each type behaves differently during specific times in each cycle. Funds are designed that way on purpose so that investors can buy a variety and be prepared for anything. Yet given the funds you have selected, at any moment in time, you might feel brilliant or like a supreme idiot. If you have a mixture of funds, you will always like one more than the other, and as the cycle changes, your favorites will always be alternating.

The 1990s: From Stock Lovefest to Disaster

Let me illustrate what I mean by stock market cycles. I want to take you back to the end of the 1990s, one of the most vivid examples of a dramatic change in cycles since the Great Depression.

The end of the 1990s was a period of euphoria for the ordinary investor. People could throw a few bucks into a 401(k) or an IRA and make mounds of money almost overnight. Peering into a 401(k) account was pure joy. Many Americans made a hobby of treating themselves to the pleasure at their computers every day. Most didn't realize it at the time, but they were simply riding a cycle up—a cycle that was bound to move from hot to cold, destroying trillions of dollars in the process.

In polls, individual investors naively said they thought the good times would last. They were expecting to keep making 20 percent returns on their money every year, even though Wall Street's old-timers knew that the 1990s were extraordinary and that 10 percent returns in the stock market are the average. Even some investing professionals who should have known better were mesmerized by the moment, leading clients to destruction. They thought the economy and stocks were in a new era when old rules about cycles no longer would apply.

Investing magazines had covers posing the question "Are You Rich Yet?" CNBC's constant stock market news was on TVs everywhere, from golf courses to Burger Kings. Giddy with their newfound wealth, people borrowed money on their homes so that they could invest in the most dangerous stocks. Many who had never analyzed a stock in their life quit their jobs to trade stocks at home computers. The mood was like the Roaring Twenties all over again—you couldn't lose in the stock market.

At the time, John Brennan, the chairman of a mutual fund company named Vanguard, discovered how far the mania had gone. He stopped in a Burger King one night after jogging, and a senior citizen recognized him from some stock market comments he'd made on TV. The man was almost trembling with excitement about the stock market and told Brennan that he, his wife, and two friends went to the Burger King every night to watch the stock market news because they didn't have cable in their homes. And the man asked Brennan to autograph his Burger King coffee cup. That's when Brennan was sure investors had gone crazy over the stock market and a cruel downturn was sure to come.

Readers of my column would call me at my newspaper office to giggle about the stocks they'd bought that had doubled or tripled in value in a few weeks. Ordinary people who told me they once begrudged the rich were calling me to get information about tax shelters because they'd made so much money.

People who knew nothing about picking stocks felt like geniuses when they selected stocks such as Cisco, even though they had no idea what technological gizmos these companies produced or what would make customers want to buy them. They didn't realize until it was too late that they'd paid about 10 times more for many technology stocks than they should have, and that ultimately set them up to lose almost everything when the game ended. Technology stocks as a group crashed about 70 percent, and many beloved Internet companies went bankrupt, leaving the stocks worthless.

But before the crash, there was one investing game in town: Buy either individual technology company stocks or mutual funds that supersized their exposure to technology stocks. Anyone who had those investments won and felt like smart investors—that is, until summer turned into autumn and, ultimately, a 2-year piercing-cold winter took hold.

Everyone Played the Game

You might not have realized any of this in the late 1990s. You might not have even imagined that you were a part of it—riding a cycle and speculating on insanely priced technology stocks. But if you had money in a 401(k), an IRA, or any mutual funds and liked the way they were behaving, you were probably part of the mania. Unbeknownst to you, the money you were making was coming from gigantic bets on technology stocks by the people who were running your mutual funds.

Amid such merriment, being cautious was the ultimate sin for a mutual fund manager. Individual investors had no patience for mutual funds that were climbing 10 percent a year while their workmate or neighbor was making 25 or 50 percent, or even more, in funds brimming with technology stocks. In 1999, the funds that invested in only technology stocks climbed an average of 134 percent—probably a once-in-a-lifetime occurrence that should have warned investors that trouble was on its way and that the cycle would have to change.

Some of the nation's most renowned professional investors who shunned technology stocks and respected the precepts of good investing (in other words, to buy only cheap stocks) paid a dear price: Their clients resented cautious investments and abandoned the thoughtful professionals so that they could give their money instead to flashy, young upstarts caught up in the tech craze.

At the time, long-time investment pro Al Harrison, of Alliance Capital, spoke at a luncheon of other investment professionals and complained that young investment managers in his office were admonishing him for his cautious approach to hot stocks, saying, "Get with it, Granddad." A few years later, his fund got with it too much and was almost decimated with Enron stock.

In the midst of the hot cycle, individuals who bought anything other than technology felt like jerks. Investments in companies that made machines, produced oil, sold food, or did virtually anything that wasn't technology related couldn't measure up. They were the ignored orphans of the stock market. Funds that invested in gold and real estate went out of business because investors wanted nothing to do with them; then five years later, as the cycle changed, investors couldn't get enough gold or real estate.

A bond, too, was nothing but a four-letter word. After all, why would people buy such a lethargic safe investment when they could double or triple their money overnight with hot technology stocks and mutual funds full of tech?

Everyone was caught up in the mania, novices and professionals alike. I went to an investors' conference for pension fund managers back then, and the presentation on bonds drew fewer than 20 people into a giant hotel ballroom. The sessions on technology stocks had standing room only in rooms that could accommodate hundreds.

The ordinary guy unknowingly bought all he could through funds operated by companies like Janus, thinking that the managers were brilliant. But Janus funds were simply riding a hot cycle for technology stocks. In 1999, the Janus Twenty grew investors' money about 65 percent by sinking large sums into technology stocks. During the next three years, investors didn't know what hit them as they lost everything they'd made and then some. Before that happened, readers got angry at me when I warned them against buying too many technology stocks and mutual funds such as Janus that were supersizing exposure to those stocks. I will never forget one person who called me and stated angrily, "You are as stupid as Warren Buffett."

Obviously, I am no Warren Buffett, one of the most renowned investors of our time. But I knew something that every ordinary investor must know: Cycles happen, moving up and down, or from hot to cold. So technology stocks couldn't keep giving investors returns of more than 100 percent a year.

The Game's Up

Then it happened. The cycle started to turn in March 2000, when astute investors decided the game was up. They came to the realization that they had paid way too much for technology stocks, and the stock prices wouldn't keep going higher every day. These savvy investors started dumping the stocks. That made stock prices nose-dive. The little guy didn't know what was happening and held on, waiting for a return of the good ol' days. But while his 401(k) was slipping lower every day, many of the pros weren't riding it out with the little guy. They were selling technology stocks before they'd lost fortunes and they were buying cheap stocks in many industries that had long been ignored during the tech craze.

The market was being set up for a new cycle, a healing phase that, at first, would hurt many who clung to the past: The cheap nontechnology stocks had become cheap because no one wanted them when technology investing was driving the cycle. Yet sharp professional investors who snapped up all the solid stocks people had been ignoring knew that, with time, the cycle would change and their bargain hunting would pay off.

It took longer than many expected, but eventually the cycle changed, just as it always does. The bargain stocks that no one had wanted amid the technology craze just a couple years earlier soared in price, and investors who had them in their retirement accounts made money almost overnight. Waste Management, for example, a company that deals with collecting garbage, was unpopular with investors as it dealt with lawsuits over its accounting in the late 1990s. As the cycle changed, Waste Management stock shot up 42 percent in a few months. Nabisco, another stock people had ignored in the technology craze, climbed 183 percent as the cycle changed.

Meanwhile, investors who loved Amazon, the Internet bookstore, in the hot technology stock cycle of the late 1990s lost 67 percent in just a few months in 2000 as the cycle turned cold. Investors who put $10,000 into technology mutual funds such as the Monument Digital Technology fund at the beginning of 1999 gleefully watched their money turn into $37,300 that year and then gasped when they checked their account in September 2001 and found only $4,888 remaining.

If in 2000 you were lucky enough to have a mutual fund in your 401(k) that held stocks such as Nabisco, Philip Morris, and Waste Management, you would have been feeling pretty good after technology stocks started blowing up. Mutual funds with those bargain-priced stocks in them soared over 25 percent. But if you were like the ordinary investor, you probably didn't know what hit you. Suddenly, your hot funds of the late 1990s mysteriously turned into losers, many destroying 50 percent or more of investors' money.

Those holding on to the past and expecting the technology cycle to continue were being slaughtered. Internet companies went bankrupt. Retirement funds bled cash. People already in retirement had to go back to work because their savings were cut in half. The overall stock market crashed because, during the mania, it had become heavily dependent on technology stocks.

Taming the Herd

All this happened because of cycles. Several economic factors cause the stock market to go from hot to cold and cold to hot over time. But simply put, a human factor plays a major role in driving cycles: Investors tend to run in herds.

Both professionals who should know better and the common investor pile into certain types of stocks that look hot. For a while, popularity alone makes stocks rise. And the managers who bought the hot stocks for mutual funds look brilliant, when all they are doing is running with the herd. At a certain point, reality catches up with people.

Stock prices ultimately are based on more than popularity: Profits are key, and if smart investors realize profits aren't going to measure up to the prices people paid for a stock, they dump the stock, the stock price falls, and people lose money.

To say it another way, when investors look out from the herd on some level-headed day and see that the herd is crazed and corporate profits can't possibly live up to investors' expectations, the herd panics and starts stampeding to dump stocks.

The old cycle cools, and ordinary investors get hurt. They hold on to their old stocks and mutual funds, waiting for them to come back. As months pass, the statements from their 401(k) and IRA look uglier. Finally the little guy says, "I've got to stop the hemorrhaging, or I'll have no retirement left."

He sells the ugliest investments at their darkest hour and then puts the money into something else. The trouble is that if he turns to another investment that looks hot, perhaps the mutual fund in his 401(k) list that has made the most money in the past year, he is likely close to the top of a new cycle.

Unknowingly, he is positioning his money to get clobbered again as soon as the cycle for that new mutual fund cools. And when that ordinary investor's 401(k) bleeds cash, the poor guy chalks up the entire fiasco to bad luck. The trouble is, it's not luck at all—it's being naive about cycles. It's about forgetting the oft-repeated precept of investing: "Buy low; sell high."

It's managing a 401(k) like playing the roulette wheel, but there's a better way.

What to Expect from the Stock Market

With the realization that cycles occur in the market, you might come to the conclusion that you will stay out of harm's way by avoiding stocks or any mutual fund that holds stocks.

That's the conclusion that almost half of 18- to 30-year-olds reached in 2011 after watching the devastation in the stock market following the housing crash. Stocks fell 57 percent between late 2007 and early 2009 as banks and the economy were poisoned by mortgage-related blunders.

It was the worst market crash since the Great Depression. Twenty-something-year-olds were horrified as one in four lost jobs and then watched their tiny 401(k) savings evaporate while their parents lost giant portions of lifetime savings as retirement age was drawing near. In a survey by MFS Investment Management, 40 percent of people under 30 said, "I will never feel comfortable investing in the stock market." Although the attitude seems reasonable after the shock of one of the worst recessions in U.S. history, avoiding stocks entirely is typically a mistake.

I do not suggest shunning stocks when you have years to go before retiring. In fact, most financial advisers think that even people late in retirement should have a small portion of their savings in the stock market. Notice that I said "small." The amount of money you hold in stocks is key, which I explain in Chapter 11, "Do This."

Perhaps if you were a multimillionaire, you could stay out of the stock market throughout your life and be fine. You could put all your savings into ultrasafe government bonds and earn a little interest on your money, and because you would have so much money in the first place, a tiny "return"— or earnings—on that money might be adequate to provide a decent lifestyle for all the days of your life.

But most Americans can't afford to rely exclusively on ultrasafe investments such as bonds or CDs. They paid only 2 percent interest as the United States was recovering from the 2008 financial crisis. Individuals need to have a sizable portion of their retirement savings invested in the stock market to earn enough to live on later in retirement.

Although bonds were a cozy security blanket for investors throughout the horrible decade that started with the technology stock bubble crash and ended with the housing financial crisis, bonds typically pay investors only about half as much as stocks.

In the unusual decade that started in 2000, investors holding long-term U.S. government Treasury bonds earned an average of 7.7 percent a year, while stocks behaved horribly and averaged a loss of 0.9 percent a year.

But during the past 86 years, from the end of 1925 to the end of 2011, the stock market was much more benevolent than bonds. Despite getting annihilated in stocks during the Great Depression, the recent housing-related crash, and other horrifying periods, the stock market has given investors an average annual gain of 9.8 percent over the 86-year period, according to Morningstar's Ibbotson research. Long-term U.S. Treasury bonds haven't come close. They have provided just 5.7 percent a year on average, and gains from intermediate-term Treasuries have been only 5.4 percent.

Stocks win because good times in the stock market have outweighed the bad over many, many years. Take a look at it in money: A person who put $1 into the stock market at the end of 1925 would have had $3,045 86 years later at the end of 2011, according to Ibbotson. But if that person had put the same $1 into long-term, safe U.S. government bonds for the same 86 years, he would have had only $119 (see Figure 6.1).

Making about $3,045 with a $1 investment might seem shocking to you if you recall some of the terrifying times in the stock market. For example, Ibbotson's numbers include the Great Depression in the 1930s, a period when an investor would have lost 86 percent of the money invested in the stock market. It also includes an awful period in 1973–1974 when stocks fell 48 percent. Most recently, there was the terrifying period between 2000 and 2002, when common folks quaked as their stock market investments fell 49 percent amid an end to the technology stock craze, terrorist attacks, a recession, scandals in corporations such as Enron and WorldCom, and preparations for war in Iraq. Then came the financial crisis of late 2007 to early 2009, when the stock market plunged 57 percent as investors worldwide worried that the entire globe would go into a depression.

Figure 6.1

If you had invested a dollar at the end of 1925, this is how it would have grown over 86 years in various types of investments.

Source: Ibbotson Associates, a Morningstar, Inc., company

Despite all those truly horrifying cycles, $1 in 1925 still turned into about $3,045. And although no one can predict exactly what stocks will do in the future, analysts see no reason why the U.S. stock market shouldn't continue to rise in the future—because it is based on a growing U.S. economy. Simply put, when you invest in the overall stock market through the types of funds I describe in the chapters ahead, you are investing in the overall U.S. economy.

Or as one investment manager once said to me, "The economy goes through recessions. Sometimes individual companies go bankrupt. But if a person contemplates his future and presumes that most Americans will go to jobs each day, and that they will eat dinner, buy clothes for school, drive to friends' homes, and go shopping at supermarkets and shopping malls, that shows an inherent belief in the U.S. economy. That belief should also foster confidence in the stock market's ability to grow." Then he added, "If the person doesn't think anyone is going to have a job and the world as we know it is going to come to an end, his problems are worse than worrying about the stock market. So who cares?"

Stocks Provide Risks and Rewards

I don't mean to make light of the possibility of losing money in the stock market or the fact that the United States has some fundamental economic problems that it must address. As many investors learned in 2000–2002 and then again in 2007 through early 2009, the threat is real. But typically people incur brutal lifelong losses only when they invest money for short periods of time, panic when conditions turn ugly, and foolishly withdraw all their money without realizing that, with time, the cycle will turn.

For example, if a person had $100,000 in a stock mutual fund in a 401(k) just before the housing bust set off the crash in the stock market in October 2007, the individual might have been horrified to see only $43,000 of his money left at the scariest point in March 2009. The stock market would have destroyed $57,000 he once thought was his to keep. But the destruction at that point was on paper, based on a moment in time, and recorded in the records he received from the firm doing the accounting for his 401(k).

He would have made the destruction real and lasting if, at that dark hour for the stock market, he awoke in a sweat one night and said to himself, "I can't take this any longer—pretty soon I'll have nothing left for retirement." If he moved everything the next day to the safety of a money market fund in his 401(k), he would have felt safe but actually would have positioned him-self for real harm. Over the past few years, his money would have earned less than 2 percent. At that rate, even 40 years later, he would not have been able to get back to even with his original $100,000 investment. The $43,000 he rescued from the stock market's destruction would have become only about $95,000 after waiting 40 years.

But if instead he had been able to fight off his fear when the stock mar-ket was ravaging his savings in 2009, and he left his $43,000 sitting in the stock market fund in his 401(k), after about three years, he would have been almost back to even. His $43,000 would have become about $98,000. That's a healing number, especially compared to the wreckage people cemented into their 401(k)s when they fled.

The investor who was scared but clenched his teeth and held on to the mixture of reliable mutual funds I describe in the next chapters gained back everything lost and then some. If he kept adding money during the scary period, his money grew throughout the upward trend in the cycle, and he's well beyond where he was before his friends fled in a panic.

Of course, it's always easier to say what you should have done with your money in retrospect. At the truly dark hour for the stock market in March 2009, no one knew that the cycle was going to turn better soon. During every low point in the market, there is never a clear signal that the worst has occurred and investors will stop losing money and start making it again.

In fact, most of the market analysts who were studying the economy in early 2009 continued to see a frightful future ahead. That's typical. Academic studies have shown that humans are very bad at seeing the future. They tend to expect the recent trend to continue. So when conditions have been bad, they expect more struggle ahead. And when the recent past has been delight-ful, they expect that to continue, too.

So what's a person to do with a 401(k) or IRA? Professionals use history as their guide. They show clients the way stocks have climbed over many years and try to prevent nervous investors from fleeing solid stock mutual funds amid panics. History doesn't provide guarantees or tell you when the good times will return, but it has shown repeatedly that changing cycles always repair the damage that has occurred if investors give the market enough time to move back into an up cycle. Because the U.S. economy con-tinues to grow, there are rough periods when businesses and investors lose money, but the long-term trend is for the stock market to continually recover from downturns and keep climbing (see Table 6.1 for how long bear markets, or severe market downturns, have lasted and how the market recovered).

Table 6.1

Bear Markets Throughout History

	Bear Market Statistics		Performance from Bear Market Low			
	Date of Market Trough	Peak to Trough Loss	Duration of Bear Market	Performance 1 Year Later	Cumulative Performance 2 Years Later	Cumulative Performance 3 Years Later
1	Nov-9-1903	–46%	29 months	59%	93%	122%
2	Nov-15-1907	–49%	22 months	66%	87%	60%**
3	Sep-25-1911	–27%	22 months	28%	13%*	–2%**
4	Jul-30-1914	–24%	22 months	44%	70%	76%
5	Dec-19-1917	–40%	13 months	25%	59%	5%**
6	Aug-24-1921	–47%	21.5 months	56%	44%*	62%
7	Jul-8-1932	–86%	34 months	172%	124%*	141%
8	Mar-14-1935	–34%	20 months	81%	127%	34%**
9	Mar-31-1938	–54%	12.5 months	29%	44%	17%**
10	Apr-28-1942	–46%	41.5 months	54%	59%	98%
11	Jun-13-1949	–30%	36.5 months	42%	59%	80%
12	Oct-22-1957	–22%	14.5 months	31%	44%	37%**
13	Jun-26-1962	–28%	6.5 months	33%	56%	59%
14	Oct-7-1966	–22%	8 months	33%	42%	27%**
15	May-26-1970	–36%	18 months	44%	60%	56%**
16	Oct-3-1974	–48%	20.5 months	38%	67%	55%**
17	Mar-6-1978	–19%	17.5 months	13%	25%	49%
18	Aug-12-1982	–27%	20.5 months	58%	62%	83%
19	Dec-4-1987	–34%	3.5 months	21%	57%	46%**
20	Oct-11-1990	–20%	3 months	29%	36%	56%
21	Aug-31-1998	–19%	1.5 months	38%	59%	18%**
22	Oct-9-2002	–49%	30.5 months	34%	44%	54%
23	Mar-9-2009	–57%	17 months	69%	95%	103%
Average		–38%	19 months	48%	62%	58%

* Notes loss in second year of recovery

** Notes loss in third year of recovery

Source: The Leuthold Group

Bear Markets Maul Investors

During bear markets, or periods when the market drops at least 20 percent, it's natural for investors to get nervous while the bear mauls their savings. In the midst of the downturns, people never know when healing will occur or when they might get back what they've lost.

Yet The Leuthold Group found that, during the many different bear markets that have happened since 1900, the median time it took for investors to recover the money they lost was two years and three months. In half the downturns, they had to wait longer.

Still, even after the worst periods in market history, investors did recover. That's what you must consider as an investor, or you will be doing yourself a disservice. Even after the Great Depression, and losing 86 percent of their money in the stock market, people came out fine if they had time to wait for a recovery. The crash would have been brutal for people who needed to retire soon, but not others. See what would have actually happened to people of various ages who invested $10,000 just before the 1929 stock market crash.

If a 55-year-old had $10,000 saved for retirement before the market crash in 1929, a full 10 years later, at age 65, that person would have continued feeling the pain, with only $6,000 left for retirement. But a 45-year-old in 1929 would have recovered in plenty of time for retirement. By age 65, she would have had about $14,500, despite the destruction the depression initially imposed on her $10,000. Younger people would have fared far better, demonstrating that time is on the young investor's side. A 35-year-old who invested $10,000 just before the crash in 1929 would have seen his $10,000 become about $95,100 by retirement. A 25-year-old would have been unscathed: She would have retired with $210,300. That's right, despite the most devastating loss in history, with $10,000 at first sinking to nearly nothing, the 25-year-old eventually ended up with more than $210,300.

Since the Great Depression, the longest it has taken Americans to recover from a bear market has been 7½ years. That long wait followed a 48 percent loss in 1973–1974. Yet people who went through the pain ended up with a delightful surprise afterward. Over the next 20 years, they averaged about a 16 percent annual return in the market.

Novices Choosing Stocks Are Gamblers

Of course, the pain in bear markets is worse if investors select certain stocks or mutual funds. For example, in the early 1970s, if you had put all your retirement savings into 50 of the most beloved stocks of the day—including

Avon, Xerox, and Polaroid—you would have crashed so hard that it would have taken you $10\frac{1}{2}$ years to recover your money. And the pain would have been particularly difficult to stomach, given the assumptions investors had made just before they took a thrashing.

Back in the early 1970s, when investors were loading up on those so-called "nifty fifty stocks" such as Avon, there was an assumption that the stocks were so strong investors couldn't miss on them. They were supposed to be the stocks people could buy at any price and make money for the rest of their lives. Those promises, like all hype in the market over the years, turned out to be false. Polaroid, for example, fell 91 percent after the herd awoke to reality, and the stock price never went back to what investors had paid for it. Others, such as Coca Cola, which fell 70 percent then, regained strength and went on to delight investors who held on.

This should show you why you should not try to buy individual stocks unless you can, and will, examine a company's financial records deeply. The stocks that fell hardest were those that were overly expensive and looked like a sure thing. Investors were sucked into the hype, falling for hot tips and promises that you couldn't lose.

Whenever investors grab for the enticing story instead of the laborious number crunching that stock picking takes, it's like going to the roulette wheel and putting your money on red. Luck might be on your side, but you will need luck. You are not investing; you are gambling.

Likewise, during the 2000s, many of the dream Internet stocks of the early part of the last decade disappeared. They never had a chance, despite the creative ideas that people thought couldn't fail. And the hurt has continued. Many of the mutual funds that invested in only technology stocks never recovered. They lost 70 to 90 percent initially, and 10 years later, investors were far from getting back to even. For the span of an entire decade, technology stocks remained down about 50 percent.

In other words, if a person had invested $10,000 in technology stocks at the point of the highest euphoria at the end of 1999, that individual would have had stocks worth just $5,000 10 years later. In fact, in March 2012, a full 12 years after that initial $10,000 investment, only $6,800 in value remained. That was better than the $3,500 in spring 2006, but a huge disappointment nevertheless on a $10,000 initial investment.

Both the 2000s and the 1970s delivered a harsh but important lesson for novice investors: A company might be popular with investors, and its product might be enchanting, but that doesn't mean that the company will survive or that the current stock price is a fair one. And if investors awaken one day and discover that the price is too high, you will get crushed if you hold on as the herd stampedes.

Getting excited about a product or a technology is not enough to carry a stock. The management in that company must also know how to raise enough money, produce a product efficiently, position it so that people will buy it, compete effectively against the competition, and survive recessions. People who can't or won't analyze corporate financial statements will get hurt if they buy stocks based on a tip or a gut feeling.

But you don't have to put yourself in this position. If you buy solid mutual funds thoughtfully, you won't need to analyze companies or do math, and you will insulate yourself somewhat from the brutality of cycles. I tell you how you can do this very simply in the following chapters. But first, a quick note about time.

Making Money Takes Time

Because cycles arrive unexpectedly in the stock market, you can never put money into any stock investment, whether it's an individual stock or a mutual fund, and assume that you will make money in the next months or even the next couple years.

Generally, there is a rule of thumb about the stock market: Don't put any money that you will need within five years into the market. The timing is based on the bear market research I mentioned previously. We know that cycles can and will happen, but if you look at history, investors who have been willing to sit tight and weather the downturns have generally come out fine if they could give it at least five years. Of course, after the Depression, it took more than 13 years, which is a sobering fact that cautious people might want to respect.

Still, if you want to live within the rule of thumb and are saving money for a down payment on a house, you wouldn't put any of that money into the stock market if you plan to buy a house within five years. If your child is going to start college in four years, you wouldn't expose money needed for the first couple of years of college to stock mutual funds.

On the other hand, if you are four years away from retirement, you can have some money in the stock market because you won't need all of it the first year. On the day you retire, you will still be investing money for 20 or 30 more years, so you can afford to have perhaps 40 to 60 percent of your money in the stock market at first and then cut it back toward 20 or 30 percent as the years go by. (This is something to discuss with a reputable certified financial planner when you are about five to 10 years from retirement.)

For now, I just want you to recognize the risk of the stock market, but not to fear it when handled wisely. Rushing into the stock market with money you will need soon is foolish. Buying an individual stock on a tip is idiotic. But avoiding the full stock market is equally foolish when you have savings that must grow during the next 20, 30, or 40 years.

Again, history helps to lay the groundwork for thinking. Although the chances of losing money in the stock market are great over a 1-year period, and possible in a 5-year period, when you move to a 10-year period, investors have lost money only twice—between 1929 and 1938, which was the Depression, and between 2000 and 2009. Investors have never lost money over 15 years or longer, according to Ibbotson research.

When thinking about risks, remember that stocks are definitely dangerous if you rely too heavily on them or cut yourself short on time. You take on tremendous risks if you try to pick them yourself by running with the herd instead of doing serious research on their profit potential.

But another risk is critically important when saving for retirement: the risk of running out of money when you are 70 or 80 and cannot go back to work. To prevent that risk, you must respect the stock market and use it to your advantage in the simple and effective ways I explain next.

7

What's a Mutual Fund?

Now that you are aware that cycles in the market will play havoc with your money, you are ready to select mutual funds with your eyes open. Instead of making foolish mistakes that will cripple your savings, you will be able to select certain mutual funds to insulate you from cycles, while giving you a chance to make money whenever and wherever conditions are bestowing wealth.

If you are like many people with a 401(k) plan, you can't tell one mutual fund from another. Don't feel bad about this. You are in good company. A few years ago, two well-known professors, Shlomo Benartzi and Richard Thaler, set out to see how people picked mutual funds in their 401(k) plans. They gave a list of funds to employees at the University of California, and their mutual fund choices were abysmal. The employees, like most Americans, didn't have the slightest idea what they were doing with mutual funds. They didn't understand what the names of the funds were telling them, so they simply chose every single fund they were offered, even though they should have ignored some of the funds.

You might do that, too—and, if so, you are probably overexposing yourself to the cruelty of cycles and potentially slicing hundreds of thousands of dollars from your future retirement money.

Other mistakes are also common. Typically, when novice investors are losing money in their mutual funds, or making less money than their friends are making with other mutual funds, they surmise that they've selected a dud and blown it as an investor.

Neither, however, may be true. You may have a very fine mutual fund that is losing money, or you could be getting richer by the day with a fund that is actually lousy. I know this is counterintuitive: If something looks good, we generally assume that it is good. In investing, the opposite often is true.

Through no fault of its own, your particular fund might simply be temporarily positioned at the top or bottom of a cycle. When that cycle turns, your loser will seem like a phenomenal choice. Instead of destroying your money, it will start making money. Meanwhile, the fund you cherish because it is making you so much money today eventually could look like garbage. Then months later, or even a couple years later, your garbage fund could turn sweet again and your favorite fund could sour.

Your Fund Is Designed for a Purpose

The reason sweet funds often turn into temporary losers is simple: Each mutual fund is constructed for a unique purpose and, therefore, is filled with stocks or bonds that are intended to be strong in certain cycles and weaker in others. This is no small matter. If you don't know this, you will give some mutual funds more credit than they are due and shun some that deserve to be in your IRA or 401(k) portfolio. About a dozen basic designs exist, and none is inherently good or bad. Each is simply unique.

Think of a bakery. It sells baked goods, but it offers a wide variety intended for different purposes. You can buy muffins, bread, and cake. All are intended to be eaten, but at different points in the day. In other words, they are all valuable but different from each other. Perhaps each is baked to perfection based on a unique recipe. Still, you probably don't want the cake for breakfast, and that doesn't mean the baker flopped when baking the cake. Based on where you are in the day's cycle, the muffin might be best in the morning, the bread at lunch, and the cake after supper.

Just as you want bread, muffins, and cake depending on where you are in the cycle of the day, you want a unique mutual fund for each point in the stock market's cycle.

And just as you might have all three baked goods in your freezer, awaiting the point in the day when you will want them, you do that with a variety of mutual funds. You keep the variety on hand in your IRA or 401(k) at all times, ready for the parts of the cycle when each will perform best.

Unfortunately, people get tripped up in this process. It seems complex, even though it isn't. So in effect, if they see that everyone wants cake, they make the mistake of buying only cake—for example, stock mutual funds filled to the brim with technology stocks in the 1990s, or bond mutual funds filled to the brim with mortgages as the housing crash turned ugly in 2008. But loading up on cake, or a mutual fund that is intended to be the dessert after the main meal, is a disaster for investors.

Want to know whether you have inadvertently been loading up on cake? If you were happy at the end of the 1990s with your 401(k) mutual funds and then hated them between 2000 and 2002, you probably were guilty. You probably were unintentionally eating too much cake at the end of the 1990s, and that made your money sick in 2000. And if you had a bond mutual fund that didn't protect you from the stock market crash in 2008–2009, you made the same mistake of overdosing on sugar.

But it doesn't have to be this way. The strange words you see on your mutual funds are intended to help you understand whether they should be a staple, like bread, or whether they are dessert, intended to be consumed in dessert-size portions.

Soon you will be able to look at a list of mutual funds and know at a glance what each fund is intended to do for you in various cycles. When you reach that point, you will never feel befuddled again as you look over names on a 401(k) list or when a financial adviser starts chattering to you in a seemingly foreign language.

All you need is a little vocabulary. The first step is to understand what your mutual fund manager does to try to make your money grow.

What Happens in a Mutual Fund?

When you select a mutual fund in a 401(k), an IRA, or any other account, you—along with hundreds of other people—are turning over your money to an expert. You know you don't have the expertise to examine more than 8,000 different stocks that make up the stock market. You have no idea how to determine which stocks have the potential to make you money or lose money. Nor can you examine the thousands of bonds available in the market. You'd probably prefer to devote your free time to your family, friends, or fun than to analyze whether a stock or bond might be a good investment.

So you turn over your money to a professional called a fund manager. In doing so, you tell that fund manager to spend every day trying to figure out which stocks or bonds will make you as much money as possible while also ducking excessive risks. Each day, the manager watches the economy and different businesses.

If the manager works for a so-called equity mutual fund, he or she will pick many stocks for your fund, possibly 100 or more. The word *equity* simply means "stocks." So every day your mutual fund manager hunts for the best stocks for you and all the other investors in your fund. Managers analyze each business they think will make you money and determine whether both business conditions and stock market conditions are in place to stimulate a stock price higher and boost the value of your mutual fund investment. When the individual stocks in your fund are going up in price, your share of that mutual fund also goes up in value, and you make money. If your fund manager is doing a good job, your tiny savings in the mutual fund should start looking like thousands—not in a month, maybe not in a year, but after a few years.

To analyze a particular stock, the fund manager tries to figure out whether the company is producing products well, whether the products are keeping up with the competition, whether new competitors are likely to take customers away, whether the employees are creative about designing new products that customers will want, whether the sales force sells well, whether managers handle money effectively, and whether the company has the money to fulfill its innovative plans and make profits grow.

The Key: Company Profits

Analyzing a company's profit potential is the name of the game. And it's not easy to do. Superficial guesses—the types that ordinary investors make when they try to pick individual stocks on their own—don't work.

Typically, when a company's profits grow—especially if profits grow more than investors thought they would—the company's stock price goes up. So if you own the stock of a surprisingly profitable company, or if your mutual fund owns that stock for you, you make money on it.

When a fund manager spots a company with potential, he or she might buy the stock—or not. First, the manager examines the stock price and compares it to the profits he thinks the company will generate. Managers want to make sure they don't pay too much for the stock, and the only way to know is to scrutinize the company's profit potential.

If the manager thinks the company is going to delight investors with more profits than anyone expected, that's a good sign that investors will make money, and the manager might buy the stock. If the manager spots a threat—perhaps a new competitor for that company—he or she might not buy the stock, even though it's been a tremendous success in the past. If the manager thinks a company might have trouble borrowing money at a low interest rate, he or she might not buy the stock because the company could have difficulty making or selling products if it doesn't have enough cheap cash. The analysis goes on and on.

Meanwhile, other investors are eyeing the same stock. If many of them are excited about the company's growing business at the same time, they will snap up the stock and the stock price consequently will soar. Under those conditions, your fund manager might decide that the stock price is too high and won't buy it.

High Stock Prices Can Be Warning Signs

This is often a shocking revelation to novice investors. Why not go for it if the stock price is soaring? However, the manager's decision isn't based solely on the quality of the company or the recent delicious gains people have made on the stock. The manager might think it's a phenomenal company with great products and smart managers, but when stock prices get too high, stocks are vulnerable. High-priced stocks fall hard, hurting investors with the slightest misstep. Managers know that a sudden unexpected turn in the economy could change the outlook for a hot company, reversing the cycle that was carrying the stock higher and higher.

So instead of buying a stock at an extremely high price, cautious fund managers might determine that they want to own the promising stock for you, but at a lower price. If you make a point of shopping for clothes only when they are on sale, you understand this concept completely. Perhaps you've had your eye on a sweater, but it's expensive. So you wait to buy it, knowing that the store will offer a sale in a couple weeks and mark down everything 25 or 30 percent. Then you will buy—you will get the same sweater you wanted, but at a more reasonable price.

As you walk out of the store, you will commend yourself for finding such a "good value." In the mutual fund world, the funds that are conscientious about shopping for "good values" actually alert you to that discipline sometimes through their names. (I tell you how to spot these so-called value funds in Chapter 9, "Know Your Mutual Fund Manager's Job.")

Fund managers are always busy looking for deals—or stocks that appear to be marked down temporarily. Shopping for them is slightly different from shopping in a store. That's because the fund manager doesn't know when the stock will go on sale. It might take months or years.

For an extreme example, consider the terrorist attacks of 2001. After the terrorists crashed airplanes into the World Trade Center and the Pentagon, investors were fleeing stocks—especially hotel stocks—as Americans stopped traveling. The stock prices plunged below bargain-basement levels. That's when Oakmark mutual fund manager Bill Nygren loaded up on stock in Starwood Hotel (Sheraton and Westin). At the time, it seemed like Americans would never fly again, but Nygren told me that he couldn't imagine Americans giving up on vacations or one-on-one business meetings with clients forever. As fears eased and people traveled again, the stock became a winner; it climbed about 55 percent in 2003 and 65 percent in 2004.

In the financial crisis of 2009, American Express stock plunged from more than $60 a share to less than $10 as investors worried that virtually every bank and financial company would collapse. Then as investors overcame their fear, studied American Express, and decided that it would not implode, the price soared 126 percent that year—a phenomenal gain as other financial companies remained suspect.

Even when the price of a stock comes down and fund managers consider buying it, they don't leap immediately. They reexamine the company to make sure that, while they were waiting for a good price, the company didn't slip in some way that might stifle profits in the future. Stock prices can fall for many reasons, sometimes because a company is making mistakes, but other times because of something less troublesome, such as a temporary downturn in the economy. For example, stores might see their sales slow during recessions, but powerful companies such as Wal-Mart and Home Depot usually come back to life when the short-term economic pressures subside.

No assurances exist, however. To make sure the company has no hidden problem when an attractive stock dips in price, the fund manager goes back to his or her original analysis and reexamines how the company produces and sells its products. Managers want to know what profits to expect so that they can determine whether the current stock price is a good deal. It doesn't matter what stock price existed in the past or what the profits were like in the past. It doesn't matter that people got rich on the stock last year or during the last ten years. Only one thing matters for the stock's future: what profits the company will generate in the future.

Novice investors who buy stocks themselves often make a major mistake with this: They look at a stock price of $20 and say to themselves, "It's a great deal because people used to buy that stock at $50." But that's flawed thinking. Stocks have no memory. Yesterday's price will never be repeated again unless the company becomes more profitable than investors are anticipating.

Want an example? In the preceding chapter, I mentioned Polaroid, a high-flying stock in the 1970s. Investors loved it with the same intensity some had for Amazon in the 1990s or Apple and Google recently. Analysts told investors to pay higher prices for Polaroid because it would never go down and disappoint them. But you know now that camera products have changed dramatically since the 1970s. Polaroid's stock hit a high in the early 1970s, crashed, and never got back to the price that gullible investors paid for it.

Repeatedly, the glorious stocks of certain periods fade when competition changes. And individuals who aren't watching closely and who fall in love with a tremendous winner get brutalized. For example, investors adored the company that made BlackBerry smartphones when the phones were first introduced to the market and every American with money wanted one. The stock price of BlackBerry-maker Research in Motion (RIM) shot up to $140 in 2008. But then came the flashier iPhone. Suddenly, the BlackBerry became passé, and investors who missed the change lost almost all their money on the stock as it fell to $7. It didn't matter that the stock price had once been at $140. What mattered was that people weren't buying BlackBerry phones, and the profits were going to Apple—not Research in Motion.

When your fund manager looks at a stock, he or she focuses on the outlook for profits at that company for the next quarter, the next year, and so on.

Fund Managers Baby-Sit Stocks

If everything checks out and the manager thinks the company is on the road to being more profitable, he or she buys the stock. Then the manager watches that stock every day, looking for warning signs that the business might be losing its footing. If any concerns arise, the manager tries to sell the stock before it plummets. If the manager fails to pick up on problems early, the stock could fall hard—and you could lose some money.

Besides watching for problems, managers are equally vigilant about the winners in the fund, knowing that stocks will climb only so far. When managers think that point is nearing, they often sell the stock and, with that money, try to buy another stock that is cheaper and, consequently, more promising for the future.

Before fund managers buy a new stock, they look at a list of stocks they've been keeping and try to identify a favorite company that temporarily has a cheap stock price compared to the profits the manager expects the company to generate in the future.

In other words, the manager tries to "buy low and sell high," a comment you might have heard about buying stocks. It's the key precept of good stock investing—and the most often abused because people are emotional. Instead of buying a cheap stock that will soar over time, people get sucked into the excitement and hype over the hot stocks of the moment. They buy expensive stocks, like BlackBerry's Research in Motion, just as the cycle for that stock is about to peak and smart fund managers are getting ready to dump them.

What's in Your Fund?

Many mutual funds contain 100 to 500 different stocks. So when you buy a share in your mutual fund with your 401(k) or IRA money, you end up owning a tiny, tiny piece of many companies. For example, if your mutual fund invests in Apple, you own a teeny piece of all the Apple stores. If your fund invests in General Electric, you own a miniscule piece of the company that makes everything from stoves to jet engines. If your fund owns McDonald's stock, you own a smidgen of the restaurants, and you hope that people continue to want to eat hamburgers or that McDonald's will figure out how to attract customers with other foods.

If, on any particular day, investors think consumers are squeamish about hamburgers or that McDonald's has lost the knack for making as much money as it has in the past, the stock price will fall, and your mutual fund will lose money on that stock that day. But you might not lose money overall in your mutual fund, because you will have dozens of other stocks to cushion the McDonald's blow. For example, General Electric and Apple might look like they've got their act down, and their stock prices might be rising nicely on the same day McDonald's is losing ground.

When you have a mutual fund, each individual stock is not as important as the mixture of stocks. So your fund manager intentionally tries to blend stocks that act differently from each other during cycles. If your fund manager buys more stocks that climb rather than fall, you will make money. But you will always have some losers. Some companies will make mistakes in their businesses, so the stocks will turn into rotten investments—maybe temporarily, maybe for as long as the company survives. Your fund manager will try to spot the problems early and sell the stock before you lose a lot of money on it. But that's often not possible.

Unforeseen shocks always arise. For example, although investors did well with hotel stocks after the terrorist attacks in 2001, the shock pulled the rug out from under airlines. Many ended up in bankruptcy.

Then there's Merck, which makes prescription drugs. It was a glamorous stock at the end of the 1990s. But in 2004 the stock plunged from about $45 a share to $33 in just one day after Merck pulled its blockbuster product, Vioxx, off the market because of evidence that the painkiller was dangerous. In other words, in a single day, an investor—whether a person or a mutual fund—lost about 27 percent of the money invested in the stock. Amid hundreds of suits over patient deaths and illnesses, the stock continued to drop. Investors lost about half of their money within months. By 2006, Merck stock was climbing again, but many investors bailed out long before that happened.

Here's the important point I want you to keep in mind about mutual funds: Your opportunity to survive a stock blow-up is tremendously enhanced if you own mutual funds than if you try to select a handful of individual stocks. If you had a mutual fund that invested in Merck, you would have lost a little money because of the Vioxx mess. If, however, you had simply purchased the individual stock and decided to flee, you would have lost about half the money you had invested in it. In your mutual fund, you had protection. You had many other stocks that were great investments at the time of the Merck fiasco, and the strong stocks buffered your loss. You probably didn't feel it a bit.

Cycles Take Stocks for a Ride

Aside from corporate disasters such as Vioxx, cycles work on the different stocks in your mutual fund in different ways. For a while, investors will be enamored with retail stocks like Wal-Mart, and that company, like other retailers, will be on a roll in the stock market, riding the cycle for retail stocks higher and higher. Meanwhile, investors might not be particularly excited about some other type of stock.

For example, investors didn't want anything to do with gold mining stocks for roughly two decades before the 2000s. Yet in 2005, those stocks shot up almost 33 percent as investors worldwide started stockpiling gold as they feared inflation and geopolitical unrest. Also, throughout the technology craze, investors snubbed energy stocks. Yet for 12 years after that, from the beginning of 2000 to March 2012, investors made more money in energy stocks than any other industry. Energy stocks gained 156 percent, while technology stocks lost 52 percent of investors' money, and banks and other financial stocks lost 41 percent. Investors didn't want to touch bank stocks as losses mounted on mortgages and mortgage-related investments.

Eventually, every cycle—no matter what is hot at the time—will turn. Mutual fund managers who seek bargains will say to themselves at some point, "Bank stocks aren't popular now, but I can find good deals on those stocks. I'll buy them and hold on to them until they turn popular again, making the investors in my fund a lot of money." Or at some point they will say, "People are going to cut back on gasoline if they lose jobs in a recession, so I'm going to sell Exxon and other energy stocks now, while I can still make a good gain."

The mixture of stocks you get in mutual funds insulates you from different cycles and also from a particular company's stumbling. At any time, some stocks in your fund will be falling, but the rising stocks will cushion the fall so that your money keeps growing or shrinks merely a little, recovering a short time later.

When your mutual fund owns a lot of stocks that are going up, you will be making money. If the fund manager makes a lot of mistakes and buys more losing stocks than winners, you will lose money—at least temporarily.

Good Funds Can Be Losers

Picking stocks is difficult, even for the most brilliant fund managers. Some of the nation's top managers have told me they regret about 40 percent of the stocks they pick. They inevitably make mistakes on forecasts for the economy and companies. Because the stock market runs in cycles, your mutual fund will sometimes lose money even though the fund manager has selected excellent stocks.

Cycles hit certain types of investments, or groups of stocks, without warning. Entire industries, or what are called "sectors," get hurt as a group. By groups, or sectors, I'm referring, for example, to all energy company stocks, or all manufacturing company stocks, or all retail company stocks, and so on. When people worry that consumers won't be shopping much, for example, everything from Costco to Home Depot and Gap might go down together. This is important to know because if, for example, you owned Costco stock and were watching only it, you might see the stock price fall and think something was wrong with your stock alone. In fact, Costco might be suffering temporarily in a cycle that will turn.

Cycles also hit various parts of the world at different times. In the late 1990s, investors ran away from Latin American stocks in terror, as companies suffered from economic and political turmoil. Investors swore they'd never put a penny into Latin America or other emerging or developing nations again because they'd been burned so badly. Yet if they were still snubbing Latin American companies in 2005, they missed out on an astronomical 76 percent return as China and the rest of Asia hungered for Latin American oil and natural resources.

As an investor, you won't get hurt by any of these cycles if you don't overdose on anything that looks overly enticing—like energy companies amid a boom or Latin American stocks riding the wave. Your future depends on recognizing what's making each mutual fund do what it's doing and knowing that cycles will affect various mutual funds differently. You need to know this whether your funds are bestowing riches at the moment or sucking wealth away from investors.

This might sound like a mammoth task. But I'll teach you an easy shortcut. It simply involves recognizing some befuddling names that currently make mutual funds appear confusing. You are about to learn how to eye mutual funds quickly and choose them with confidence.

I'll start walking you through the process.

8

MAKING SENSE OF WACKY
MUTUAL FUND NAMES

When I started going to physical therapy for a back problem a few years ago, word spread quickly that I was a new patient there. One of the therapists, Mark, told me while strapping me into a weight machine one day that he and other therapists were trying to edge their way onto the schedule so they could get me as a patient and grab a little investment advice.

He apologized for "taking advantage of a client" but then persevered anyway.

It wasn't unusual. I'm used to being cornered at parties, at doctors' offices, at the hair salon, and even in the gym by apologetic people who are perplexed about investing and desperate for help. I can almost predict their questions before they ask them.

Nothing prepares Americans to invest money for their futures. So everyone, from doctors to hair stylists, commits similar, devastating mistakes that they could easily avoid if they simply knew about stock market cycles, picked up about a dozen vocabulary words, and had a few basic tidbits of information about making mutual fund choices.

So I told Mark I was happy to assist him or anyone else.

At the therapist's office, there was a sense of urgency. The staff, like so many ordinary investors, had been badly bruised by the 49 percent plunge in the stock market during the technology stock wreck. They had no idea how to rehabilitate their long-lost savings.

Mark, for example, was a therapist by day and a blues musician at night. When he looked at his list of mutual funds, he saw nothing but "wacky words." None of them made sense, so he made the same mistake that masses of other novice investors do. He looked over his list of 401(k) funds and saw one that was making more money than any of the others. Figuring that it had to be the *best* one, he put all his money into it.

Picking the big money maker, the fund that looked the best, had led him into a dangerous snare. By selecting the champion among his fund choices, he had set the groundwork for a disaster, but he didn't know it. For a while, he was ecstatic. Every time he eyed the account, he saw more thousands. The sum was getting so big that, at one point, he had visions of retiring rich and devoting his time to his music. Then one day the cycle changed, and thousands of dollars vanished for some seemingly mysterious reason. Every day he peeked at his 401(k), it was worse. Instead of retiring rich, he began envisioning himself forever setting up weight machines for sweaty people.

When Mark told me about his missed fortune, he looked like he was in more pain than I as I struggled to finish my 19th repetition on the weight machine. Then he asked me the same naive question thousands of others have asked me: "I've lost so much money in my mutual fund. Should I sell it?"

"What fund is it?" I asked. And the answer he gave to that critical question was totally predictable, an area where most investors get tripped up unnecessarily. Like the average person with a 401(k), Mark didn't know the name of his fund, and, of course, didn't have the slightest idea what the fund manager's job was. All he knew was that he was losing money.

"Knowing what the fund manager has been hired to do is essential," I told Mark. "The clue often comes from the fund's name."

Then I delivered the shocker: "I know it's awful to be losing money, but the loss alone tells me nothing about whether your fund is good or bad. Your fund might simply have suffered along with others in a bad market cycle."

Poor Mark! He looked like he had just edged his way onto the physical therapy scheduling list for nothing. Yet when I returned for my next therapy session, Mark was primed. He knew the name of his fund and gave me his full list of 401(k) choices.

"Which is the best fund?" he asked. He was making another toxic mistake that virtually every novice investor makes.

"That's the wrong question," I told him as I watched his earnest face turn disappointed once again. "There is no single best or right fund in your 401(k) plan—or anyone else's 401(k) or IRA. If you rely on just one fund again, your retirement dreams will probably implode one more time. Instead, what you have in your 401(k) are several funds that you need to combine.

"Think of it like baking a cake. Flour is one of the right ingredients, but if you leave out sugar, eggs, and a few more ingredients, your recipe is going to be a flop. You have a retirement fund disaster now because you tried to make a recipe using only sugar.

"So now look at your 401(k) list," I told him. "I will give you a quick recipe for retirement investing success. To start, I am going to help you understand the wacky words, because everyone needs to recognize them. They are invaluable. They tell you whether you are selecting flour or sugar," I explained.

"Next, I'm going to tell you how to mix them together. Proportions matter a lot. You can ruin a 401(k) or IRA by using too much or too little of an ingredient, just like you will ruin a cake by using only a tablespoon of flour when the recipe calls for a cup."

Mark was wearing his hopeful, earnest face again. And in less than an hour, I gave him all the basics he—or anyone—needs to be a successful investor in a 401(k), an IRA, or any other retirement account.

This is what I told him, and I offer it as a roadmap for you now and in the next couple chapters. It is your guide to maneuver through cycles and make sense of the befuddling language. It's what people pay financial advisers to handle for them. But regular people can master it, regardless of their background. It's your recipe for a decent retirement. I promise.

Avoid the Traps

When employers create 401(k) plans for their employees, they typically provide about a dozen mutual fund choices—but that doesn't mean they are all for you. Some people like to tinker with their mutual funds more than others. Some want to take more risks than other people. Some will be retiring in a couple years, and some have decades to go. Consequently, a few of the mutual funds in the 401(k) will be essential for you, and others are available so that there is something for everyone. You need to zoom through the mess and focus on what you need—not what looks like a winner.

The mutual fund with the best return is often not the essential one. In fact, you can think of it as a decoy or trap, perhaps distracting you from the mixture of funds that ultimately will be best for you. If you throw all your money into the enticing fund, it will likely hold you hostage from a decent retirement. Falling into the trap seems to be human nature. In a recent study, Harvard students were given a list of mutual funds, and almost everyone fell into the dangerous snare.

Instead of falling for it, when you see the highest return, remind yourself about cycles. The fund that is attracting you is probably riding a cycle that could be about to end. This was the case with Mark's choice, a stock fund on steroids, filled with technology stocks. He was attracted to it when it was on its last legs.

Instead of focusing on the hot fund, there's another way—the only way that works: Make your way through categories.

The Three Main Choices: Stocks, Bonds, and Cash

Having a dozen or more choices of mutual funds can be overwhelming, but while they make your head spin, the pros see it much more simply—and you can, too. Realize that virtually all the funds before you in a 401(k), and almost all available for an IRA, fall into three basic categories: stocks, bonds, and cash.

When you know that, your choices will start to dwindle. Instead of feeling like you have to make sense of a dozen funds with strange names, now you are focusing on just three simple categories.

Even discerning between stocks and bonds on a 401(k) list might seem hard at first because investment pros muck up those easy words by using their own lingo. When they mean stocks, they sometimes use the word *equity*. When they mean bonds, they might use the words *fixed income*. The same might happen when you go to a broker to open an IRA. But your choices ultimately come from the same three basic categories.

To the pros, the special language has extra meaning, but just speak English to yourself. Say, "Okay, I have a choice between a fund that will buy stocks for me and a fund that will buy bonds for me."

In addition, just about every 401(k) has something in it called a money market fund. When you see one, consider it like a piggy bank for cash. That's your relatively safe place to store money when you are trying to decide what investment to use next. It's similar to a savings account at a bank, although not as safe as a bank account because no FDIC insurance guarantees your money.

After you recognize the difference between stocks, bonds, and cash, you are halfway home. You don't need to use the money market fund, but you will need to put a good chunk of money into stock mutual funds and another chunk into a bond mutual fund. Using both stocks and bonds is what the professionals refer to as diversification. That's important, and I will explain how to do it right and simply.

First, I must teach you a few more vocabulary words so that the "wacky words" help you rather than hurt you, and so that your mutual funds no longer act in mysterious ways. The wacky words sound strange, but they alert you to how each fund will behave in cycles. The words guide you to the variety of funds you need to weather all cycles.

If you put money into a stock mutual fund, you will own stocks—maybe 100 of them, all within that one mutual fund. So when people are making money in the stock market, you will likely be making money in your fund. When people are losing money on stocks in a rough cycle, it's likely that you will be losing, too. This is why it was not relevant that Mark's mutual fund was losing money. It was natural that he would be losing when the stock market was dropping 49 percent. In fact, losing some money, though unpleasant, doesn't necessarily mean a mutual fund is defective.

What mattered was whether Mark's mutual fund was losing *more* money than other funds like his and whether he'd given himself enough protection from inevitable market cycles by investing in a variety of mutual funds instead of just the one. Without knowing the name or the description of his fund, he was in the dark, absolutely unable to make a smart decision. His quandary is almost universal among people with a 401(k) or an IRA.

By the end of my session with Mark, he realized where he'd gone wrong. He had not known about cycles, so in his attempt to be prudent and pick the *best* fund, he had chosen a dangerous one: a fund posing as a mild-mannered large cap fund but hyped up on an overdose of technology stocks. That overdose made it exceedingly vulnerable to cycles. His fate was sealed the moment the tantalizing fund lured him in.

There was a better way to pick funds, I told Mark. I gave him all the tools he needed to assess whether a certain fund is better or worse than others. I will provide you with that same ability. In addition, I started with the most essential of investing lessons: To avoid grief in the future, Mark could not depend merely on a single stock mutual fund. He needed bonds, too. He needed to start diversifying. In other words, he needed to start mixing and matching mutual funds into an appropriate combination so that cycles wouldn't hurt him badly the next time conditions turned brutal.

That strategy would save him from the destruction that was about to brutalize others between late 2007 and early 2009, as people from throughout the world feared a global depression.

Why You Need Bonds

Mark was a lucky guy. After holding me captive in a weight machine for an hour a week for a few weeks, he would never have his money ravaged again the way it had been in the technology stock wreck that ended 2002. I gave him the antidote against stock market poisoning: a good dose of bonds.

Unfortunately, too many people didn't learn early in the decade that they needed bonds for protection. So they were completely defenseless a second time when once again the stock market devoured half their money, this time from late 2007 to early 2009, in the worst crash since the Great Depression.

When you lose half your money twice in a decade, you wise up. People learned through the school of hard knocks that stocks can turn cruel. As a result, many dumped stocks completely and figured they would hide in bonds.

Yet they still didn't really understand how bonds work. They didn't realize that people can lose money in bonds as well as stocks. So many naive investors inadvertently made a move with their money once again that would potentially bring on hardship.

I explain later in this chapter how bonds can hurt you. Now I simply want you to know that bonds are critical to your future. Yet they work best for people saving for retirement when they are combined with stocks instead of being used as your sole investment.

You can think of bonds like shock absorbers, or protection that you always want installed in your retirement savings. When the stock market suddenly starts to bang you around, bonds soften the blows and return you to a smooth ride. They reduce the damage stocks alone can inflict on your money.

Because you keep that protection in place all the time, you can have more courage day in and day out with your money. Stocks, while potentially destructive, also can be benevolent, growing your money far more than bonds alone. When you have the security of holding bonds all the time, you can dare to also own stocks. That way, you have the best of all worlds: protection provided from bonds, but the possibility of enjoying the huge growth spurts that only stocks deliver.

Let me walk you through an example of how bond protection works. Let's go back to 2007. You might recall that the year started blissfully, with no inkling of the horror to come. The economy was booming, people were still making money on homes, stocks were soaring, and Americans were feeling secure about the future. They had forgotten the devastation of the technology stock wreck in 2000–2002. Since that 49 percent decline in the stock market, stocks had soared more than 70 percent.

Fear was gone. People trusted stock funds in their 401(k) again to do the heavy lifting for their meager savings. One in four baby boomers was rushing to catch up for lost time by keeping 90 percent of 401(k) money in the stock market.

This cozy feeling wasn't unusual. Before every major market crash, the last thing people imagine is trouble. Everything around them points to prosperity. That very comfort level drives excessive risk taking and, ultimately, ends badly in a crash.

That's why, in good times and in bad times, people need bonds constantly in their 401(k) and IRA. Bonds are protection when horrible stock markets sneak up on investors.

So observe the outcome.

Imagine that it is that comfortable time in 2007, and you take a look at your 401(k). The money in your stock fund has increased 16 percent since the previous year. At the same time, however, you've had a bond fund—a huge disappointment, by comparison. It's gained just 2 percent in a year. So you figure, "Why let my money languish in the lousy fund that pays just 2 percent?"

You don't realize that there is absolutely nothing wrong with that bond fund. It has been behaving exactly as bond funds do. In good times, bonds usually pay you less than stock funds—often significantly less.

Naively, you snub that bond fund and put all $10,000 that's in your 401(k) into the stock fund that's been so sweet to you. You figure that you've been pretty clever with your money by moving all of it where it will grow more.

Then investors throughout the world start getting spooked by the mortgage mess in the U.S. and stocks start falling. You ignore it at first, but then it's early 2009—the nation's unemployment rate is spiraling, businesses are crippled, banks have been collapsing, and investors throughout the world are panicking. You imagine losing everything, and you are horrified when you look into your 401(k). Your original $10,000 in stocks has turned into only $4,300.

From that point, the stock market starts climbing. But you don't see relief coming. At the ugliest point, nothing calms your nerves. Virtually, every Wall Street talker you hear on the news predicts doom and gloom ahead.

You might have felt more calm if you hadn't relied on stocks alone and had been holding bonds for protection. Instead of putting everything into a stock fund in 2007, if you had divided your retirement savings in half—with 50 percent in the stock market fund and the other half in bonds—the outcome would have been ugly, yes, but significantly better.

With bonds and stocks together, you would have had $7,700 at the scariest point in the cycle instead of a mere $4,300. You would have still been way below your original $10,000, so even $7,700 probably would not have been reassuring.

But then came the healing. The fact that you retained $7,700 instead of only $4,300 while the stock market was plunging positioned your money to recover relatively quickly and start growing again. By the end of 2011, about 2½ years after the scariest period in the market, you would have had about $12,500—or $2,500 more than your original $10,000. Not bad at all for the most dreadful period for investors since the Great Depression.

Yet if you had not used bonds and had relied 100 percent on stocks, by the end of 2011, you still would have been in sorry shape. You would have recovered somewhat from the point when only $4,300 of your original $10,000 remained. But as 2012 began, you would have had just $9,000 and still would have been wondering when your original $10,000 might reappear.

In other words, here's the moral of this story: When you mix bonds in with the stocks, you get a smoother, more reassuring ride. You don't have to know when stocks will be kind to you, or cruel to you. Bonds become your lifesaver.

What's a Bond?

Bonds generally are safer than stocks for one basic reason. When either a person or a mutual fund buys a bond, a specific promise is made—one that doesn't exist for stocks: The promise is the following: If you buy an individual bond, you will loan money temporarily to a corporation, to the U.S. government, to a city, or to some other entity. (The entity's name appears on the bond.)

You know the concept if you've ever given a reliable friend a loan and been paid interest for doing it. The bond itself works the same way. It's simply an IOU for a loan that you make to a stranger instead of a friend. At some specific date in the future, the loan will end and the corporation or government will give all your money back to you. Until that date arrives, however, you will get a certain amount of interest on a regular schedule. It won't change; it will be like a tiny paycheck that comes regularly.

This promise is why people buy bonds. They want to earn interest on their money, and they like the safety of knowing that the interest check will arrive like clockwork. They want to earn more interest than they would in a savings account. They especially like the assurance that eventually they will get all their original money, or principal, returned to them.

If you own an individual bond, you will get your interest payments directly on a specified date. But if you instead invest in a bond mutual fund, your fund will hold the bonds for you and hundreds of other investors in your fund. The interest payments will go into your fund, not directly to you. In effect, you will be sharing the interest payments with all the other investors who put money into your mutual fund.

Regardless of whether you buy a bond directly or your fund manager buys a bond for your fund, the same process occurs. When you loan money to a corporation or governmental entity by buying a bond, that entity tells you up front when it will return that money to you. It might be 5 years or even 30 years.

Take, for example, the hypothetical Nimble Pots and Pans Company. It needs money to develop some new pan factories around the world, so it decides to borrow the money by selling bonds to many different people. You hear about it from a broker and decide that you will buy one of the bonds so that you can earn interest. Nimble sells you a $1,000 bond through your broker. The bond is like an IOU. You turn over $1,000 to your broker, she gives it to Nimble, and then Nimble promises to give you back the full $1,000 on September 15, 2023. Meanwhile, to make it worth your while, Nimble also promises to pay you interest for the next ten years. In this case, let's say it's 5 percent, paid semiannually. That's $50 a year, or $25 paid in September and $25 paid in March every year until September 15, 2023.

As the years go by, you rely on Nimble to keep its promise. After 10 years, you assume that you will get your original $1,000, or what's called your principal, returned to you.

How to Lose Money in Bonds

Although bonds are your insulation from painful stock market cycles, they are not absolutely safe. You need to know this so that you don't bail out of your bond fund at the first sign of a loss. I've had people call me horrified over a dip in a bond fund. "There's something wrong with my bond fund— it's losing money," they say, unaware that losses can occur even in relatively safe bond funds during a few months or even a year.

Combined with a stock fund over many years, your bond fund will protect your money. The losses in bonds aren't nearly as intense as those in stocks and typically don't last as long. Whereas the worst single year in stocks has been a downturn of 43 percent, the worst for U.S. government bonds has been 15 percent, according to Ibbotson Associates. With less lost, recoveries come faster. So expect bumps from bond funds, and understand why they occur so that you don't dump a fund you should hold.

You face two types of risks in bonds. I start with what's called credit risk. You need to know the concept, not the term.

It works like this: When you or your fund manager buys a corporate bond such as a Nimble Pots and Pans bond, you take a risk that you won't get all your money back. Remember, when you buy an individual bond, you are making a lengthy loan—maybe for five years, maybe longer. Sometimes during that time, business conditions change and companies can't keep their promise to pay you back. Say that, a few years down the road, Nimble has built new factories all over the world, and suddenly customers don't like the pots and pans anymore. Nimble's business starts to deteriorate, and eventually the company is having trouble paying its bills. With time, it ends up filing for bankruptcy.

This is one of the scariest prospects for people, or mutual funds, that invest in individual corporate bonds. When companies go into bankruptcy, they usually don't pay back all the money investors were promised. If you are lucky, you might get a portion, but your bond definitely is not the safe investment you anticipated.

When you invest in a bond mutual fund, however, you have a lot more protection from bankruptcies than if you had gone to a broker and bought a single corporate bond. Because your fund manager has selected hundreds of bonds for you, you might not even sense one bad bond. Most of the bonds in your fund will continue paying interest. Your bond fund manager should be studying bonds constantly and steering clear of a lot of dangerous companies, like Nimble, so that blowups like Nimble don't happen often.

Also, if you invest only in U.S. government bonds through government bond funds, you don't have to worry about bankruptcies. No matter how financially stressed the government gets, it can always raise taxes and use the money to pay back you and other investors. It does that because it needs the entire world to be confident that it will always pay its bills.

Even with ultrasafe bonds such as U.S. Treasury bonds, however, you are not completely safe if you invest in a bond fund. Another risk applies even to the safest of bonds, and people who depend on bonds fear it greatly. It's called interest rate risk. Again, you don't have to learn the term, but you need to understand the concept so that you don't look at your bond fund in your

401(k) someday and panic when you see that you've lost a little of your money.

The risk works like this: Whenever you hear in the news that the Federal Reserve is raising interest rates or you notice that mortgage rates are rising, it usually means that your bonds or bond funds are vulnerable to losing some value. Bonds that you purchase today will always lose value tomorrow, next month, next year, or years later if interest rates end up higher then.

This might sound complicated, but it's not. Think of it this way: Say that I want to borrow $1 from you for a week, and I tell you I will pay you either a nickel or a dime when I return the dollar to you. The nickel will be 5 percent interest, and the dime 10 percent. Naturally, you want to make the most money you can, so you want the dime—in other words, you want 10 percent in interest.

Well, when you invest in bonds, you are always examining the interest that bonds will pay you, and you always hunt for the most interest you can get. That's why you will be disappointed if you buy a bond that will pay you 2 percent interest during the next 10 years, and then a few months later, interest rates go up and other investors are able to buy new bonds that will pay them 4 percent interest.

At that point in time, you are stuck with money in a lower-interest bond, and although you can sell it, no one else is going to want your 2 percent bond when he or she can simply buy new bonds paying 4 percent. Consequently, your bond will lose value. If you wanted to sell it to someone else, that person would pay you less than you paid for it. In other words, you would lose money.

If you keep holding that bond instead of selling it, you might not care that the value has dropped. You will continue to get your 2 percent interest, and at the end of 10 years, your original money will also be returned to you, as promised. So you won't lose a penny. But the situation is different if you have a bond fund.

If your bond fund manager bought a lot of bonds paying 2 percent, and new bonds become available at 4 percent, your fund manager might want to sell those old, low-interest bonds. At that point, however, no one is going to pay full price for them. So you are going to look at the bond fund in your 401(k) one day and discover that you are losing money.

You might find that unsettling. If it happens, however, do not assume that your bonds are as dangerous as stocks. With time, your fund manager will adjust to the higher interest rates by buying newer higher-interest bonds, and you will stop losing money.

In other words, you are affected by changing cycles in bonds as well as stocks.

The Trade-Off Between Seeking Safety and Making Money

I want you to understand an important point about safety and investing. It's a fact of life that is central to all the investing choices you will make.

When you choose a safer investment, you also choose to be paid less for it than you would for taking more risks. So stocks have the potential to pay you the most—perhaps more than 20 percent in a year and averaging 9.8 percent a year if history repeats. But they also smack you the hardest—maybe dropping more than 37 percent in a single year like 2008. That's part of the bargain. You are supposed to know it and go in with your eyes open.

Bonds aren't as risky, so they pay you less than stocks. The lower returns from bonds don't just happen by accident. Governments and businesses that sell bonds know they don't have to pay you as much as stocks pay because they are giving you a special promise instead of big returns—the promise to repay all your money, plus interest.

Stocks, on the other hand, never make promises. You buy a stock for the *potential* of making money. There is never a "sure thing" with an individual stock, no matter what anyone tells you. You can win; you can lose. Of course, with a stock mutual fund, you have a better shot at winning than if you pin your hopes on one stock because mutual funds hold dozens of stocks.

Although bonds generally are safer than stocks, they come in different varieties. Some are safer than others, and they pay you accordingly based on the risks you take. They don't do this out of the kindness of their hearts. They do it because they know they have to pay you extra to get you to accept greater risks.

The U.S. government doesn't have to pay you much interest on U.S. Treasury bonds because you can be sure that you will get every cent back. So historically, that's meant about a 5.7 percent average annual return for long-term bonds. Corporate bonds are more risky because of the possibility of bankruptcy, so they pay more to entice investors to take the risk—about 6.1 percent, on average, according to the 2012 Ibbotson SBBI Yearbook.

If you reach for the highest return in bonds, you will select what's known as a high-yield bond fund, or a junk bond. Beware! This fund might say "bond" on it, but it is not mild mannered. It is almost as dangerous as a stock because it purposely picks bonds from companies that are in financial trouble and might go bankrupt.

You might be attracted to a 12 percent return in a high-yield bond fund when a safe U.S. government bond fund is paying only 5 percent. But because you get paid to take risks, that 12 percent return should serve as a red flag. Instead of picking it for the juicy temporary return, you must try to picture that same fund losing 12 percent during a bad cycle and ask yourself whether you want to take the risk of losing money in it then. If your goal is to use bonds for safety, you'd be wise to pass up the high return.

An Easy Bond Fund Choice

Here's an easy solution for your 401(k) or IRA. Look through your bond mutual fund choices. You might see a short-term bond fund, a long-term bond fund, and an intermediate-term bond fund. The diversified intermediate-term fund is a solid all-around choice. It usually invests in bonds that mature in about ten years or less, so it generally won't fall as hard as a long-term bond fund when interest rates rise. It also usually yields more than a short-term fund. (By "mature," I mean that the loan ends and the government or corporation returns the investor's money, or principal, to the investor.)

If you buy a diversified intermediate-term bond fund, your fund manager buys a mixture of bonds for you—some safe U.S. government bonds, some riskier corporate bonds, and maybe a small number of risky high-yield bonds to boost your return just a little. Mixing bonds cautiously, while relying mostly on safe government bonds, is a sound strategy.

In the words of the investing profession, you balance out your risk and return. You are diversifying your bonds. That means you will get a little jolt from a small quantity of riskier bonds but will protect your money with the safer choices. Such a fund is a good choice for one-stop bond shopping.

You now know how to use bonds to reduce your risks in your retirement savings. You have progressed a long way. You know how to spot a mild-mannered bond fund among 401(k) choices and how to ask for a diversified intermediate-term bond fund for your IRA. You are already better off than most people with 401(k) plans and IRAs. If you went no further, you would be to the point that you'd have a healthier retirement. But you can do even more for yourself. To build up enough money for retirement, you must hold more stocks than bonds.

So next, you are ready to learn how to spot the risks in stock funds, too. Then you can deliberately choose a mixture that will blend different levels of risk and help you weather the cycles that will come your way.

As with bonds, stocks don't come with just one level of risk. Some can give you explosive growth but also can explode into nothing. (Mark had these.) Others are more mild mannered. You don't have to guess about which are which or find out in the middle of a scary cycle. Stock mutual funds have specific names that alert you in advance.

Now on to the "wacky words" that help you spot stock funds you will need, along with an introduction to your fund manager's job.

9

KNOW YOUR MUTUAL FUND
MANAGER'S JOB

One reason people make so many mistakes with their stock mutual funds is that they and their mutual fund managers have a totally different understanding of the fund manager's job. This ends up in awful marriages and painful divorces between investors and their mutual funds. Destructive relationships batter retirement savings.

Most novice investors put money into a mutual fund with a dangerous false assumption. They assume that they hired their fund manager to make money for them, no matter what. Consequently, if they start to lose money, investors figure that their fund is a flop and that they should unload it and find a better one before all their money disappears.

The fund manager, on the other hand, is operating with a totally different mind-set. Managers don't want to lose money, either. They tend to be fiercely competitive people who love to leave other fund managers in their dust. Yet they know there will be times when losing money is inevitable simply because of the specific job they've been assigned and the cycles of the market that will temporarily spoil their specialty.

This is no small matter. Fund managers are specialists hired to pick a precise type of stock and ignore all other investments. It means that some managers are expressly hired to take on huge risks with your money, and others are hired to take only modest risks. It means that if a manager's specialty is being battered by a nasty cycle, the manager usually won't be allowed to pull away and channel your money toward safer stocks and bonds, even when the cycle is being gracious to those alternative investment choices. You read that right: By design, your fund manager will have to shun stocks or bonds that could be moneymakers for you.

Under certain cycles of the stock market, you will lose money in particular funds no matter how brilliantly the fund manager handles stocks. That's true even of lower-risk stock funds. All stocks get battered by cycles, but not all stocks suffer at the same time. As cycles change, sometimes the risky ones will get hurt and other times the safer ones will take the beating. In general, though, the riskiest stocks get throttled the most.

Novice investors are usually shocked to find that sometimes even the savviest stock-picking pro will fail to save a mutual fund from harm. But your fund managers assume that you know all of this. They figure that you are consciously choosing mutual funds with your eyes open and that you can distinguish one fund from another by recognizing the wacky names most people find so befuddling.

In other words, if you buy an aggressive, risk-taking fund, the manager assumes that you bought it on purpose. With more than 8,000 other funds available, you could have purchased other funds instead. So the manager takes his marching orders from you. When you bought the fund, the manager assumed that you were instructing him or her to take sizable risks for you and that you are prepared for the extreme highs and lows that come with the territory. So instead of fleeing from the strategy in the midst of a scary cycle, the manager forges ahead, completing the job that he thinks you want done and preparing you for the next upturn in the cycle.

This is why Mark, the physical therapist I mentioned in the preceding chapter, might have had a perfectly capable mutual fund manager, one worth keeping despite losing thousands of Mark's savings. After all, the manager was doing exactly what he'd been hired to do: to buy the riskiest stocks. Mark just couldn't stomach the ride down, even though it was part of the original bargain—a natural trade-off for the superior gains Mark had loved previously.

Everything would have been fine for Mark if he had understood what he was getting into at the outset. He could have stayed out of the dangerous fund or bought less of it, using it as spice in his investment portfolio instead of the main ingredient. With a small portion of the risky fund, he could have added larger portions of safer stock funds and bonds. The combination would have insulated his money from the brutality of the high-risk stock fund.

Because he was like most investors, however, Mark naively poured all his money into the one fund that seemed like a winner and ended up in a position he couldn't stomach.

The Cost of Ignorance

Unfortunately, novice investors routinely repeat messes like Mark's, and they are costing people dearly.

In 2006, a mutual fund consulting firm named Dalbar analyzed how mutual fund investors handle their money. The findings were enough to make you cry.

Over the previous 20 years, investors would have gained about 11.9 percent a year on average if they'd simply put money into a mutual fund that reflected the stock market and stayed the course. Instead, Dalbar found that people moved from fund to fund, looking for the elusive better fund. And they earned a measly 3.9 percent a year.

Take a look at this disaster in dollars: At the end of 20 years, investors would have had about $398,500 if they had invested $5,000 a year in the stock market, or what's called the Standard & Poor's 500, and stayed with it through thick and thin. Instead, by running away from one disappointing mutual fund after another, the ordinary mutual fund investor ended up with only about $153,100.

This is why you must know your fund manager's job before you pick a fund. That way, you will be able to discriminate between funds and protect yourself before it's too late. You won't need to bolt when your fund does just what you should have expected.

I'm sure you are wondering now how a person like you can ever know what a fund manager is hired to do. It's actually quite simple, and you don't have to know the intricacies of the job. You merely have to pay attention to the wacky words in your mutual funds and know what they actually tell you. It's not just gibberish. Fund names and each fund's description usually tip you off to the risks you will take and how the fund will act in cycles.

Although there are more than 8,000 different mutual funds, you must recognize only a few specific types, or categories. Just as you gave yourself an easier task by breaking down a list of 401(k) choices into just three categories—stocks, bonds, and cash—you can now break down the stock category into a few manageable types.

When you do that, you will be able to spot what you need fast and know how to mix and match riskier and less risky stock funds so that you can whip up a hardy recipe for your retirement fund and save yourself from grief.

Focus on the Right Words

I'm talking about terms such as *small cap* and *large cap,* the stuff they throw at you in TV ads to make investing seem more complicated than it has to be. I'm not talking about company names such as Fidelity, Vanguard, American, T. Rowe Price, or hundreds of others. People get lost in those less critical words. They call me and say, "I have a fund that's doing bad—should I get rid of it?" When I ask the name, they might say, "Fidelity." But that's totally deficient information.

Names such as Fidelity and American just tell you what company is running a fund. That's not where I want you to focus. This illustration will help you understand what I mean: Picture yourself walking into a large electronics superstore. The variety of merchandise can be almost as overwhelming as a 401(k) plan. The store carries televisions, computers, camcorders, smartphones, and so on. You are in a hurry and want to go quickly to the section of the store you need.

You want a television. So when you walk into the store, you don't want to waste a minute. You go to the clerk by the door and ask her to point you in the right direction. Do you ask the clerk where to find the Sony? Of course not. Sony makes loads of products. If you focused on the brand name, you could bounce around the store all day, seeing everything from computers to digital cameras, and never find what you needed. With the brand name alone, the clerk wouldn't know where to send you in the store.

What's relevant is to ask where to find the televisions. After you get to the television section, you might want to discriminate between the Sony and Samsung brands, but the key for you is to at least find and buy a television. Even if you picked a television that was somewhat inferior to another, any one of the televisions would do the job for you—it would let you watch your favorite shows.

It's exactly the same with mutual funds. Fidelity, Vanguard, and hundreds of other companies make dozens of mutual funds, but the key to your selection is to find a certain type of mutual fund that will do a specific job for you. That's a small-cap fund, a large-cap fund, a bond fund, an international stock fund, and so on.

Soon you will look at a list of mutual funds and be able to focus in on a key term, such as *large caps*, and say instantly and with certainty, "That's like a television. It's what I came to buy."

Or to go back to the investing recipe analogy I want you to keep in mind, you will look at a list of mutual funds for your 401(k) plan, ignore the brand names, and scan the list for the term *large cap*. When you see it, you will say to yourself, "That's like flour, the main ingredient for cooking a solid retirement fund. I need a fairly large amount of it." Then you will scan the list a second time, and you will say, "I see a small-cap fund. That's like sugar. It will sweeten my retirement fund, but I have to be cautious about adding too much."

This quick recognition will determine whether you make a lot of money or lose it. So hunt for the following words in mutual funds and know both the worst-case and best-case scenarios they can deliver. Pay serious attention to what they will do for you over many years, not just one or two. The idea is to never be taken by surprise, to know what you are getting into so that you can avoid bailing out after losing a bundle at a frightening point in a cycle.

Often you will find the few words you need buried right in the mutual fund's name. Other times, you will have to look a little further at the description of a fund. You can always find the description in a booklet called the prospectus. There's one for every mutual fund, and you are supposed to receive a copy whenever you buy a fund.

Unfortunately, prospectuses are written in too much legalese, so reading them from cover to cover is impossible. But in a simple paragraph, usually labeled "Investment Strategy," you will spot the keywords I'm about to teach you.

Look for the keywords so that you will know whether you are buying flour or sugar for your retirement fund recipe. Then you will be ready for the next chapter, knowing how to mix and match all the ingredients in the right quantities so that you enjoy the brew you've created—even when the stock market is acting cruel.

Stocks Come in Three Sizes: Know Your Size

Three key terms in stock mutual funds relate to sizes of companies: *large cap, midcap,* and *small cap.* Don't be put off by the word *cap*; it's an abbreviation for the word *capitalization.* It's simply a way of telling you how big a company is. The word doesn't relate to how much a company sells, but rather tells you what investors think the company is worth. It's the market value of the stock, or what all investors together are willing to pay for all the shares of stock in a company.

That might be confusing, but don't worry about it. What matters to you as a mutual fund investor is that *cap* instantaneously helps you identify a category. And that is important.

Categories help us in everything we do. For example, if we are thinking about animals, the word *mammal* helps us start focusing on a certain type of animal. But it's still a broad word, or category—it includes everything from dogs to lions. Knowing the specific names of the animals will clue you in to how they will behave.

Likewise, the word *stocks* is broad, including stocks that act more docile like dogs and those that are fierce like lions. So the fund world tells you more about stocks with more specific terms such as *large cap* and *small cap* so that you can anticipate distinct differences in the behavior of stock categories.

As stocks, large-cap stocks and small-cap stocks are somewhat alike, but with differences that increase or decrease your risks during various cycles in the market.

When you start recognizing the distinct label for stock categories, it will help you keep track of where your mutual fund manager will be hunting for stocks to buy for you and the risks he or she will take with your money.

That might not sound like much. After all, a novice investor often thinks, "A stock is a stock; I know nothing about them and just want my manager to buy me the best one." But categories matter.

Different sizes of stocks behave differently, just as different animals, such as dogs and lions, behave differently. With stocks, those differences come out dramatically during various cycles in the market. The risks between different sizes vary a lot.

In other words, when you recognize categories of stock, you will know whether you are getting into a cage with dogs or lions. In the next chapter, I tell you how to corral dogs and lions together to remove the lion's fury. Together they act like man's best friend.

Using the Remainder of This Chapter

Use the next part of this chapter to become acquainted with the categories of stocks. Don't expect to absorb the details all at once. I figure that you will familiarize yourself with categories now, learn how to mix and match them in the next chapter, and then come back to this chapter in the future whenever you need to choose a fund for an IRA, a 401(k), a college savings 529 plan, or some other kind of investment account.

As you go through the categories here, I've put a quick note at the end of each about how to use funds in that category. You will get complete recipes— or step-by-step models to follow—in the next chapter. But in the future as you make mutual fund choices, the quick notes in this chapter should be a fast reminder of how to use each type of mutual fund. If you have a list of 401(k) funds in hand and then compare your funds to the following list, you should be able to make choices in less than five minutes.

Also, you will see some suggested funds. The list doesn't include every fine fund, but I've given you some reliable ideas for IRAs or other investment accounts. If you have a 401(k) plan, do not be dismayed if you look through my suggestions and your 401(k) funds aren't among them. Remember, the most important job you can accomplish with your 401(k) is to use the proper categories—rather than specific funds—and then mix and match them.

That's what you will accomplish in the next chapter. Now you learn once and for all what those wacky words are telling you.

Large-Cap U.S. Stock Funds

If you have a fund with *large-cap* in its name or description, your fund manager will look only at the largest companies in the nation. In other words, he or she will sort through companies that are household names, firms such as Apple, Microsoft, General Electric, Exxon, Wal-Mart, Johnson & Johnson, McDonald's, JP Morgan, Procter and Gamble, Coca-Cola, and so on.

These are established companies that might be known as "blue chips." They are solid firms that aren't likely to go bankrupt. Of course, as time goes by, business conditions change and even great companies sometimes flop. Just consider firms such as Kmart, Lehman Brothers, and United Airlines, goliaths that succumbed to bankruptcy. However, it's less likely that a large, established company will fail, compared to a small, young company that is still trying to figure out how to get customers to buy its products. Larger companies are considered safer investments than small companies—not as safe as bonds, but among stocks, they are the safest.

Your fund manager must still study them carefully to make sure that each company will be growing its profits and that the stock price will rise. But over many, many years, a mutual fund holding a broad variety of solid large company stocks is likely to behave a lot like the overall stock market—or what you might hear called the Dow Jones Industrial Average or the Standard & Poor's 500 on the news.

Understanding Your Risks in Large Caps

Over the past 86 years, the Standard & Poor's 500, which is just a shorthand way of referring to many of the largest stocks of the stock market, has given investors an average annual return of 9.8 percent. So with a mutual fund that invests in large stocks, you might anticipate making about 10 percent a year, on average, if you keep the fund for many years. But don't expect it each year or even in the next 10.

Remember the past: Large-cap stocks have fallen as much as 43 percent in a year, if you go all the way back to the Depression. They also have climbed as much as 54 percent in a single year, according to Ibbotson. In the past 30 years, the largest loss in a single year was 37 percent in 2008. The largest increase was 37.6 percent.

What does that tell you? It's not a guarantee, but if you look at your large-cap mutual fund someday and see that you have lost 10 percent, or even 30 percent, of your money, and news reports are saying that the stock market is down like that, too, you should be able to calm yourself and say, "This is within the realm of possibilities for this type of fund. I thought about this when I bought it, and history tells me that cycles will change. If I stick with it, I could still average a 10 percent return—or something like that—over the next 20 or 30 years."

Investment professionals use history as a guide to anticipate the future. It's not perfect or precise, but it's all we have to go on. You should use the past for insight but realize that the future could be somewhat different. Some analysts, for example, are telling investors to expect only about 4 to 8 percent returns on stocks over the next decade as the U.S. works its way out of its debt problems.

On the other hand, at the start of the decade that began in 2000, few experts imagined what was actually going to happen. Instead of gaining any money in the stock market during a 10-year span, investors lost an average of 0.9 percent per year. Notice I used the word *average*. During some years in the decade, people did well. For example, in 2006, they earned about 16 percent in large-cap stocks. But when all the good years and the awful years were blended together, the good times seemed to evaporate and people averaged the 0.9 percent loss per year over the 10 years.

In other words, the outcome was very different than the 9.8 percent average that history suggests people will get in large stocks over many, many decades.

Also, keep in mind that historical averages apply to large-cap stocks in general. Your particular mutual fund might not act just like the average. Maybe yours will be a couple percentage points higher or lower than the average for funds in its category. (You should check your funds every year to make sure they are roughly on course, and I give you the tools to do so at the end of Chapter 13, "Index Funds: Get What You Pay For.")

What's important now is to realize that your fund isn't going to deviate much from the average fund because the category of stocks you have tends to dictate how you will do during cycles of the market. One large-cap fund will behave much like another. Keep this in mind so that your mutual funds don't seem so mysterious.

When large caps are popular, your fund probably will be making money. When they are unpopular, you probably will be losing money or just crawling along lethargically—not making much or losing much. You will be doing this along with people who have chosen hundreds of other large-cap funds.

Their managers might be smart, but depending on the cycle, they probably won't be able to protect investors if it's a losing time for large-cap stocks in general. Just as you can't expect a dog to act like a cat, you can't expect a large-cap fund to act like a small-cap fund or a bond fund.

Still, your fund manager will try to pick the best stocks for you out of the bunch—ones he or she hopes will give you an extra edge over the average. If the manager picks a lot of technology stocks, such as Microsoft, when tech is popular, you might do better than investors on average in the large-cap fund category. But if the manager guesses wrong about what will be popular, and stocks such as Exxon become popular, you might not do as well as the average.

What to Do with Large Caps in Your Retirement Fund

Because large caps are the most stable companies, a large-cap fund should serve as your core investment in stocks at all times. By "core," I mean that the largest portion of your stock money should go into large caps and stay there year after year. It's your staple, like bread in a meal.

Financial advisers frequently rely on a simple guide to determine how much of a client's money to invest in large-cap stocks or large-cap funds. First, they channel some of their client's money into bonds. Then they focus on the full U.S. stock market. When they consider the composition of the entire U.S. stock market, they see that large-cap stocks make up roughly 70 to 75 percent of the total. So when investing in U.S. stocks, they simply put 70 to 75 percent of an investor's stock investments into large caps. You can do the same. I give you more guidance in Chapter 11, "Do This."

Some Large-Cap Funds Ideas

Hundreds of large-caps funds exist, and an excellent choice is usually what's called an index fund. You find the names of several here, and I provide more information about them in Chapter 13. I also provide a couple other well-respected fund names so that you can make comparisons. Don't worry if you don't see your 401(k) funds here; this list does not include all the quality funds available. Also remember that whenever you select mutual funds from any list (whether this one or a list in a magazine or newspaper or on TV), you should check them out using the techniques provided at the end of Chapter 13. Fund quality is not static; it can change over time.

For now, here are some ideas you can use as starting points when digging through thousands of funds: Vanguard 500 Index (VFINX), Oakmark (OAKMX), T. Rowe Price Blue Chip Growth Stock (TRBCX), Fidelity Growth Company Fund (FDGRX), Fidelity Contrafund (FCNTX), Sequoia (SEQUX), Vanguard Dividend Growth (DVIGX), T. Rowe Price Equity Income (PRFDX), Mairs & Power Growth Fund (MPGFX), Standard & Poor's 500 exchange-traded fund (SPY), Fidelity Spartan Total Market Index (FSTMX), Vanguard Total Stock Market Index (VTSMX), iShares S&P 500 Index (IVV), and Fidelity Spartan S&P 500 (FUSEX).

Notice the capital letters in parenthesis. These are called the tickers, or symbols. They are a short-hand way to look up a fund on the Internet or to order one from a broker. To identify more funds, try the "gold rated funds or the fund "screener" at www.Morningstar.com or the Fund Finder at www.moneycentral.msn.com. Find it under "Investing" and "Funds." Don't set the finder on "Top Performers." Being on top for a few months, or even a year, means nothing. Those with a top rating over three to five years are more reliable. But before you pick a fund from a list, also pay attention to the expense ratio and loads, which I discuss in Chapter 12, "How to Pick Mutual Funds: Bargain Shop."

Small-Cap U.S. Stock Funds

Small-cap funds are the dessert, or the funds you use to sweeten your results. As with dessert, however, you should not rely on them for a healthy diet unless you are very young and can accept a loss as painful as 58 percent in a single year.

In their best years, nothing compares to small caps. As a group, they have climbed as high as 143 percent in a single year, but they've also destroyed a lot of wealth during periods when they have been unpopular. In the worst year, they've dropped 58 percent, according to Ibbotson Associates. Over the past 86 years, all those ups and downs have turned into an average annual return of 11.9 percent, significantly higher than that of the large companies, at 9.8 percent.

Small-cap funds invest in small companies, such as Columbia Sportswear, Revlon, Pandora, or Krispy Kreme Doughnuts. You might not think of them as small. After all, Krispy Kreme has about 700 stores in the world and sells donuts in 10,000 grocery stores and gas stations.

Remember that, when I'm talking about size, I'm talking about what investors think a company is worth, or what's called their market cap. For small caps, that generally means companies worth about $2 billion or less. By comparison, large companies are worth about $10 billion or more.

Small companies can be fragile because they are often young or struggling and are consequently making mistakes. Their products might be hot, but if the corporate leaders can't make the business work out right, all the excitement about what they sell might be for naught.

Consider Krispy Kreme Doughnuts. People loved the donuts, so they paid high prices for the stock in the early 2000s. Then the company had serious operating problems and legal battles with the independent business people, or franchisees, who ran many of the donut shops. Government regulators also questioned whether investors were misled with faulty financial reports. The stock, which soared in 2003 to about $49, fell below $4 and was at only $7 in early 2012. An investor who got excited about donuts and bought the stock at $49 would have lost almost all of his or her money.

Small-cap stocks have a high probability of problems. It's an area of the stock market that can make you rich if you spot a rare winner such as Apple or Microsoft in its infancy. But more often than not, small businesses fail. They might depend on a single customer, and if that customer encounters financial trouble and goes out of business, the small company might be sunk. Likewise, if another company offers a better price than a small company, all the customers might shift their business to the competitor, and a great small company could be toast.

In addition, small companies can have trouble getting banks to loan them money, or they might have to pay higher interest to get loans. If interest payments are expensive, the small company might be short on cash and might not have enough money to make top-notch products or advertise and market them. The company might not be able to hire the best employees if it can't afford to pay people what a large company would. A fund manager for a small-cap fund must hunt for companies that will excel, knowing full well that a number of factors could work against them.

Because small caps, such as Microsoft in its infancy many years ago, can make extraordinary gains, investors who find well-managed small-cap companies can do extremely well. But risks are especially great during downturns in the economy or during some of the cruel cycles that pound small caps for months or even years.

A large company can trim fat during economic stress, but small companies often don't have fat to cut. Think of Wal-Mart and a neighborhood store. If people lose their jobs in a recession, they might buy less from both types of stores. Wal-Mart might have to lay off some people or cut some advertising; the neighborhood store might not even be able to pay the electric bill.

Consequently, investors should put some money into small-cap funds for the extraordinary growth that young upstarts enjoy—but they should do it with care because the downside is dramatic, too. Your fund manager must be exceptional as he or she tries to identify the great firms and survivors. Because the risks are great, avoid a steady diet of small caps. Dessert-size portions will sweeten returns over many years.

What to Do

Financial planners generally recommend that investors put about 20 to 30 percent of their U.S. stock money into smaller company stocks. The definition of "small" is somewhat imprecise, though. Often when professionals talk about small caps, they are referring to the stocks that are smaller than large ones, so medium-size companies might be included in the mix. If a financial planner focuses more specifically on small companies, the adviser might suggest putting only about 12 or 15 percent of your U.S. stock money into small-cap funds.

These are all ballpark figures. Some advisers are more liberal with daring investors, if they are confident the people won't panic and flee small caps during a brutal cycle.

How do you know whether you should be more daring? You know that small caps have fallen close to 60 percent in a single year. So look at your money. Maybe you have $1,000. Ask yourself, "Could I stand to lose all but $400, knowing that, over the next 20 to 30 years, I will be likely to make more money after that loss than I would if I invested only in large stocks?" Then revisit the issue one more time and think of it this way: "If that $1,000 goes to $400, I won't know at $400 whether it will turn into $200, and I won't know when the bleeding is going to stop." If history still comforts you, you might have the stomach to hold more small caps than the average person.

One more warning before I move on: The closer you are to retirement, the less you can afford to risk. If you are 20 and lose half your money, you can earn it back—maybe in 5 years, maybe in 15. But if you are 50, you don't have enough working years ahead of you to keep investing new money while waiting for the old money to rebuild after a substantial loss.

Here's an example: If you would have put $10,000 into the ordinary small-cap growth fund in March 2000, you would have lost all but $5,787 by October 2001. By March 2006, or about six years after the crash, you would have regained most, but not all, of your money. You would have had $9,707, according to mutual fund research firm Lipper.

Put that into perspective by thinking of people in various age groups. For a 20-, 30-, or 40-year-old, the effects of the crash would be about gone after six years of waiting, and there would be years ahead to enjoy the high growth that historically has come from small stocks. But if you were 60 and about to retire, having $10,000 turn into less than $6,000 would be a harrowing experience. After you stop working and stashing away new money, catching up is difficult to do. In retirement, you remove money from savings instead of adding to it. You might not have six years to let your original $10,000 come back to where it started.

Some Small Cap Ideas

Consider Royce Special Equity (RYSEX), Wasatch Small Cap Growth (WAAEX), Artisan Small Cap Value (ARTVX), T. Rowe Price Diversified Small Cap (PRDSX), Vanguard Small Cap Index (NAESX), Vanguard Small Cap Value Index (VISVX), S&P SmallCap 600 exchange-traded fund (IJR), Bogle Small Cap (BOGLX), or Russell 2000 Value exchange-traded fund (IWN).

Midcap U.S. Stock Funds

Now that you understand large and small caps, this one should be easy. These are medium-size companies, those between about $2 billion and about $10 billion in capitalization. Examples you might recognize are Saks, Black & Decker, Panera Bread, and H&R Block.

Midcaps generally are companies less vulnerable than small caps. The businesses might be more established. They still are not the goliaths that large caps are, however. Some might have been large companies at one time and stumbled.

As a group, the companies tend to be a little more risky than large caps and a little less risky than small caps.

What to Do

A financial adviser might have people put about 14 percent of their U.S. stock money into midcap stocks if that choice is available within a 401(k) plan. Until a few years ago, advisers simply focused on large and small caps, not considering midcaps as a significant category of stocks. Some advisers still don't bother with midcaps. So if you don't have a midcap choice in your 401(k), don't worry about it. Instead, put some of the midcap chunk of money into your large-cap choice and put slightly more than you otherwise would into small caps.

Keep the basic makeup of the stock market in mind: It's roughly 70 to 75 percent large caps, 14 percent midcaps, and about 12 percent small caps. Why roughly? Because different analysts see the borders between the sizes somewhat differently. For example, some say small cap companies become midcaps once they are larger than $1.5 billion in size. Others don't consider small caps appropriate for the midcap category until the company reaches $2 billion in size. Regardless, feel free to copy the general mixture—putting roughly 70 to 75 percent of your money in large caps and 25 to 30 percent into smaller companies (roughly half of that 25 to 30 percent would go into small caps and the other half midcaps).

Some Midcap Ideas

Consider Weitz Partners Value (WPVLX), Westport (WPFRX), Longleaf Partners Small Cap (LLSCX), Fidelity Spartan Extended Market Index (FSEMX), Osterweis (OSTFX), Vanguard Mid Capitalization Index (VIMSX), or Standard & Poor's MidCap 400 exchange-traded fund (IJH).

Recognizing the Tortoise and the Hare: Growth Versus Value

You can make money with stock mutual funds in two basic ways. You can buy funds that try to pick stocks because they are expected to be very fast winners, similar to the hare in the story the "Tortoise and the Hare." Or you can buy funds that try to pick the slow but steady, dependable stocks, or the tortoise.

When you see a list of mutual funds, you sometimes see the word *growth* in the name or description. When you do, that's the hare. The fund tries to pick stocks similar to Apple, which has grown its profits at a phenomenal pace—consequently, its stock has climbed sharply.

If instead you see the words *value* or maybe *equity income*, that's the tortoise. The fund might pick companies such as Procter & Gamble, a company that's been around for a long time and keeps growing, but at a slower and steadier pace than fast growers. It makes dependable products for the household, so whether the economy is weak or strong, people are going to need them—it's a relatively dependable stock.

Stocks that grow at a startling rate can't keep it up forever. So growth stocks tend to be hot for a while and then maybe lose their momentum or do something that disappoints investors greatly, as Netflix did in 2011. At the point when momentum fades or the growth spiral fails, stock prices often drop, leaving investors bruised. Value stocks are less exciting and can include companies that have seen better days. As a group, however, they tend to be more dependable.

In the famous story, the tortoise wins the race. In investing, academic studies have shown that the tortoise is also the winner when the race lasts for many, many years. But with stocks, the hare wins a lot of sprints—and those short spurts can be very lucrative to investors. Consequently, most financial advisers have their clients invest in some growth funds, which pick stocks that are expected to grow fast, and some value funds, which pick relatively cheap stocks that are less likely to nose-dive. Neither growth nor value is inherently good or bad; both behave very differently during market cycles.

At the end of the 1990s, investors were infatuated with growth stocks, especially technology stocks. The growth funds that contained those soaring technology stocks climbed a remarkable 40 percent a year. But in the 2000s, it was a totally different matter. Growth stocks fell close to 40 percent. Then investors got scared and didn't want to touch the growth funds, particularly those with money-destroying technology stocks in them. As investors soured on technology stocks, they wanted the safety of the steady value stocks. The cycle had made a dramatic change, from growth being popular to growth being unpopular. With that change, value became popular.

Between February 2000 and the end of 2005, the tortoise left the hare in his dust. In other words, value stocks climbed with gusto: up 59 percent. Meanwhile, the hare was out of gas. Growth stocks lost so much money between 2000 and 2002 that investors holding them were still suffering a 38 percent loss at the end of 2005.

All these statistics can make your head spin. I present them now just so you realize that what's hot for a while doesn't stay hot, even though you might have the illusion at any point in time that excitement for a certain category will last forever. When investors are very confident, and love stocks, growth funds tend to soar. When they are nervous, they tend to pick safer, more dependable stocks, and then value has the edge. Yet the fate of these funds is not as simple as evaluating the confidence level of the moment. Growth funds tend to pick technology and healthcare stocks, and value funds tend to pick industrial and financial stocks, so their fate tends to depend on phases in the economy and popularity of those types of stocks at any given time.

An extreme example appeared in 2008. Value funds went from being the popular choice for three years to being the most detested of mutual funds. Why? They were stuffed with bank stocks, and people throughout the world were terrified about banks collapsing in 2008. That year, value funds plunged 45 percent.

Don't drive yourself nuts trying to figure out whether a growth fund or a value fund will be a potential winner in any single year. Having a mixture of growth and value gives investors a chance to make tremendous gains during hot cycles but protect themselves somewhat during down cycles.

How to Recognize the Fund

A growth fund is likely to have the word *growth* in the name. Its name also might suggest some forward-looking idea, as in "new era." Growth funds also often use the words *aggressive* or *emerging*.

Value funds often include companies that pay dividends because older, established companies tend to pay dividends. (Dividends are small regular payments—somewhat like an interest payment—that some companies send to stockholders.)

So a value fund's name might include the word *income* to reflect the dividend payments. But if you see *income*, look at the description to make sure it's talking about stocks. The word *income* often refers to bonds, and you won't get the stocks you need if you buy a bond fund by mistake.

What to Do

Let's assume that you put 50 percent of your entire stock portfolio into funds that invest in large stocks. Divide that with an equal portion in a large-cap growth fund and a similar portion in a large-cap value fund (so 25 percent large-cap growth, 25 percent large-cap value).

Do the same with small-cap stocks. Say you have 16 percent invested in small company stocks. Divide that equally into a small-cap value fund and a small-cap growth fund (8 percent each).

On the other hand, if you get nervous about losing money, sometimes cutting back on growth stocks will reduce some risk, and choosing value funds that emphasize dividend-paying stocks can help.

If you would rather not have to bother figuring out whether a fund is value or growth, look for a fund that is called a blend or core fund. Blend funds mix value and growth for you. Often 401(k) plans offer a large-cap blend fund.

Because small-cap growth funds can be so volatile, and because some research shows that small-cap value funds have had an edge during long periods, some financial planners use only small-cap core funds and small-cap value funds, not small-cap growth funds. But the decade that started in 2000 shows clearly that investors can be caught by horrible surprises in either growth or value. It's why you hedge your bets by holding a combination of fund types instead of relying on one type.

Some Core Fund Ideas

Consider Vanguard 500 Index (VFINX), Fidelity Spartan Total Market Index (FSTMX), Schwab Total Stock Market Index (SWTSX), Primecap Odyssey Growth (POGRX), T. Rowe Price New America (PRWAX), or Yacktman (YACKX).

Check Value and Growth Funds for Worst-Case Scenarios

Still not sure whether value or growth is best for you? If you want to understand what your mutual fund is likely to do in the worst of times, go to www.morningstar.com, type in the name of the fund in the Quotes box, and, when you get to the snapshot of your fund, click on Performance. Pay particular attention to the years 2000, 2001, 2002, 2008, and 2009—five terrible years in the stock market. You can get a glimpse of the damage investors endured. It's not a perfect look at the future, but it gives you a recent example of a major bear market. Also click on Risk Measure and notice the Bear Market Rank. (A score of 1 is best and 10 is worst.)

International Stock (Equity) Funds

When you have an international stock fund, you hire a fund manager to search the world for the best stocks for you. Perhaps the fund manager will pick Toyota in Japan or Samsung in Korea. If his or her fund looks for small foreign companies, you might not recognize the names of the businesses.

If your fund is a truly broadly "diversified" international fund—one not focused on one particular country or region—your fund manager will search for good buys on every continent. That's the type of diversified fund that is best for investors instead of one focused on only one country or region. Find the fund by looking for the word *diversified* in the fund's name or description.

Sometimes novice investors will see news about a booming economy somewhere in the world and think it has to be a great investment. But their timing tends to be atrocious. They tend to jump in after a cycle has been climbing for a long time, and then their money gets decimated.

Most investors are not ingrained enough in foreign cultures to anticipate events that can zap company profits. How your stocks perform depends on the management of particular companies, politics, and economic conditions. A change in political leadership in a country, for example, could bring about government regulations that could turn a profitable company into an unprofitable one. Competition from another country with low-cost labor could take customers away from a country that previously was known for a certain product. Reading a newspaper in the U.S. doesn't provide a deep enough insight.

Stay away from funds that invest only in Japan, only in China, only in Latin America, or in any other single country or region unless you can tell yourself honestly that you know what will happen with the Yuan currency in China or how the next election will turn out in Venezuela. Leave those judgments up to a fund manager who travels the world to spot strong companies in places where political, regulatory, or economic conditions will help them profit. Even the pros make mistakes on these complex factors.

If you have a good fund manager for a diversified international fund, the manager might move you into Australian stocks, for example, when he or she sees potential there. Later, when growth seems to be peaking in Australia and potential emerges elsewhere, your manager might move some of your money away from the lackluster area to a region of higher potential.

As in the United States, each country or region of the world goes through economic cycles and times when local stock markets are weaker or stronger. In 1998, for example, underlying problems in overheated Asian economies suddenly became undeniable, and stocks went from red hot to scary losers fast. During just three months, Asian stocks dropped 40 percent. Yet at the same time, large European stocks climbed 35 percent.

You could have lost 40 percent of your money if you had invested only in an Asian fund then. But if you had a diversified international fund that made a practice of investing money all over the world, your European stocks would have buffered the blow you took on Asian stocks at that time. Yet like all cycles, European stocks turned weak down the road and needed buffers too. In 2011, investors became terrified that severe debt problems in Greece, Spain, Italy, Portugal, and other European countries would cause the Euro zone to collapse. Over only a two-month period, European stocks plunged 20 percent. So at that point in time, a person who had simply selected a European stock fund would have lost 20 percent of his or her money.

Although it's tough to guess which country will be the best investment at any particular moment, investors must also be aware of another choice that can be enticing during certain cycles. When investors are given a selection of international funds, they sometimes see what are called emerging market funds. Fund managers for these funds invest in less stable countries than the United States—in places such as Russia, Brazil, China, Indonesia, India, Lebanon, Turkey, and Egypt. The economies are developing and move in fits and starts that make them volatile. They soar and crash, often with little warning to an outsider.

If you look at an emerging market fund during a hot period, it might look like the wisest investment at the time, maybe providing a 40 percent return one year. But don't be fooled. These are volatile, and although they might be red hot for a while, they have been known to drop 80 percent.

Still, impressive growth is happening in many developing parts of the world—growth that you don't want to miss. Franklin Templeton Investments, for example, has estimated that Asia's middle class will make up 59 percent of the world's $56 trillion in middle-class spending by 2030, compared to 23 percent in 2009.

Given the opportunity, plus the risk of volatility, instead of merely picking an emerging market fund, a more conservative approach is to pick a diversified international fund in which your fund manager can dabble in emerging markets. The more stable stocks the manager has in your fund will buffer any surprise disaster in a corner of the globe. Typically, the international fund manager might put 5 to 20 percent of your money into the volatile areas of the world, or emerging markets.

What to Do

Search for what is described as a diversified international fund or world fund with a manager who has been investing in foreign markets for years. This is no area for a newcomer. Check on a fund manager's background by reading a prospectus, or the pamphlet you are given when you select funds. For an easier approach, call a toll-free number for your fund and ask about the fund manager's background. Another easy approach is to go to www. morningstar.com, type in the name of your fund, and read the quick description under Management.

You want your manager to have at least five years of experience running your fund or an international fund just like the one you are considering. Think about it: If managers are new to the international arena, are they going to be equipped to appreciate cultural nuances?

Checking a manager's background should actually be a part of your research on any fund. I bring it up for foreign funds, however, because some fund companies dump managers into these complex funds before they've had adequate experience abroad.

You can put about a third of your stock portfolio into international funds. But you should know that investment managers have been having a spirited debate about the right proportions. Some argue to invest as much as 50 percent of your portfolio outside the United States because international markets make up about 53 percent of the world's market value. But investors such as Warren Buffett have claimed there is no need to invest any money abroad because large U.S. companies do so much business in foreign lands. Even Buffett, however, changed his mind recently as he spotted investment opportunities in other countries.

I have been persuaded by those who argue that it is worthwhile to be invested in the best companies everywhere. And although the economies of the world are intertwined, cycles will play out differently in various parts of the world. So you diversify your stocks by investing at home and abroad.

Sometimes U.S. stocks do better; other times, your foreign funds will do best. That's the idea. Because it's impossible to predict cycles accurately, you don't guess. You simply keep some money in international funds at all times, just as you would use with small caps and large caps constantly.

Some International Fund Ideas

Consider Oakmark International (OAKIX), Oakmark International Small Cap (OAKEX), MSCI EAFE exchange-traded index fund (EFA), Masters' Select International (MSILX), Tweedy Browne Global Value (TBGVX), Vanguard Total International Stock Index (VGTSX), MSCI All Country World Index ex-US (ACWX) or (CWI), Vanguard World Stock Index (VT), or Vanguard MSCI Emerging Markets (VWO).

Balanced Funds

These are easy-to-use funds that enable you to hedge your bets and cut the risk of losing money because they combine stocks and bonds for you. Although they are typically called balanced funds, they might also have a name such as asset allocation funds. Typically, they invest about 60 percent of your money in stocks and 40 percent in bonds.

Increasingly, employers are automatically depositing their employees' 401(k) contributions into balanced funds and target-date funds, which I explain in Chapter 14, "Simple Does It: No-Brainer Investing with Target-Date Funds."

So don't be surprised if you look at your 401(k) plan and see your matching money, or all your 401(k) money, going into a balanced fund. This is about as simple an investing approach as you can pursue.

During good cycles in the stock market, your stocks will help you make money, but you won't make as much money in that single fund as if you had chosen a mutual fund that invested only in stocks. During bad cycles for the stocks, your bonds will insulate you, keeping you from sharp losses.

For example, 2008 was an awful year for the stock market as people worldwide worried about a potential global depression. If your money was in mutual funds that invested only in stocks, you probably lost at least 37 percent of your money in that single year. But if you mixed stocks and bonds through a balanced fund, your losses were not nearly as extreme.

You did lose about 22 percent in a balanced fund in 2008, and, of course, that's a painful loss. Even worse, the damage intensified over the next few months. But the balanced fund continued to mitigate some of the stock market's damage so that you got back to even and started making money again relatively quickly.

Let's say that you originally invested $10,000 in a balanced fund in 2007 when the stock market looked promising, and you had no inkling of the coming crash. At the scariest point in the financial crisis in 2009, you would have had only about $7,100 of your original money left in the balanced fund. That's a lot of devastation, and you might have been worried. But if you had chosen only stocks, not a balanced fund, at the worst point in 2009, you would have had only $4,300 of your original money. The shock absorbers in the balanced fund clearly served you well.

From that point on, the balanced fund continued to help you recover from your pain. Since you had insulated yourself from some of the brutality of the stock market, your money in the balanced fund started to heal well once stocks hit bottom and began climbing again after March 2009. By the end of 2011, your balanced fund probably contained $11,800, or about $1,800 more than your original $10,000 investment.

It was certainly a better place to be than with stocks alone. If instead of a balanced fund you simply had a stock market mutual fund, your pain would have been long-lasting. By the end of 2011, the stock market mutual fund would have contained just $9,000, or $1,000 less than the original $10,000 invested.

Yet if the insulation from a balanced fund is attractive to you, it's important to realize from the outset that sometimes that fund might be a letdown for you. During cycles when stocks are hot, people around you will be talking about gigantic gains in stocks alone. Your gains will be more modest because you took a more conservative approach.

Again, take a look at what happened in early 2009. After the stock market hit bottom in the financial crisis, it made a sharp about turn. Stocks went from being cruel to investors to being extremely generous. This typically happens after fierce destruction in the market. Between March 2009 and the end of 2011, the stock market gained 67 percent. So if you had dared to put $10,000 into a stock market mutual fund at the scariest point in 2009, a little more than 2½ years later, you would have turned that $10,000 into about $16,700. Not bad, especially after the beating the stock market had delivered before that time.

In contrast, a balanced fund would not have gained as much. During the same time period, it would have gained about 53 percent and turned $10,000 into about $15,300. Of course, that's a pretty delightful sum. Still, it is not as large as the sum from stocks alone.

There's a significant point here: When you use balanced funds to take some of the sting out of stock market crashes, you improve your chances of healing faster if a brutal period arrives. On the other hand, if you happen to enter a period when everyone around you is gaining huge amounts of money in stocks, do not envy their fortune and dump your balanced fund. You picked a balance fund for a reason: to reduce your risks in the destructive periods that show up in the stock market without warning. The tradeoff for that protection is to be satisfied with somewhat smaller gains when stocks are hot.

What to Do

Although I told you previously not to rely on one mutual fund alone, a balanced fund is the exception. You cannot rely on a stock fund alone because it provides too much risk. You cannot rely on a bond fund alone because it won't grow your money enough for retirement.

However, you can hold a balanced fund alone because it is designed to be fairly well diversified. It gives you stocks and bonds, so the stocks help your money grow and the bonds insulate you from risks.

If you want a simple one-stop solution as an investor, a balanced fund could be your easy choice, although I prefer a little more diversification if you are willing to do it. A balanced fund typically doesn't give you many, if any, international stocks or small-cap stocks. A greater variety of investments usually gives you more opportunity. So if your only easy choice for a combination of stocks and bonds is a balanced fund, by all means, don't hesitate about using it.

But you might have access to a relatively new invention that has the entire panoply of investments in it: stocks of all sizes and from many countries, plus bonds. These so-called "target date funds" are ideal easy investments, and I've devoted all of Chapter 14 to them.

Some Balanced or Asset Allocation Fund Ideas

Consider Vanguard Wellesley (VWINX), Fidelity Balanced (FBALX), Dodge & Cox Balanced (DODBX), Vanguard Wellington (VWELX), Bruce (BRUFX), FPA Crescent (FPACX), T. Rowe Price Spectrum (RPSIX), or Mairs & Power Balanced (MAPOX).

REITs (Real Estate Investment Trusts)

These are funds that invest in real estate—shopping centers, warehouses, apartment buildings, office buildings, and companies that manage and finance them.

A study by Ibbotson shows that it makes sense to put a little money into REITs because they tend to act differently than stocks and bonds—maybe rising while the others are falling, or vice versa. In other words, they diversify your holdings.

Still, the ordinary person often has a huge investment in real estate through a home. So some financial planners argue that you already are diversified, without also buying a mutual fund that invests in real estate. Others insist that clients put about 5 to 10 percent of their portfolio into a REIT fund.

What to Do

If your 401(k) plan doesn't have a REIT in it, don't worry about it. If you do have one or are investing in an IRA, you can diversify your stock and bond investments by putting no more than 5 to 10 percent of your total portfolio into a REIT fund. REITs behave somewhat like small-cap stocks but also tend to provide a consistent stream of income from dividend payments, similar to bonds. People like dividends because they can buffer the impact of a stock decline.

Gold

Investors became infatuated with gold during the 2007–2009 financial crisis because it was the only investment other than bonds that protected investors from the wrath of the stock market. But many investment experts have had little long-term experience with gold and are debating whether people should always be holding it as a diversifier.

Although stocks lost 57 percent of people's money in the financial crisis, gold gained 24 percent and, by the end of 2011, had climbed 100 percent. People new to gold investing assumed that there was something special about gold and that they could always count on it to be a money maker. They were making the same mistake that people made about technology stocks in the late 1990s and homes in 2005.

Gold runs in cycles just like stocks, bonds, and homes, and the losses can be intense. Up to 1980, gold had soared almost 2000 percent over seven years; then it hit $850 an ounce in 1980 and became a loser for two decades. By 1999, the price had fallen to $254 an ounce. At that point in time, no investor wanted to touch the stuff.

So if you are in the midst of a cycle when gold is glistening, you must realize that it has its cycles, too. It's not always a one-way street, like the climb from nearly $600 an ounce in 2008 to $1,920 in September 2011. When investors realize that gold doesn't provide a guaranteed Midas touch, but they want it to diversify their investments and to protect them from inflation and market panics, they are in the right frame of mind for holding some gold on a constant basis. An adviser typically recommends no more than 5 percent of a portfolio.

Still, beware of how to invest. Gold mining stocks are sometimes used for gold exposure in IRAs, but mining stocks often do not behave like gold itself. If you want gold exposure, the best way to get it is to buy gold bullion or a fund that invests directly in gold bullion. The SPDR Gold Trust (GLD) is the oldest and best known.

Sector or Specialty Funds

You probably won't find these funds in a 401(k) plan. But you might make the mistake of following the herd into these in your IRA.

My advice: Stay away from them. Sector funds or specialty funds invest in only one type of business—maybe just energy, or maybe just technology, or maybe just consumer products, and so on. The common person gets lured into one of these sectors when they are hot but doesn't have enough inside knowledge to know when to get out. In fact, even professionals lack that knowledge. It's tough to guess when a cycle for any particular sector will start or end.

So buyer beware. You are likely to get throttled in these funds.

Instead, choose a diversified mutual fund that invests in all industries, and let your fund manager choose sectors for you. In a diversified stock fund, the fund manager is always looking for hot sectors. When he or she spots one, the manager might buy a few more stocks than usual in that sector to give your fund some extra oomph. But he or she will also be watching closely to try to get you out of the way when the party ends.

When a diversified fund makes a bet, it tends to be with a small amount of money—maybe 2 percent of the fund's total investments. When novices do it, they jump in with both feet, a very dangerous endeavor.

Stable Value Fund

This fund is more like the bond funds or money market funds covered in the preceding chapter. It is not a substitute for a stock fund. Instead, it can be used as a temporary holding tank for cash at times when you might be nervous about both stocks and bonds—perhaps when interest rates are rising and people are losing money in bond funds.

As its name suggests, it is a stable choice. It will pay you a very low interest rate that you can count on. It might be just 3 or 4 percent.

This is not a place for young investors to stash their money on a long-term basis. It simply won't grow enough. You might see a stable value fund as a "no-risk investment," and it typically has been just that. But in the financial crisis, investors grew worried about them because the guarantees they provide depend on insurance, which could fail in a crisis.

There's another risk too. Remember, the biggest risk Americans face is not having enough money for retirement. So young people must be willing to invest in stocks, despite dramatic losses. Earning just 3 or 4 percent interest in a stable value fund will present the risk of running out of money in retirement.

For a person within five years of retirement, however, a stable value fund can be appealing when both stocks and bonds are falling. But remember, if you withdraw from stocks completely while they are plunging, you won't be positioned to grow your money when the cycle suddenly turns up.

What to Do

To provide stability in your 401(k), you might have 5 percent of your money in what's called cash. You could consider either a stable value fund or money market fund, because they are your only cash-like options in a 401(k). Be aware, however, that neither is as safe as actual cash or a bank savings account.

If you work for an employer that automatically puts matching money into a 401(k) for you, the employer might deposit your money into either a stable value fund or a money market fund. If that occurs, it doesn't mean that the fund is your best choice. Employers deposit money in stable value and money market funds because they are afraid to invest any of your money in stocks and risk a suit if you lose money and panic.

But you cannot count on this fund to grow your money enough for retirement. If your employer has put your money there, contact your benefits office and make a change—sign up for some stock funds and bond funds, too. The next chapter helps you with quantities.

Company Stock

You might have one choice in a 401(k) that is not a mutual fund. Your employer might give you the opportunity to buy stock in the company where you work. If so, make sure you don't overdose on it.

One of the most frequent mistakes people make with 401(k)s is assuming that they will be safe if they invest in the company that employs them. People tend to feel more comfortable with what they think they know. So they see people going to work every day and assume that the stock in their company must be just fine.

However, looks can be deceiving with stocks. Even companies with thousands of employees around the world can end up in bankruptcy or get pummeled by a new competitor. When companies go into bankruptcy court, stocks usually become worthless.

Don't get burned the way people did at Enron in 2001, believing that their retirement was safe with stock Wall Street loved before fraud was discovered.

What to Do

Take a lesson from the professionals who run pension funds: Because single stocks are too unpredictable, pension funds never put more than about 5 percent of their money into one stock, no matter how stupendous it looks.

If you have more than that in your 401(k), sell some of the shares and transfer the money to diversified mutual funds instead. If it's painful to do all at once, do it in stages.

Bond Funds

Bond funds invest in bonds, which tend to be safer than stocks. For a detailed explanation, see the preceding chapter.

What to Do

Investors should hold some bonds to buffer the blows of the stock market. A classic combination of stocks and bonds puts 40 percent of the portfolio in bonds and 60 percent in stocks. Young investors don't need to keep 40 percent in bonds unless the stock market scares them. For a brave 20- or 30-year-old, 10 to 30 percent in bonds might suffice.

Consider a well-diversified bond fund that invests in a combination of U.S. government bonds and corporate bonds. Generally, an intermediate-term bond fund is a good selection. Often there are three different diversified bond fund choices: intermediate, long term, and short term.

Intermediate means that the bonds in the fund will tend to mature in about 5 to 10 years. That makes them safer than long-term bonds, or those that might not mature for about 20 or 30 years. Bonds are considered riskier when investors must wait a long time to get their money returned to them— so 20 years is riskier than 10 years, 10 years is riskier than 5 years, and 5 years is riskier than 2 years. Short-term bond funds typically choose bonds that mature in about two years. Although that makes them less risky than intermediate bonds, they usually provide a lower return.

When interest rates climb, all three types of bond funds lose money. Long-term bond funds will lose the most and short-term funds lose the least. A solution for retirees is to buy individual U.S. Treasury bonds, rather than bond funds, and hold onto the individual bonds until they mature. When you buy individual government bonds, you only lose money in a rising interest rate environment if you decide to sell the bonds.

Ideas for Bond Funds

Consider Harbor Bond Fund (HABDX), PIMCO Total Return (PTTAX), Loomis Sayles Bond (LSBRX), Vanguard Total Bond Market Index (VBMFX), or iShares BarclaysAggregate Bonds (AGG). You can also buy individual bonds for an IRA from a broker. High-quality bonds include U.S. Treasury bonds or corporate bonds that are rated A, AA, or AAA.

10

THE ONLY WAY THAT WORKS: ASSET ALLOCATION

Stay calm.

I threw a lot of information at you in the preceding chapter, and you might be in the mood now to toss it aside and simply try to pick the one right mutual fund.

Please don't.

You will certainly find plenty of temptation in the marketplace. Potential investors are bombarded with ads beckoning to them to trust a winner, and TV shows, publications, and Web sites make stars out of a handful of investing pros. So when faced with more than 8,000 different fund choices for an IRA or a dozen in a 401(k), busy people often want to find a shortcut. They spot a fund manager being lauded in the news media and think their problems are solved: They will hand over their money to that one remarkable genius and be done with it; they'll trust someone who clearly knows his or her way around the stock market or bond market.

Usually, they end up disappointed, face to face with the unpleasant truth in investing: No single magic fund or investment savior will always grow your money, keep you out of harm's way, and outsmart the other pros who are trying to be outstanding.

In fact, college finance professors have studied at length whether stars truly exist in the investment world, and the academic research is discouraging. It comes down to this: Fund managers shine for a while, bask in public attention, and attract a lot of headlines and millions of dollars in new money to manage as investors glom onto a winner. Then, often after only a year, the fund ends up fairly mediocre, or even worse.

There's actually a joke about this among investment professionals. It revolves around a coveted award that is handed out every year to an exceptional mutual fund manager. The award comes from a firm named Morningstar, which is well respected for analyzing mutual funds. At the end of each year, Morningstar anoints someone "The Manager of the Year," the equivalent of the Academy Award in the fund business.

If a fund manager is named "Manager of the Year," it's a tremendous tribute. Firms that receive the honor make a fortune on new money coming through the door as investors seek the Midas touch. But the joke among fund managers is that it's a dubious honor: Often the "Manager of the Year" falls from stardom the next year. A few have held on or returned to stardom a few years later, but more often than not, all the excitement ends in mediocrity.

Academic studies come to this bitter conclusion: Winners only appear to be winners for a while, but they rarely keep it up. Luck, or being in the right place at the right time during a cycle in the stock market, seems to be why fund managers stand out temporarily. That's very different from possessing unusual investing prowess that lasts. One or two years of amazing returns simply create an illusion of outstanding skill.

Why Star Funds Fade

When you think about it, an apparently great fund can fizzle into a so-so fund for good reason. If a fund manager has only a little money to handle, investing it is a lot easier than when he or she has millions or billions to deploy. If you doubt this, think about what it's like to make a meal for a couple friends, compared to 100, or consider how well you handle one project at work versus many dumped on you simultaneously by multiple bosses.

In investing, it's even more complicated. If a fund manager is famous, he gets flooded with money. Other investors also try to copy him. A rumor mill circulates in the investing business, and if someone gets wind of a star manager buying or selling a stock, news travels fast. You might think that having copycats would be flattering. But it messes up a fund manager's life and, ultimately, the money you make in the fund.

If traders (who buy and sell stocks for investors) spot the renowned manager buying a stock, they tell clients and their bosses. Those people want to make money, too, so they rush to buy the same stock. The result: The stock price goes up because of the volume of buying. So while the fund manager is in the process of buying the stock, he has to pay a higher price for the stock than intended. Likewise, if the manager starts to sell a stock and is noticed, others will copy him and bail out, too. So the stock plummets before the manager can sneak away from it. Consequently, if you own the fund being copied, you might make less money than you would if your manager was inconspicuous and could buy and sell stocks at the best prices for you.

More importantly, each manager has a certain style acquired over time in selecting stocks or bonds. Perhaps a fund manager understands how small company stocks generally act during cycles, so she can maneuver through good cycles with skill. She buys the promising stocks and avoids blowups, making mutual fund clients adore her. But she might not be as adept with large caps and might not even be allowed to buy them when they are the beneficiaries of a specific cycle. Or perhaps for years she's been assigned to invest in healthcare stocks, and she looks brilliant while they are the popular stocks. But then along comes a cycle when investors hate healthcare stocks and are grabbing energy stocks. In that environment, her intuition and knowledge fail her, so she doesn't shine during that particular cycle.

If you owned a Janus fund in 2000, you know what I mean. The funds seemed to be tremendous masters during the growth stock mania in the 1990s. But they became ugly losers in the early 2000s when investors ran away from technology stocks and other growth stocks and wanted safer value stocks—or companies that made widgets and drilled for oil. Janus managers lacked background in value stocks then. Growth stocks of all sizes outperformed value stocks from December 1997 to June 2000, with growth up 164 percent and value up only 41 percent. After 2000, the trend was the opposite. Growth stocks dropped 44 percent, and value stocks climbed 60 percent. That, of course, left even the savviest growth fund managers licking their wounds. Table 10.1 shows the fluctuations in the cycles of large-cap growth stocks and large-cap value stocks.

This might bring you to the conclusion that all you need to do is find the all-around pro. But the academic studies suggest that the odds of finding the Warren Buffetts of the investing world are against you.

Table 10.1

Good and Bad Investment Cycles in Large-Cap Growth Stocks and Large-Cap Value Stocks (Annual Total Returns Through 2011)

Year	Large-Cap Value	Large-Cap Growth
1993	15.48	−1.96
1994	−1.94	3.82
1995	45.22	39.68
1996	20.02	20.11
1997	37.63	32.87
1998	19.87	57.52
1999	14.65	50.59
2000	14.02	−19.03
2001	−1.26	−27.73
2002	−12.76	−28.83
2003	29.35	38.06
2004	12.42	3.29
2005	5.98	8.3
2006	21.6	4.0
2007	5.5	14.2
2008	−44.8	−33.3
2009	42.2	30.3
2010	14.8	17.3
2011	−8.5	1.5

Table based on data from The Leuthold Group.

The One Proven Way to Success: Asset Allocation

Instead, the studies point to another investment approach that truly does work. And I'm going to teach you how to use it step by step so that you can make money over a lifetime without devoting more than a few minutes a year to the effort.

To get ready for it, I want you to start thinking the way you would when selecting doctors. When you need a doctor, you don't pick one brilliant doctor and expect him or her to care for your every need. You pick one with the specialty you need. In other words, you wouldn't go to an eye doctor if you needed heart surgery. And when you needed to have your eyes checked, you wouldn't want the heart surgeon.

Both types of doctors are skilled; both are trained in the basics of the body. But one cannot step in for the other. As you go through life, you need a variety of doctors, with various specialties for all the needs of your body.

The same holds true for mutual funds. That's why, if you went to a qualified financial planner with your list of mutual funds from a 401(k) plan and asked for help, the adviser wouldn't focus on finding you the one *right* fund or the most brilliant fund manager. Your planner would check for well-managed mutual funds, but his primary focus would be on mixing and matching the funds on your list. He'd aim to hold a little of this and a little of that for you so that you would have all the specialties you needed: large-cap stocks, small-cap stocks, international stocks, and bonds.

The mixing process is called asset allocation. And although asset allocation is not nearly as glitzy as finding an investing whiz kid, it's the one approach that studies have shown works over time.

Money manager Gary Brinson did a crucial study on this in 1986. He analyzed pension funds and found that the key influence on 94 percent of an investor's return came from how the money is divided among stocks, bonds, and cash—or asset allocation. Only 4 percent depended on how well a manager selected stocks. Only 2 percent came down to how the manager "timed the market," or figured out when to buy stocks and when to bail out.

Forget Heroes—Just Match

In other words, novice investors have the entire process backward when they focus on trying to find one brilliant stock picker with the Midas touch. And if you think you can't be a good investor because you don't know how to pick stocks, this should give you great confidence: Asset allocation is fairly easy—much easier than analyzing a stock. You don't have to scrutinize company operations, follow the economy, or do any complex math.

It's as easy as playing a matching game or following a recipe. Think of the matching games you played as a child. On one page of a workbook, you'd see a picture of a two-story brick home. Then you had to match that picture to one of four words in an adjacent list: *car, house, girl,* and *dog.* You'd draw a line from the brick home to the word *house.*

You don't need much more than the ability to match in order to do a fairly good job investing your retirement savings—really! That's why I taught you the terms in the preceding chapter: large-cap stocks, small-cap stocks, international stocks, and bonds. Those are the words you match to the names of funds on a 401(k) list, or the words you use to make a recipe fit for an IRA, a 529 college savings plan, or any other investment fund.

You combine the various types of funds into a mixture because each fund acts differently in cycles. When you jumble them together, one or two tend to buffer the blows from the fund that inevitably will be getting hurt or lagging.

Maybe the large-cap fund or the small-cap fund saves you from harm— or it could be the international fund or the bond fund. The point is that, right now, neither you nor anyone else knows which it will be. So when you buy the entire mixture and continue to hold on to the fund you adore and the fund you despise, you should be ready for the unpredictable changing seasons of the stock market. You will always have a fund that helps you relax while you wait for a rebirth of a laggard.

Start the Sorting—It's Asset Allocation Time

Say that your employer gives you a list of funds for your 401(k) plan, or your broker gives you a list for an IRA. You have no idea which to choose. You see the Best Ever Large-Cap Fund, the Go Anywhere Small-Cap Fund, the Better Than Best International Fund, and the Wonderful Bond Fund. They all sound outstanding. Which do you select?

In the past, maybe you would have looked for one fund with a stock picker who had been touted in the news, but now you know that finding a hero alone is unreliable. So next, maybe you look at the returns for all the funds in your 401(k), hoping that one fund will stand out. You see that the Go Anywhere Small-Cap Fund was up 20 percent last year, whereas the Best Ever Large-Cap Fund gave investors only a 5 percent return. And the Wonderful Bond Fund was up only 1 percent.

So maybe you think the choice is easy. You will go with the winner, the one that gained way more than any of the others last year: the Go Anywhere Small-Cap Fund. That's what many novice investors do. But you know now that's the wrong decision, the road to destroying hard-earned money.

Instead, the right answer is to pick all four funds—large caps, small caps, international stocks, and bonds. The Best Ever Large-Cap fund might just look like a dud at the moment because the cycle at that particular time is not being kind to large caps and is bestowing wealth on small caps. But history shows that, with time, fortunes will reverse, and large company stocks will be the winners while investors temporarily shun the small company stocks.

You need all four types of funds to be ready for whatever the market cycles throw your way. That's what the investment world calls asset allocation, or dividing your money into a variety of specific types of funds.

And that's why you play the matching game, looking for the words you need on your fund list. Extra words in the fund names always get in the way. So as you play the matching game, you hunt for the keywords I taught you in the preceding chapter. You'll find them within either the fund name or the fund's description that accompanies the fund.

Within the name Best Ever Large-Cap Fund, for example, you merely focus on two words, *large cap,* and you match that fund to the amount of large caps that I give you in Chapter 11, "Do This." You are going to start pouring fund types—or ingredients—into a recipe that will make your retirement savings grow.

After you have matched the large-cap fund to your recipe, you go back to your 401(k) list and then hunt for your small-cap choice. And there you find it. Buried within the name Go Anywhere Small-Cap Fund, you find the most important words: *small cap.* You are going to match a certain amount of that fund to the small-cap proportion of your recipe.

So let's say that you've thrown an approximately correct amount of small caps into your 401(k) retirement success recipe. Then you move to the international fund and the bond fund, dropping the right quantities into your retirement fund.

That's the process.

But what if you see a fund that doesn't have keywords such as *large cap* or *small cap* in the name? That happens sometimes. Funds have names such as Fairholme and PIMCO Total Return. In that case, you have to probe a little deeper into the fund's description in your 401(k) materials, maybe using the prospectus (the pamphlet that comes with the fund) or going to www.morningstar.com. At the Morningstar Web site, you can enter the name "Fairholme" or the symbol "FAIRX" for Fairholme in the white Quotes box at the top of the page. After you press Enter, you will see a page with a lot of information about the fund. Toward the top of the page, you will see Category and, next to it, Investment Style. Both tell you that Fairholme is a "large value" fund. In other words, you know that the manager picks large companies that he thinks are cheaply priced, or value stocks. You will also see four out of a possible five stars nearby and a 10-year history of solid performance. So if you wanted a large-cap value fund, this could be your choice. You would match it to your recipe.

Getting the Proportions Right

But now you might be wondering how to get the proportions right when you do the matching. That's not difficult, either, given all the asset allocation models (or recipes) that are available to you. If you have a 401(k) plan, your employer might have a Web site or printed material with pie charts. A broker or financial planner might show you these, too. The charts might be identified in a brochure or on a Web site under the heading "Asset Allocation." These are the recipes to follow, and the slices on the pie charts show you how much of each type of fund to use.

You might have seen these charts in the past and found them meaningless. They won't be confusing anymore because now you can recognize the mutual fund names and will know how to match names on your mutual fund list to the corresponding slice on the chart.

Still, you might get somewhat overwhelmed because there are many different pie charts. You see a variety for a reason: How you divide your money depends on when you will need it and how nervous you get when the stock market goes through nasty cycles. In the next chapter, I help you identify the pie chart (recipe) that might be appropriate for you.

First, I want you to be aware of one important point: If you went to various financial planners, each would have a slightly different recipe, or asset allocation plan, for you. That might be unsettling; perhaps all the variations would make you worry about making a mistake. Maybe one says to put 35 percent of your money into large-cap funds and another says 38 percent. Instead of being nervous about imprecision, let it comfort you and empower you.

Asset allocation, or mixing and matching types of mutual funds, is essential. You must do it to be a successful investor. But the theory behind it is not so refined that professionals agree on precise portions of the various types of mutual funds. In other words, professionals generally agree that you need large caps, small caps, international stocks, and bonds, but they might deviate on the amounts by a couple percentage points.

Think of it like using a recipe that calls for a rounded teaspoon of sugar. Just what is "rounded"? It's more than a teaspoon, yet whether you rounded the amount of sugar a lot or just a little, the recipe would probably turn out okay.

The critical point is that you use sugar. You don't just leave sugar out of the recipe, and you don't use a cup when the recipe calls for a teaspoon. So as an investor, what's vital to you is that you use the full mixture—the sugar, or small caps; the flour, or large caps; international stocks, for variety; and, of course, bonds. The blending of the ingredients will make your money grow effectively over time.

It's called diversifying. All it means is this: You don't overdose on a single type of investment, but you hold a blend of investments so that you are ready for any cycle.

The Logic Behind "Diversification"

If you handed your money to most financial planners, they would not try to predict when the cycles would come and go or when a certain mutual fund would win or lose. Studies convince investment professionals that guessing tends to be folly. Instead, they simply decide on an appropriate "diversified" mixture of mutual funds for clients based on research showing that small caps, large caps, international stocks, and bonds take turns soaring and plummeting during cycles.

They figure that if they buy the right mixture for an IRA or 401(k), their client will get the advantage of the 47 percent upturn in small-cap funds in years such as 2003, when the good times just happened to hit without warning. After all, who would have expected such a windfall then? The previous year, a person with the same fund would have lost 20 percent and perhaps dumped the fund in disgust.

Likewise, large-cap funds can deliver delightful surprises and insulate people from losses that small-cap funds deliver as they go through vicious phases. For example, in 2006, small caps were sweethearts, growing money 18 percent and tempting investors to channel all their savings there. Then without warning, small caps made a Jekyll-and-Hyde move and started destroying money the next year. Large caps saved the day as they gained 5.5 percent and insulated people from the damage that would have hit their money if they had depended on small caps alone.

But it's not always the large-cap stock funds that save you from destruction. The stock heroes of the entire decade that began in 2000 were small-cap value stocks. They gained 10.6 percent a year, on average, while large caps went through 10 years without recovering fully from the viciousness of technology stocks early in the decade and the barbarity of bank stocks late in the decade.

One piece to this approach might shock you. As cycles occur, and as any one of the mutual funds in an investor's retirement fund takes a beating in a day, a month, or a year, most financial planners do not fixate on the moment or let it deter them from a well-conceived plan.

Planners just hold tight to the mixture of funds they created. They focus on historical studies showing that after many, many years, the large stocks in the mixture should climb about 8 to 10 percent, on average, annually—even if they are being brutalized at the moment. The small stocks should average around 12 percent, even if they are soaring much more than that at that point in time. And the bonds should smooth out the worst bumps, climbing at about 5.5 percent.

The professionals concoct the mixture based on historical studies that demonstrate how blending all the different categories provides a decent retirement after 20, 30, or 40 years of letting the mixture sit intact through ups and downs.

Proportions, however, are the key for the long-term outcome. Financial advisers determine which proportions are best for certain types of clients by using historical data. It shows them what various concoctions of stocks and bonds are likely to do.

They know that a person who relies only on stock funds during a five-year period could lose as much as 12 percent a year or make as much as 28 percent, because there already has been a point in history when this happened.

They know that they can soften the impact of a cruel stock market by putting 30 percent of a client's money into bond funds and 70 percent into stock funds. With such a mixture, history tells them the worst loss during five years could be 6.3 percent a year, and the upside could still reach a delightful 22.7 percent.

To be even safer, planners know that they could put half a client's money in bonds and half in stocks. Then the worst anticipated loss would be 2.7 percent a year during five years, if history repeats the worst cycle. And there still would be an upside of potentially 21 percent if history repeats the best period.

Could the future be somewhat different than the past? Absolutely. But the past is the best tool available to provide a guide to the future.

With this type of historical data, investment professionals pinpoint the combinations that best fit people at different points in their life. A 25-year-old needs a lot of stock to harness the power of compounding early and build a fortune. A 60-year-old needs to be more careful—perhaps dividing her money half in bonds and half in stocks to make sure she doesn't lose a fortune in a stock market disaster on the verge of retirement.

This Isn't About Math

This might sound like a complex endeavor, but it isn't. Financial advisers don't have to do elaborate calculations to incorporate history into plans for these various age groups. Brilliant professors and math geniuses have fed years of stock market data into computers and turned out some simple models. Those models show up in colorful charts with 401(k) and IRA materials, and they are all over the Internet.

Professionals and people like you have access to these so-called asset allocation models and can follow them without any more math than you learn in elementary school.

Although most people think they can't handle any of this because it must require a math brain, what's actually involved is quite different. If you went to a financial planner, he or she probably wouldn't be doing equations. Instead, that planner would be trying to figure out your psyche.

Planners want to know whether you are going to panic in a market downturn and run away from the combination of mutual funds that they assembled for you based on a simple model. They know that, if you panic, you could lock in a tremendous loss and perhaps need decades to recover. That's too costly for you, and they don't want it to happen.

Consequently, if planners think you might flee your stock funds, they tweak one of the typical models for your age group a little, maybe reducing your exposure to stock funds by 5 or 10 percent.

This is critically important. Novice investors usually get this wrong. They tend to go for all or nothing—either all small caps or no small caps, all stocks or no stocks. In contrast, the professional tweaks—maybe up 2 to 5 percent or down 2 to 5 percent in a category of stock funds.

The same goes for scary periods in the market. The professional might move 5 to 10 percent of a person's money out of stocks and into a money market fund to soothe a nervous client. But the professional tries to talk clients out of moving every cent to safety because the pros know that the cycle will change when you least expect it. And being there, ready for the change of seasons, is the sure way to make money.

11

Do This

Now you know how professionals think and what they try to do with your money. It's time for you to do the same—to master the finishing touches. Asset allocation, or mixing and matching a variety of funds, is the most important move you will make as an investor. And you now have all the tools you need to do it well.

You already know what's inside various mutual funds, what makes them soar and plummet in cycles, and how to match key terms such as *large cap* and *small cap* to your list of mutual funds. Now I'm going to show you how to select the appropriate proportions, and you will then be done. You will be a skilled investor.

We start with a classic mixture of funds. Investment professionals agree that a moderate asset allocation model divides retirement savings like this: 60 percent into stocks and 40 percent into bonds. This investment blend is comparable to the porridge that's "not too hot, not too cold" in "Goldilocks and the Three Bears."

From now on, think of the 60 percent stock/40 percent bond combination as a reliable asset allocation model that is just right if you aren't greatly adventurous. Then venture off from that point, if you'd like, into a model that might be even better for you. As you read further, you will become competent at adapting the model to your particular age, years to retirement, and temperament.

The 60:40 mix is a good starting point in learning asset allocation. Over the years, knowing this classic allocation model will give you your guidepost for investing decisions. It can always be your fallback position if you are ever confused.

If you use it continually, you will be on a better track than most people. The math whizzes have shown that you can lose money with a 60:40 mix in a single year. But losing money for even two years in a row is unusual.

Asset Allocation Is Simply Matching

Let's say that you have decided to sign up for a 401(k), or you want to overhaul a retirement account you have neglected.

Your employer hasn't given you a recipe, or model, to follow. But it doesn't matter. You now have the classic 60:40 stock and bond asset allocation model in your head, and you are going to use it as your recipe. You have your list of mutual funds on your desk, and you have a form to fill out. It asks you how much of your paycheck to invest in the retirement plan. It also asks you how you want to divide that money among the various mutual fund choices. You need to state your preferences in percentage terms.

Let's say that you decide to put $100 from each paycheck into your 401(k) plan. So as you fill out your 401(k) form, you think of your $100 as 100 percent of your recipe's mixture and start from there.

The next step is to hunt through the mutual funds on your 401(k) list, to start the mixing-and-matching process. Your 60:40 recipe calls for bonds. So you peruse your list of mutual funds and find only one diversified bond fund. It's called the Wonderful Bond Fund.

"Wonderful!" you exclaim. "I've found it." The only question is, how much? So you simply match that fund to the quantity you need in your recipe. Your decision is easy because the recipe tells you exactly what to do. You already decided you were going to use a classic 60:40 mixture for your recipe.

So you write on your 401(k) form that you will put 40 percent of your 401(k) contribution into the Wonderful Bond Fund. That's $40 every payday.

You now have assembled 40 percent of your recipe. The bond portion is done. Next, you return to your list of 401(k) mutual funds to complete the second part of your recipe: pouring in the right amount of stocks. You know the quantity from your recipe—it's 60 percent. You also know from the preceding chapter that a well-diversified large-cap stock fund is a key ingredient, a core investment to hold year after year.

You find one large-cap stock fund on your list of funds, the Best Ever Large-Cap Fund. You select it and follow your recipe by putting 60 percent of your 401(k) contribution into that fund, or $60 a payday.

You now have a classic 60:40 asset allocation—60 percent of your money is in stocks, and 40 percent is in bonds.

Your recipe is complete, and your 401(k) form now looks like this:

Wonderful Bond Fund: 40 percent

Best Ever Large-Cap Fund: 60 percent

As you go through life, you will have different actual funds in 401(k) plans or IRAs, but whatever they are, you can put 40 percent into a diversified bond fund and 60 percent into a diversified large-cap fund. If you keep this approach intact, with 60 percent of retirement savings in stocks and 40 percent in bonds, you will be more successful than most 401(k) investors.

But let's say that you feel comfortable taking this a little further, and you should. We are going to fine-tune that 60 percent piece you put into stocks, making a slight change in your recipe so that you are ready for more cycles in the market. The basic recipe of 60 percent stocks and 40 percent bonds is going to stay intact. But you realize that sometimes small-cap stocks do well and large caps are disappointing, and other times large caps win and small caps are scary. So you want to be prepared for both cycles.

I assume now that your 401(k) plan gives you a choice of one large-cap fund and one small-cap fund. Not all do. But say that you have those two choices. Then go through your list of stock mutual funds and find those that match the two basic U.S. stock categories: large caps and small caps. You will choose both based on a common practice in the investment profession: Typically, a financial adviser wants you to put about 70 to 75 percent of all your U.S. stock money into large caps because they are less volatile and make up a larger portion of the overall stock market than small caps. In fact, large caps make up roughly 70 to 75 percent of all the stocks in the stock market, so that's where the recipe originates. You can simply copy it. When you have tucked large caps neatly away, you dump the remainder into small caps, which make up roughly 30 to 25 percent of the stock market.

Here's how you would follow the recipe and sign up for 401(k) mutual funds—again, starting with the original $100 for your 401(k) plan contribution.

First, remember that the basic recipe is 60 percent stocks and 40 percent bonds. Begin by selecting bonds, filling 40 percent of your recipe with a bond fund. That is $40 on every payday.

Then you move to stock funds in the 401(k) list and decide how to allocate the remaining $60, or the 60 percent, that your recipe says should go into stocks. You state on your 401(k) form that you will put 45 percent of each 401(k) contribution, or $45, into a large-cap fund, and 15 percent, or $15, into a small-cap stock fund. (This might not look like 75 percent large caps and 25 small caps, but it is. Remember, you are simply dividing up your stock money, or $60, into the 75 percent large cap and 25 percent small cap concoction.)

That takes care of 100 percent of your contribution into your 401(k) plan. With the combination of large stocks, small stocks, and bonds, you are well diversified and ready for most cycles in the U.S. stock market.

For that 60 stock and 40 bond asset allocation, your 401(k) selection form now reads like this:

Whatever Bond Fund: 40 percent

Whatever Large-Cap Fund: 45 percent

Whatever Small-Cap Fund: 15 percent

All right, but let's say that your 401(k) also includes an international fund; you know that sometimes foreign stocks do best, and in other cycles, U.S. stocks do best. You want to be ready for anything worldwide and partake in the global economy—smart!

In this case, let's start fresh with your $100 contribution. First, put 40 percent, or $40, into a bond fund. But now you are going to think of your $60 stock portion with a fresh approach. You will think of dividing your total stock money, or 60 percent of your full 401(k) contribution, into two major categories: U.S. stocks and international stocks. And I recommend that you put roughly a third of all the stock money into international stocks.

With many countries going through a growth spurt recently, financial advisers have become increasingly interested in foreign markets. But advisers are debating how much money to channel there. Some say 50 percent because foreign markets make up about 53 percent of the globe's stock market value. A few say no foreign investment is necessary because large U.S. companies sell products everywhere.

So feel free to tweak your foreign allocation a bit, if you'd like. But let's say that you decide to put a third of your stock money into a solid, well-diversified international fund that insulates you from regional shocks by investing in many countries throughout the world. Then, given your $100 contribution to your 401(k), you would put $40 into a bond fund, $20 into an international fund, and the remaining $40 into the large-cap and small-cap U.S. stock mixture I previously described.

In other words, you'd put about a quarter of your U.S. stock money in small caps and the rest in large caps. Now your 401(k) form looks like this:

Whatever Bond Fund: 40 percent

Whatever Large-Cap Stock Fund: 30 percent

Whatever Small-Cap Stock Fund: 10 percent

Whatever International Stock Fund: 20 percent

You are nicely diversified and ready for cycles. With every paycheck, you will put $40 into bonds, $30 into large-cap stocks, $10 into small-cap stocks, and $20 into stocks throughout the world.

If you are offered a midcap fund, you can use that to diversify even a little more. In that case, leave everything intact on your recipe except your small-cap allocation. Divide the small caps in half, putting a 5 percent allocation of small caps into the mixture. The remaining 5 percent goes to midcaps.

You have a complex, well-diversified portfolio. Your 401(k) form would look like this:

Whatever Bond Fund: 40 percent

Whatever Large-Cap Fund: 30 percent

Whatever Small-Cap Stock Fund: 5 percent

Whatever Midcap Stock Fund: 5 percent

Whatever International Fund: 20 percent

That's it. You've got the basics. You write those percents on your 401(k) form provided by your benefits office at work, and you can be done with the task. With every paycheck, your orders will be followed, and you will be ready for the various cycles of the market. You will stay with the plan regardless of market conditions, forging ahead even if one or more of the funds happens to be bleeding cash during an awful cycle.

Picking Within Categories

But what if you have more than one large-cap fund on your 401(k) list? How do you choose between them? If you find one fund that is described as a core fund, that makes your choice easy. It means your fund manager will blend various types of large stocks for you so that you will be ready for a variety of cycles and won't be overly risky. You will have some risky, fast-growing stocks but also more dependable, slower-growing value stocks.

To find such a fund, look for words such as *core* or *blend* in the fund's name or description. But you might not be lucky enough to see that simple language. The fund description for a core fund might instead tell you that the fund looks for capital appreciation and selects both growth and value stocks.

If you are lucky, you will find a fund called a "Standard & Poor's 500 Index Fund" or a "total stock market index fund" on your fund list. If you do, either of these will serve you well as a core fund. In the next chapter, I explain more about why these two particular funds are usually excellent choices.

But if you don't have a core fund, you will probably have to choose between a large-cap value fund and a large-cap growth fund. The growth fund will be more daring. In certain years, you will make more money, and in others, you will lose more money than you would in a value fund. Generally, the value fund gives you a more stable ride, with less shocking losses than in a growth fund.

As I said in Chapter 9, "Know Your Mutual Fund Manager's Job," the value fund—or the tortoise in the "Tortoise and the Hare" race—wins over many years of investing. But even if you can't figure out whether you are looking at a tortoise or a hare, don't get hung up on this decision and fail to act. Get started with a well-diversified large-cap fund, and you will be headed in the right direction.

Still, if you are up to the task and willing to fine-tune your choices more completely, start trying to identify which of your choices is large-cap growth and which is large-cap value. Let the matching game begin. Look in the fund name or description for these words to find a growth fund: *growth,* or maybe *maximum growth* or *aggressive growth*. Typically, a maximum growth or aggressive growth fund is riskier than a growth fund.

Value funds often have words such as *income* or *low cost* in the name or description. The description might also tell you that the fund selects stocks that pay dividends. Typically, when stocks pay dividends, that gives you a certain level of stability—insurance against wild ups and downs. (Think of dividends a little like the interest you get on a savings account, except that dividends are never guaranteed. The company can increase a dividend, leave it the same, or take it away. (In the financial crisis and recession of 2008, companies were under financial pressure, so many took away the dividend or stopped paying as much to investors as they had previously. So just when investors desired the insulation dividends can provide, they lost it.)

Okay, let's get back to the matching game. You will find the same *growth* and *value* labels on both small-cap funds and large-cap funds. So what do you do now that you can spot them? If your head is spinning with growth and value, and you are asking what's best for you, take a deep breath again and be assured that there is a simple way to handle all of this. In fact, if you went to a financial planner for help, he or she would likely take the simple route. The planners don't know any better than you do whether the cycle in a single year will favor a growth or a value fund. So they don't try to figure it out. Instead, they get the stock portion of portfolios ready for any cycle. They simply divide it half growth and half value so that the investor will be ready for the ups and insulated somewhat from the downs.

So let's say that your 401(k) plan doesn't have any core funds in it. Instead, you are given two large-cap fund choices: a large-cap growth fund and a large-cap value fund. Likewise, you are given two small-cap fund choices: a small-cap growth fund and a small-cap value fund. What do you do? You can just divide your large-cap money 50 percent into growth and 50 percent into value. Do the same with small caps.

Here's what it looks like in money: If you are putting $45 into large caps, $22.50 will go into a large-cap growth fund and another $22.50 will go into a large-cap value fund. If $15 is going into small caps, you will put $7.50 into the small-cap growth fund and another $7.50 into the small-cap value fund.

That's the process. That's as elaborate as you have to get.

You Don't Need to Use Every 401(k) Fund

Your 401(k) might give you more choices than I have described here. You don't have to use them all. The key is to match the necessary categories, not to use all the funds. Just to reiterate, the necessary categories are bonds and stocks. And for stocks, you want international, large cap, small cap, and maybe midcap. Fill each of the categories with one core fund that blends growth and value stocks, and you will be on the right track. So that's four or five funds. But if your plan doesn't offer a core fund, you can pick one fund for large-cap growth, one for large-cap value, one for small-cap growth, and one for small-cap value.

If you do this, you are far beyond the average person. You are assembling your retirement savings the way a financial planner would if you went to one for help.

What's Your Age: 20, 30, 40, 50, or 60?

Depending on your age and how you will feel when conditions get really ugly in the stock market, you might want to alter the quantities in your recipe somewhat. Think again about the rounded teaspoon for your recipe—a close but inexact measurement. Again, there are no absolutely exact measurements with investments because only you can figure out just how much nerve you will have during scary cycles.

But here are some rules of thumb. If you are in your 20s and 30s, and if history makes you comfortable that you will recover from the scariest of stock market downturns, deviate from the classic 60 percent stocks and 40 percent bonds portfolio I have described. Go right ahead with a more aggressive approach to stocks: cutting back on bonds. True believers with no fear of the stock market can even eliminate bonds altogether in their 20s, but should add bonds a little at a time each year as they age so bonds provide insulation from a market crash.

Before the 2008 stock market crash, financial advisors were pushing young investors to put 90 to 100 percent of their retirement savings in stocks. They argued that when people are in their 20s, they should be more worried about running out of money in their old age than incurring maybe a 20 or 30 percent loss in the stock market when young. And stocks tend to be the way over many years to give the biggest boost to your money.

Yet the 57 percent crash in the stock market between the end of 2007 and early 2009 was sobering for just about everyone, including financial advisers. Many had been blinded by the unusual grandiose gains of the stock market in the 1980s and 1990s and ignored the fact that stocks are capable of furious losses at times. As reality hit in 2008, most individuals lost their nerve as stocks were careening toward what looked like oblivion. Many people went to financial advisers begging for a quick route out of stocks. So advisers now tend to recommend some bonds even for 20-somethings, to keep them calmer in brutal times.

If you came through the crash confidently, you might be among those who can take substantial risks, perhaps putting all or almost all of your retirement savings into stocks.

Yet that doesn't mean investing in just one specific stock or one type of stock fund. That's asking for trouble and leaving you way too vulnerable to a corporate mishap or bad cycle in the market.

It does mean taking steps to cushion the impact of cycles—in other words, dividing your money into large caps, small caps, and international stocks. It also means keeping a mixture of growth and value, not the hot mutual fund of the day. You can get growth and value blended into core funds, or you can select growth and value individually.

So if you are 22 and signing up for a 401(k) plan for the first time, and you want to be 100 percent in stocks, your mixture of funds could look like this:

Large-Cap Core Stock Fund (maybe a Standard & Poor's 500 Index Fund): 50 percent

Midcap Core Stock Fund: 8 percent (or Midcap Growth 4 percent, Midcap Value 4 percent)

Small-Cap Core Stock Fund: 8 percent (or Small-Cap Growth 4 percent, Small-Cap Value 4 percent)

Diversified International Stock Fund: 34 percent

Sometimes, with gutsy 20-something-year-olds who have seriously contemplated the effects of an awful stock market, financial advisers lean toward more small caps. Instead of putting about 75 percent of the U.S. stock portfolio into large caps and 25 percent in small caps, the advisers might go to 30 percent in small caps or even somewhat higher. Some also favor small-cap value funds over small-cap growth funds because, historically, value has outperformed.

Regardless, of these alterations, the closer you get to your retirement years, the more conservative you should become. The idea is to cushion your savings so that a stock market tsunami doesn't do so much damage that you will have trouble recovering in time for retirement. So as you go into your 30s, you slowly add some bonds to your investment portfolio.

By age 35, your 401(k) mutual fund selections and IRA would look about like this:

Large-Cap Stock (maybe a Standard & Poor's 500 Index Fund): 38 percent

Midcap Stock: 6 percent

Small-Cap Stock: 6 percent

International Stock: 25 percent

Bonds: 25 percent

During each year after age 40, consider moving another 1 percent into bonds and taking it out of stock funds. The process of slowly moving money away from stocks continues into retirement. Remember as you do this to stay diversified, following roughly the portions of large, small, and international stocks I have provided.

At about age 55 or 60, financial advisers often suggest a classic combination of 60 percent stocks and 40 percent bonds, although since the 2007–2009 market crash, there is a focus on being even more conservative with stocks close to retirement. I lean toward putting half your money into stocks and half into bonds at around age 60. To be even safer in troubled times, consider only 40 percent in stocks and 60 percent in bonds, but realize that, by cutting your risk in bad times, you impede the growth you will get in good times.

Consider the full cycle of the 2007 crash—both the horrible period and the healing period that comes after every stock market panic. People with a classic portfolio of 60 percent stocks and 40 percent bonds lost about 29 percent of their nest egg by the worst point in the 2007–2009 crash. A $10,000 investment became only about $7,100. People with half in stocks and half in bonds lost 22 percent; their $10,000 turned into $7,800.

Both approaches insulated people from the 57 percent decline that stocks delivered, but many were horrified at the extent of their losses nevertheless. They imagined they'd be eating cat food in retirement. Yet those who dared to hold on to their 60:40 mixtures of stocks and bonds learned a valuable lesson. Although the crash conjured up images of irreparable devastation, within about 18 months of the scariest point, people regained all that they had lost. By the end of 2011, they had about $11,800. Those with the 50:50 stock and bond mixtures had about $12,500.

In other words, diversification works, and ratcheting back on risk close to retirement works, although it does not insulate you completely from damage during awful cycles. Unfortunately, not enough baby boomers realized this ahead of the 2008 crash. One in four close to retirement had 90 percent of their money in stocks and suffered the full fury of the market storm.

Individuals close to retirement must realize that they are in a very different position than people saving for retirement in their 20s, 30s, 40s, and even 50s. Once you retire and stop working, you typically have to remove money regularly from your savings to pay for your living expenses. That means that the money you remove cannot wait for the healing cycle that will inevitably arrive in the stock market. So the destruction from the stock market is multiplied by the fact that you are also removing money from your savings at the worst possible time, robbing your nest egg of the opportunity to let that money heal.

That's a very different situation than for people who are saving for retirement in their 20, 30s, 40s, and 50s. Because working people aren't touching the money in their 401(k) or IRA, it remains there to heal completely.

Furthermore, if they keep adding money during scary periods, that money usually gets the benefit of gigantic gains when the healing process begins. On average, the stock market climbs about 48 percent within a year of hitting bottom.

Because you can be so vulnerable after you start spending money for retirement, I suggest that, about five years prior to retiring, people meet with a certified financial planner to make sure their finances are positioned for good times and bad times.

I recommend going to a fee-only financial planner, and I provide tips on selecting one in Chapter 15, "Do You Need a Financial Adviser?"

Doing Your Gut Check

As you look at asset allocation models that are appropriate for your age and the number of years you have remaining until retirement, don't delude yourself about your personality. Try to force yourself to consider how you would actually act under certain stock market scenarios.

People have difficulty forcing themselves to do this when they are making money in the stock market. Yet every time the market falls sharply, my phone mail system fills up with calls from anxious people.

In June 2006, for example, Carol, a 50-year-old Chicago psychiatrist, was among the terrified callers. She had just looked at her international fund, and she had lost about $5,000 in a few days. She wanted to know whether she should flee.

It was only natural that her fund would be down. The international markets had gone through a sharp downturn. In just two weeks, stocks in emerging markets of the world, such as Pakistan, Malaysia, and Venezuela, had crashed about 20 percent. It was troubling to investors, but it should have been expected. For two years, emerging market stocks were the sweethearts, bestowing great gains on investment accounts. The herd had piled in and then awoken in May 2006, concluding that the world was growing, but not enough to support the stock prices people had paid. So the stocks fell for a while as investors became more realistic.

Carol didn't know about cycles and didn't understand that she had been a part of an international stock craze during the previous couple years. All she knew was that she had put almost half of all her retirement money into an international fund, and it was quickly performing a disappearing act.

I told her about cycles and explained that the economies of the world would keep growing. Then I also explained that she had overdosed on international funds during the best of times. She needed to make a change—but not because of the loss she had just taken. She simply did not have the gut for the beating investors take whenever they've concentrated heavily on a certain investment.

Typically, about a 20 percent allocation in international funds would have been about right for a person like Carol, about 15 years from retirement. Yet the market had just forced her to do a gut check, and it demonstrated that perhaps even 20 percent in international stocks might be too much for her.

I told Carol not to flee her diversified international stock fund entirely, but to tweak the usual 20 percent model so that she would feel better, maybe using a 15 percent allocation in a foreign stock fund. With that approach, she would still diversify her stocks, tapping the world and the United States, but she would be less susceptible to the shocks she could not stomach.

When you do your gut check, you can use market history to quiz yourself about how you might respond. Go back to Chapter 9 and look at the best- and worst-case scenarios for the different types of mutual funds, and look at Table 11.1. Ask yourself how you would deal with the worst shock, such as losing an average of 12.5 percent every year for five years in an all-stock portfolio, or 10.3 percent with almost all stocks. Realize that, when it's happening, you don't know when it will end.

Also consider the mixtures I have advocated. Say that you put 70 percent of your money into stocks and 30 percent into bonds. The worst year for that model has been a 32 percent drop. If there is about a 30 percent drop in the future, your $1,000 will turn into about $700. I hope you now know enough about cycles and history to hold on to diversified portfolios of mutual funds, knowing that, with time, you will recover.

Table 11.1 should help you focus on the long run so that you can get through tough times and make your money grow. But be honest with yourself now rather than amid the carnage. If you tweak your 70 percent stock allocation—maybe to 65 or 60 percent—that could take the edge off of downturns, allowing you to stomach them and come out better in the long run.

Table 11.1

How Stocks and Bonds Work Together—Compound Annual Rates of Return in Percents, 1926–2011

Portfolio Makeup	Historical Average Annual Return	Average Year During Worst 5 Years	Average Year During Best 5 Years
100% large company stocks	9.8%	–12.5 %	28.6%
90% stocks/10% bonds	9.6%	–10.3%	26.6%
70% stocks/30% bonds	9.0%	–6.3 %	22.7%
50% stocks/50% bonds	8.3%	–2.8%	21%
30% stocks/70% bonds	7.4%	0.12%	21.3%
100% Long-term government bonds	5.7%	–2.14%	21.6%

Source: Ibbotson Associates, a Morningstar, Inc., company

A Reality Check for Fear: The Losses of the 2007–2009 Crash

I just allowed you to peruse the averages because averages tend to be the favorite method used by the financial industry to show good times and bad. However, I think that averages fail people. When individuals are in the midst of seeing their futures exploding in a horrifying stock market, they don't think in averages. They think in real dollars—or maybe I should say that they feel their losses in dollars. They observe their money disappearing. They contemplate utter devastation.

So I am going to take you through a journey that will let you see a horrific scene in real dollars. I am going to walk you through the scariest time in the stock market since the Great Depression so that you can feel the pain, see the ultimate outcome, and give yourself a chance to test your gut in real dollars.

I think of the stock market crash of late 2007 to early 2009 as the period in which virtually all Americans with 401(k)s and IRAs lost their innocence. It unveiled with brutal force the naive thinking of two prior decades, when people ignored the wisdom of combining stocks and bonds. Too many believed in the 1990s that they could plop a little cash into just about any stock mutual fund, earn 20 percent a year, and assume the money would be theirs for life.

When the illusion burst in 2008, and people saw carnage in their 401(k)s and IRAs, my telephone rang continually at my *Chicago Tribune* office. People sobbed as they asked me how to salvage their retirement and college funds. One woman told me she had just vomited. Another told me she didn't know if she should worry more about the stock market or her weight because she'd been eating chocolates constantly to calm her nerves. Almost every caller blurted out, "I've lost everything."

In fact, they had not lost everything, but it felt that way—partly because the losses seemed unbearable financially and partly because there was no end of the devastation in sight as the cycle played out on its own hidden schedule. Perhaps most important was the shock as their 401(k) and IRAs were doing the unimaginable.

Because individuals were taken by surprise, they panicked. They lost confidence in their ability to handle their own investments, they lost trust in their advisers, and, in many cases, they swore they'd never touch stocks again.

But the reality wasn't as bad as some people assumed. If they followed the precepts of good investing and combined stocks and bonds, most combinations saved people from ruin and positioned them to get back to even and start making money again within 18 months or less of the horrific losses. Even people who had invested 70 percent of their savings in the stock market were back to even by the end of 2010.

So I show you here exactly what happened to various mixtures of stocks and bonds during this unnerving period so that you see that each combo behaved differently during one of history's worst cycles. My hope is that it will help you decide what mixtures of stocks and bonds might fit your gut. By looking at these mixtures, you will see that blending stocks and bonds together matters a lot. You will see that bonds insulate your money from destruction, but not entirely. Most important, you will see how investment combinations allow you to recover with time.

Nothing ever plays out in the future exactly like the past, so keep that in mind as you review these combinations. Also realize that if you ever live through an alarming period, you won't know at the time whether your losses will be as bad as 2009 or even worse. You won't know when the decline in your money will stop, but at some point, the decline *will* stop.

So take a look and test your resolve. The numbers you are about to see here are real. I am providing very simple portfolios I assembled using actual months from Morningstar's database. The stock portion simply is the Standard & Poor's 500 Index of 500 large companies ranging from Apple to Exxon, Procter & Gamble, and Wal-Mart. The bond portion is long-term U.S. government Treasury bonds, or bonds that mature in 20 years.

Assume that it's late 2007, you have no idea what's about to happen, and you invest $10,000 in one of the eight ways you see here. This is what actually would have happened to you.

The Scary Period

First, look at the market collapse. I assume that you invested $10,000 at the start of October 2007 and held on all the way to the worst month, March 2009. At that scary time, you would not have had any inkling that the market was done falling and the pain was about to end. Here's what would have been left of your original $10,000 at the worst point.

100 percent in stocks: You lost roughly 50 percent and your $10,000 became about $4,980.

80 percent in stocks and 20 percent in bonds: You lost about 40 percent, and $10,000 became about $5,980.

70 percent in stocks and 30 percent in bonds: You lost about 34 percent, and $10,000 became about $6,540.

60 percent in stocks and 40 percent in bonds: You lost about 29 percent, and $10,000 became about $7,140.

50 percent in stocks and 50 percent in bonds: You lost about 22 percent, and $10,000 became about $7,780.

40 percent in stocks and 60 percent in bonds: You lost about 15 percent, and $10,000 became about $8,480.

30 percent in stocks and 70 percent in bonds: You lost about 3 percent, and $10,000 became $9,705.

100 percent in bonds: You gained almost 18 percent, and $10,000 became about $11,775.

The Healing

Next, look at where you would be if you had allowed your money to heal. These numbers include the same mixture of stocks and bonds that you just saw. But now I run your $10,000 through the cycle, from the very beginning of the downturn in 2007, through the worst losses, and finally through the healing phase.

I assume that you put $10,000 into the stock market when there was no sign of trouble at the beginning of October 2007. Then you rode the market all the way down and maybe were scared almost senseless in March 2009. But instead of yanking your money, you simply let it sit there to go through the healing phase. Three years after the scariest point, you had taken advantage of stocks soaring about 98 percent. As a result, your original $10,000 would look like this by March 2012:

100 percent in stocks: Your $10,000 would be about $9,865.

80 percent in stocks and 20 percent in bonds: Your $10,000 would be about $11,110.

70 percent in stocks and 30 percent in bonds: Your $10,000 would be about $11,725.

60 percent in stocks and 40 percent in bonds: Your $10,000 would be about $12,340.

50 percent in stocks and 50 percent in bonds: Your $10,000 would be about $12,945.

40 percent in stocks and 60 percent in bonds: Your $10,000 would be about $13,530.

30 percent in stocks and 70 percent in bonds: Your $10,000 would be about $14,100.

100 percent in bonds: Your $10,000 would be $15,660.

In other words, an all-stock portfolio was still down 1.4 percent after all that time, but despite the terror on the way down, every other combination was growing your money again.

Beware now of jumping to the conclusion that you might as well invest 100 percent in bonds because they did better than stocks during this period. If you come to that conclusion, I have failed you. Instead, recall a critical lesson of investing: Cycles happen in every investment—stocks, bonds, gold, homes, you name it.

I showed you these combinations of stocks and bonds so that you see how the mixture pulled you through this cycle and ended up growing your money. It's important to know that this cycle yanked stocks and bonds in unique ways, but combining them worked.

Bonds were abnormally strong because panicky people poured massive amounts of money into bonds when they got scared, and that caused the value to soar. Also, the Federal Reserve helped by tinkering to help the economy.

So don't expect bonds to always deliver gains as robust as during this period. More often than not, stocks grow your money more than bonds over long periods of time, and bonds hold up better than stocks amid trouble.

Even in the period after the stock market crash, stocks left bonds in their dust. As is typical after a crash, stocks soared as fear started to fade. Over three years, stocks gave people gains of about 98 percent, while bonds delivered 33 percent. But remember, the average for long-term Treasury bonds is a 5.7 percent gain annually, not the huge jumps that happened during this unusual time period. Most important, know that bonds suffer losses, too. In 1999, for example, investors lost 9 percent in bonds.

So I hope the message you take away from this is that stocks and bonds act differently in cycles, and that's why you hold them both. The only question is, how much of each?

The Easy Rule of Thumb

As the years go by, sometimes you won't have an asset allocation model to follow. You might see articles that refer to an old-style, easy rule of thumb that people use as a guide. The approach is to subtract your age from the number 100. That tells you what percentage you should invest in stocks, while placing the rest in bonds.

So say that you are 60. That would mean only 40 percent in stocks and 60 percent in bonds. Currently, with people living into their 90s, the old rule of thumb is considered somewhat outdated and too conservative. Some advisers argue that you should subtract from 120; others claim that subtracting from 100 still makes sense.

You could follow another rule of thumb, too: Tweak your typical asset allocations up 5 percentage points if you think you are braver, or down 5 percentage points if you feel more scared than the ordinary person. Again, there's not an exact answer. There's only an answer that's close to appropriate, one that will make you comfortable. The portfolios of stocks and bonds I provided earlier will help you feel your way through your comfort zone.

Just avoid these common mistakes: waiting to invest because you can't decide, being overly conservative when you have years to go before retirement, or swinging for the fences at any age—especially when retirement is just 5 or 10 years away. In other words, depend on diversifying your investments instead of counting on one stock or type of fund. Remember to tweak the proportions by a few percentage points instead of betting all or nothing.

Starting an IRA

Choosing mutual funds for your IRA isn't as easy as for a 401(k), because your choices are vast. In a 401(k), your employer gives you maybe up to a dozen choices, so your selection is relatively easy if you play the matching game I just described. It's as easy as looking at your list of maybe a dozen funds, spotting words, and slotting five to 10 of your funds into the pieces of an asset allocation model.

With IRAs, if you look at all the mutual funds available, you might indeed be overwhelmed. After all, more than 8,000 different funds exist. But you don't have to bother with most of them. I give you some shortcuts in the next chapter, and you might want to go back to Chapter 9 for some mutual fund suggestions.

For now, I just want you to understand that the same step-by-step approach I laid out for mixing and matching funds in a 401(k) applies to an IRA. So if you don't have a 401(k) and you skipped the previous explanation, go back and read it. The principle of using asset allocation and mixing and matching types of stocks applies to all your retirement savings. It's easy, and academic research proves that it's the one approach to investing that works.

You play the matching game with large caps, midcaps, small caps, international funds, and bond funds whether they are in your 401(k), your IRA, or any other account that is aimed at retirement saving. The key isn't the label on the account. The key is the purpose it's destined to accomplish. In other words, you are saving for retirement, so use the models I've provided for any IRA.

If you are in your 20s and starting your first IRA, however, you won't be able to follow the model I have provided you from the outset. With time, you will position your savings in line with the beginning model.

Say that you are starting with just a $1,000 contribution. There's no need to divide that into four different mutual funds. In fact, many mutual fund companies won't let you because most don't accept $250 contributions. Begin the first year by investing in a fund that will serve as your core investment for your lifetime, a mutual fund you will buy and hold year after year. In other words, start with a diversified large-cap U.S. stock fund, preferably a low-cost Standard & Poor's 500 index fund or a Total Stock Market Index fund, described in Chapter 13, "Index Funds: Get What You Pay For."

Then the next year, you might put another $1,000 into that same large-cap core fund in your IRA. You could do this again the third year. But after that, you'd take another $1,000 and buy your next fund: a diversified international fund. Then the next year, you could take another $1,000 and buy your next fund: a diversified small-cap fund. If you originally bought a total stock market index, you wouldn't need a small-cap fund because you would already have large stocks and small stocks in your single fund. (Learn more about this topic in Chapter 13.)

Over time, you will be working toward having a portfolio made up approximately like this:

Large-Cap Fund (perhaps a Standard & Poor's 500 Index Fund): 50 percent

Midcap Fund: 8 percent

Small-Cap Fund: 8 percent

International Fund: 34 percent

You don't have to get any more elaborate than this if you just buy diversified funds. But if you want to fine-tune even further, as the years go by, divide each of the pieces in half, putting one half into a fund with a growth approach and one half into a fund with a value approach.

Remember, although you might start out in your 20s or 30s with just stock funds, you should begin buying individual bonds or a bond fund as time goes on. So in your 50s, having 60 percent of your retirement savings in diversified stock funds and 40 percent in bonds would be a solid approach.

If all this mixing and matching is driving you nuts, you will find a shortcut in Chapter 14, "Simple Does It: No-Brainer Investing with Target-Date Funds." What's important before you head to that shortcut, however, is to understand the keys to investing that I am laying out first so that they always steer you away from an explosive investment, calm you at scary moments, and guide you into an appropriate mixture of funds.

Avoid Market Timing

When investors discover that the market goes through cycles, they come to a fairly logical conclusion: They vow to keep their eyes open and bail out of stocks as soon as they see hints of danger emerging.

Avoiding trouble works well in many aspects of life. But it's virtually impossible in investing, even for the savviest of professional investors. If you doubt this, consider September 11, 2001. Who would have predicted that terrorists would attack the World Trade Center and that the stock market (Dow Jones Industrial Average) would fall 14.2 percent in just five days? Or consider March 2000, when the stock market was shooting straight up. Investors thought investing was a no-brainer, that they would make money in the stock market forever. People were taking equity out of their homes to put it into the stock market just before it crashed. Little did they know that the stock market was about to fall 49 percent.

Perhaps you feel that you were the only fool in this debacle and that the pros know better. But it's not true. Professional investors who manage people's money might be skilled at asset allocation or shine at picking stocks and mutual funds. Yet even the best of them are lousy market timers—in other words, they don't know when to get into stocks or when to flee.

College finance professors have done numerous studies to see whether market timing works. And they have come up with little evidence that it can be done successfully over time. In one study, a researcher examined the track record of 32 market-timing newsletters over a 10-year period. Not one beat the broad stock market. The reason is easy to understand. Even if you are astute enough to get out of the way of trouble initially by withdrawing from stocks, you probably will miss the next surge up. And that's no small matter. Typically, investors make most of their money over a very few days. If they have put their money into safekeeping outside the stock market, they might miss those very few days.

If you think a couple days might not matter, consider research done by respected investor and author Peter L. Bernstein. In *The Portable MBA of Investment*, he notes that if the average investor missed just 10 of the very best days in the stock market over a 9-year period in the 1980s, his or her return would have been reduced by a third. Removing just 30 of the best days would have cut returns by 70 percent.

Most people make a terrible mess out of their own money by practicing market timing—or trying to catch what's hot or moving away from a falling stock market. They think that the market is safe when it isn't. They think that they should stash money in safekeeping when it's time to invest again, or they move from one fund to another trying to find the elusive best one.

In March 2009, after the stock market had declined 57 percent, the widespread view among professional investors was that doom and gloom was far from over. That view was wrong, and most fund managers that I interviewed months later said they wished they had been braver when there were stock deals of a lifetime in early 2009. As they waited for signs that the stock market was recovering, brave investors bought stocks, so the great deals were gone by the time most investors felt safer.

The Impact of Market Timing

Fear of having a mishap as an investor sometimes keeps people from doing what's prudent. They wait for the right time to invest and then end up waiting forever because they can always spot a potential threat. If you are among them, you might be reassured by some research done by Charles Schwab. Analyst Mark Riepe looked at four different hypothetical investors who took different approaches to market timing during 20 years from 1976 to 1996.

First, he looked at the person who ignored market timing and just put $2,000 into the stock market every year on December 31. At the end of 20 years, that person had accumulated $265,308. Then he looked at the person who had perfect timing and just happened to hit the best time to invest during each of the past 20 years. The results were good: $283,445. But the person who tried to buy stocks only during periods that looked promising and then accidentally blew it by investing just before a crash each year did the worst: $242,182 after 20 years of investing.

The lesson is this: If you knew you could time the market right, it would be worthwhile. But since you can't, automatically investing money each month or each year should provide you comfort. Having $265,308 after 20 years isn't bad when you are simply investing $2,000 a year. Also keep one more of Riepe's findings in mind: The person who was afraid he'd make a mess of his money in the stock market and just put his $2,000 a year into safe U.S. Treasury bills ended up with only $85,708 at the end of 20 years.

So instead of trying to time the market, do what financial planners do for their clients: Decide on the asset allocation that seems right to you, keeping in mind that if you use a teaspoon rather than a heaping teaspoon, you will still be fine. If you get nervous during a downturn and can't take it, make small changes, maybe shifting 5 or 10 percent out of stocks and into a money market fund instead of yanking all your funds and cowering in a money market fund that pays almost no interest.

I can't emphasize this enough. As novice investors have called me over the years, they have repeatedly made one common mistake: betting too much money on either ups or downs in the market. If they think times are great, they put everything in hot stocks. If they think times are scary, they naively move everything to safety. Instead, think of tweaking, using what professionals sometimes call "tactical" changes, with 5 percent or 10 percent of your money. Do it if it makes you feel better, but realize that your timing will probably be off.

Also be aware that the stock market does fall. In fact, it falls at least 10 percent or more every nine months, and 20 percent or more every 3–4 years. It can get very ugly, as with the 2000–2002 drop of close to 49 percent and the 2007–2009 drop of 57 percent. But throughout the past 86 years, the market has been climbing, not dropping, about 70 percent of the time. And that has turned $1 into close to $3,045.

Dollar-Cost Averaging

Because investors get nervous during the periods when the market falls just after they have invested money, financial advisers often tell people to follow a process that is less nerve-wracking than simply dumping a large sum of money into the market at one time. The approach is called dollar-cost averaging.

This is the process that's ingrained in the 401(k) system. Dollar-cost averaging means that, with every paycheck, you put a little money into your investments.

Because you do this with each paycheck over 20, 30, or 40 years, sometimes you will get great deals during low points in the stock market, as in early 2009. That's when the stock market was just about ready to start climbing about 100 percent. If you invested routinely in early 2009, you captured that gain even if you were afraid and had no insight into the stock market. Of course, with dollar cost averaging, sometimes you will be putting money into the stock market at times when you will lose, as in 2007. That's when the stock market was about to plunge 57 percent.

Investing in 2008 was traumatic, and many took a break and avoid losses. But over a lifetime of investing dollar cost averaging tends to be a sound approach. It is done more for emotional reasons than any other purpose. It forces investors to keep investing money when their gut says no. And in the long run, that pays off.

Rebalance

Instead of market timing, a discipline that professionals use increases the chances that you will benefit from highs in the market and not suffer severely in lows.

It's called rebalancing. To do it, you look over your retirement accounts once a year to see which funds have surged in value and which have lagged. Then you remove some of the money from the hottest funds and move it into the slowest funds.

You go back to your original recipe, or asset allocation, to see whether you need to do this.

Let's say that you were working off a very simple model, the classic 60 percent in stocks and 40 percent in bonds. And say that, during the past year, bonds have been the place to be and stocks have been lousy. You have lost so much money in your stock funds that your stock allocation is now down to 50 percent, and your bond allocation has grown to 50 percent of your overall portfolio.

You rebalance by taking your bond allocation down to about 40 percent again by removing some money. You move that money into your stock funds so that you have 60 percent of your money in stocks, matching your original model.

At that point in time, making a move like this will be hard to stomach. You will think that stocks are going to be scary because they have been scary. But if you think of cycles, you will appreciate the concept behind rebalancing. Eventually, the cycle is going to turn—and when it does, you will get the benefit of having 60 percent of your money in stocks. Best of all, you moved some money into stocks when they were cheap and neglected. In other words, you bought the stocks low and will get a chance to sell when they are high during the upturn in the cycle. It's a bargain hunter's delight.

What You Can Control

Ironically, a common practice that makes novice investors feel cozy is, in fact, one of the riskiest mistakes.

When they look over their list of 401(k) choices, they see one unfamiliar fund after another, so they go with what they think they know best: the stock of the company that employs them. They load up their retirement fund with it.

It's like playing Russian roulette with retirement savings. Academic studies show that choosing a single stock frequently sets you up for disaster. Typically, the person looks around his surroundings—seeing machinery, offices, and thousands of people hard at work all over the country or even around the world—and says to himself, "What could go wrong?"

Need I say it? United Airlines once looked like a corporate titan to its employees and to investors. Yet it had to file for bankruptcy, making its stock worthless. Kmart once looked like the most powerful retail chain in the country, but it went into bankruptcy a few years ago, leaving investors with worthless stock.

Enron was one of the hottest stocks of the 1990s. The press wrote glowing stories about the company, and employees at Enron filled their retirement funds with the stock, figuring they could retire at 50. Corporate executives encouraged them to do it, singing the company's praises even when it wasn't true. Then reality caught up with the company. Much of the glowing news was based on fake numbers, and the company collapsed. People who once thought they'd retire at 50 were wiped out. Their dandy nest eggs had turned to zero.

So if your employer lets you buy the company's stock in your 401(k), follow the lead of experts who know more than you: Pension fund managers don't put more than 10 percent of their portfolios into any single stock, no matter how impressive its prospects look. Mutual fund managers often won't exceed 5 percent, even with the stocks they most adore.

If you have a 401(k) and have loaded it up with your company stock, see whether you can sell some of the shares and move your money into diversified mutual funds, using the asset allocation models I have provided. If you can't sell the stock, stop buying it. And put all new money into diversified stock funds.

As a novice investor, you should also avoid buying individual stocks in your IRA—that is, unless you will devote the hundreds of hours it takes to study them and make sure they remain growing, profitable businesses. Only about 30 percent of professional stock pickers do well enough to beat the stock market. So why do you think that, acting on a hot tip, you are going to do any better?

12

How to Pick Mutual Funds: Bargain Shop

It's enough to drive a control freak crazy.

You can't control the stock market as it goes through unpredictable cycles. There's no way to know which mutual funds will be outstanding or disappointing in the years ahead. The most acclaimed investing stars in the mutual fund business tend to fizzle with time.

Those realities might be making you feel a little out of control at this point, perhaps wondering just what power you have over your money.

You actually have quite a bit—just not the type people imagine when they think their future depends on picking a hot stock or a top mutual fund. Remember, asset allocation—or mixing and matching categories of mutual funds—sets you up to grow your money well if you've matched the ingredients in your recipe diligently.

But beyond that, you can control one other factor as an investor. And you should, because it's the one "sure thing" you can count on to make a huge difference in the money you will accumulate over a lifetime.

I'm talking about fees, or the expenses you pay when you invest. You might not know that you are paying anything; most people don't realize it. But whenever you buy a stock, a bond, or a mutual fund, you pay fees, and costs vary greatly. If you don't pay attention to them, they will rob you of the easy money you could make—not just nickels and dimes, but thousands of dollars.

Suppose that you are 22 and you invest $1,000 for 40 years in a mutual fund that keeps your expenses low. If your fund averages 8 percent annually after you've paid all the expenses, in 40 years, your $1,000 will have become about $21,700. Contrast that with a high-priced fund, charging you only 2 percent extra in expenses over the low-cost fund. In 40 years, you will have only about $10,300, or just half as much as you could have if you'd been attentive to fees.

To most people, the costs they pay for their mutual funds are invisible. If you have money in a mutual fund now, the fund company is removing fees automatically from the money you have invested. When you pay the fund company, the money goes toward everything from the fund manager's salary to advertising costs. That's right; you pay the fund company to lure potential new investors. You pay fees whether the fund makes you rich or loses your money.

It's all part of the deal, the way the fund industry operates. But fees also differ significantly between funds, so you can save yourself a bundle if you just notice two simple numbers: the expense ratio and loads. Don't get nervous over the math-sounding word *ratio*. You don't have to do any math, and being aware of these two numbers takes less than a minute of attention—yet it can save you thousands of dollars over a lifetime of investing.

I explain more about how to do it later. For now, I just want you to understand the control you have over the fees you pay. When you see a fund charging you 0.18 percent, you have found a good deal. When you see another charging 2 percent, you need to be on guard.

Tiny Percents Have a Huge Impact

Although 0.18 percent and 2 percent sound like tiny, insignificant numbers, the difference between them ends up being gigantic over time. That's because of the power of compounding, which you can review again in Chapter 2, "Know What You'll Need." Compounding helps your money grow, and the more money you have invested, the more it can grow. When you give up money by paying unnecessary fees day after day, it sets you back for life. Every year that you pay an extra percent, you reduce the money you earn that year and every other year afterward—you rob your nest egg forever.

Let me illustrate this using some research done by Edward O'Neal, a professor at Wake Forest University. O'Neal examined 5,000 mutual funds in 2004 and determined that the average fund then was charging investors 1.41 percent a year on their money.

In other words, if you had $10,000 in the average mutual fund, you were paying $141 a year in fees. That doesn't sound so bad. But consider the alternative: You can get funds that charge just 0.10 percent, or about $10. You tell me, if you went into a store and saw two identical shirts, one for $141 and one for $10, which would you buy?

In his study, O'Neal took a modest approach, focusing on the low-cost funds charging an average of 0.314 percent, or about $31. If you chose one of those low-cost funds and invested $10,000, and the investment earned 10 percent annually, you would have about $63,200 in 20 years. If you instead held on to the fund charging 1.4 percent and earned the same 10 percent return on the investments, fees would shortchange your future by more than $12,000. You would have only about $51,000.

It has always shocked me that people will drive for miles across town to save $50 on some household item but will throw away thousands on their mutual funds without giving it a second thought. I think they do this because numbers such as 1 percent sound so small and because mutual funds are so confusing that people just want to get the job done.

Mind Your Money: Your Broker Might Not

Also, brokers and many of the mutual fund companies have no incentive to tell clients that they are paying more than they need to pay for their mutual funds. The higher your fees and commissions, the more money the fund companies make, and the more the brokers make.

Talk about a conflict of interest: If the broker sells you what's best for you, it very well might hurt him by reducing his compensation.

Controlling costs is easy. And here's what might shock you: Cheaper funds generally do better than those that charge you more.

You might find that surprising because, as consumers, we generally are taught that "you get what you pay for." Some financial advisers use that line to justify the exorbitant fees they charge clients. But the assertion simply is not true when it comes to investing in mutual funds.

Cheap Funds Work

Morningstar, known for its mutual fund research, has studied fees in depth. The firm's director of research, Russel Kinnel, says, "Each move up in price greatly lowers the likelihood that a given fund will be able to beat a corresponding low-cost index fund."

Index funds generally are the cheapest funds, and I explain more about why you should use them in the next chapter. For now, I just want you to understand why you should not be led astray by sales pitches for expensive funds.

According to the Morningstar study, if you have money in a fund that charges you more than 1 percent, you probably won't even keep up with the cheapest funds you could have bought. So you *are* throwing money away. Your expensive fund has only a one-in-seven chance of doing as well as the cheap fund.

Why does this happen? Because investing money is difficult, even for the top fund managers. I've talked with many of the nation's pros, and they are thrilled if they can generate a return for you that's even 1 percent higher than the stock market as a whole. Because it's so tough to do, fund managers who do beat the competition, even by a little, get paid bonuses.

So realize when you buy a fund that a half of a percent (0.50 percent) is a big number in the fund industry. If a fund manager excels by even that much, he or she might earn a bonus for outstanding performance. It's also enough to take thousands from your nest egg, and paying it doesn't necessarily get you anywhere.

Let's say that you have a mutual fund that has an excellent year, with a return of 11 percent on the stocks in the fund. During the same year, another mutual fund has a return of only 10.5 percent on its stocks. Your fund manager is superior—at least, that year. But the fund is outstanding only before your fees come out. Let's say that your fund charges you 1.5 percent of your assets. In other words, your return dips from the 11 percent you would have earned on the stocks in the portfolio to just 9.5 percent after paying your fees. And if the fund that earned 10.5 percent on the stocks charges investors only 0.50 percent, that fund turns out to be a better deal after the fees are paid. The fund's return, or the money the investor gets after fees, is 10 percent.

The bottom line: A clever fund manager who picks stocks and bonds skillfully might end up doing you little good if a fund is gouging you on fees.

It gets worse. Morningstar has found that funds that charge high fees also take exceptional risks with your money, apparently to try to boost returns to overcome the effects of the fees. It doesn't work, and it puts you in danger of losing more money than other funds do, on average, according to the research.

So here's a no-brainer strategy: To stretch each dollar you invest as far as possible, try to select low-cost mutual funds.

Watch Out for Loads

First, try to avoid paying loads, which are nothing more than a fee you pay a broker or financial adviser to select funds for you. Instead, select no-load funds—in other words, they don't charge you for advice.

If you pay a load, it works like this: Say that you are putting $10,000 into a mutual fund with a 5.75 percent load. That means that you give your broker $10,000, and she keeps $575 of the money as her commission and puts the remaining $9,425 of your money into a mutual fund for you.

Instead of earning a return on your hard-earned $10,000, you earn it on only $9,425. The result: Compounding works on $575 less than what you intended to invest. So over 35 years, if you average a 10 percent annual return, you end up with about $265,000. Not bad. But it could have been about $16,000 more if that $575 had gone into the fund originally.

Try the calculation yourself on your own loads using a cost comparison calculator at www.sec.gov/investor/tools/mfcc/holding-period.htm. Perhaps an easier calculator is www.dinkytown.net/java/FundExpense.html. To look at loads at the Dinkytown site, insert the sales charge (or load) and add no operating expenses to the calculation. It's easy and takes half a minute. You will probably be shocked by the impact.

Most mutual funds sold by brokers and many financial planners include either conspicuous or inconspicuous loads. Be aware of this so that if a broker assures you that you aren't paying anything up front in fees, you also realize what you will pay later—perhaps what's called a back-end load. Many funds that don't charge you up front (or front-end loads) end up costing you more because they charge you a lot for operating your fund year after year.

To protect yourself, you can ask a broker to show you all fees, loads, and mutual fund expenses you will pay, and ask him or her to do the math for you, showing you what you will pay and what that will do to your earnings over a lifetime of investing. This calculation should include both loads and what's called the expense ratio. When you have the figures, you can also plug them into the calculators I mentioned previously.

Your broker won't be eager to talk about fees and commissions because they are the bread and butter of the profession. But you are entitled to know the information, and you can ask to receive it in writing.

Also, to avoid loads, you can skip a broker, take your money directly to a mutual fund company, and buy what are called no-load funds. These funds do not charge you for a broker's advice. To buy funds directly, you call a mutual fund's toll-free telephone number and say that you want to put money in a certain fund.

Even if you buy no-load funds directly from a mutual fund company, you still have expenses and must pay attention to them. It's easy to examine them without doing any math. Aside from loads, everything you pay is blended into one number, called the expense ratio. It sounds like a complicated term, but it isn't. You will spot it in the materials, or the prospectus, you are given when you buy a fund; you also can get it from the telephone staff at your fund's toll-free number or ask a financial adviser to point it out to you.

Every fund charges you to pay for the manager of your fund, the paperwork for running your fund, and even the fund's advertising. All those expenses are bundled together and reported in the expense ratio. Examining that one number alone shows you what percent of your money goes to pay all your various costs.

Whenever you buy a fund, take a quick look at that one number. If the expense ratio is 1.41 percent, you have average costs. With $10,000 in the fund, it means you will pay $141 a year for the privilege of being an investor.

Although that's the industry average, most investors are paying less because many of the largest mutual fund companies have reduced fees. The ordinary investor pays about 0.77 percent for U.S. stock funds, according to Morningstar's Kinnel. For international funds, the average is 0.97 percent, or $97. For bond funds, expenses average 0.64 percent, or $64.

Generally, there's no reason to pay more than those numbers, Kinnel says. And some fine U.S. stock funds, called index funds, charge only 0.18 percent, or $18. Contrast that with some of the higher-priced funds at 2.5 percent, or $250.

To see the impact, go back to the mutual fund expense calculator at www.dinkytown.com that I mentioned previously. Let's assume that you put $10,000 into a fund with no sales charge or load and an expense ratio of 0.18 percent. (The Web site uses the phrase "operating expenses" for the expense ratio.) Over 35 years, your investments average a 10 percent annual return. You end up with about $264,000. But along the way, you had to pay about $5,000 in total fees as your cost of doing business with the mutual fund. If you hadn't had to pay anything, you would have ended up with about $281,000 because each penny would have been earning a return for you.

Still, $264,000 isn't bad at all. Now let's assume that you paid 2.5 percent every year after making your original $10,000 investment. You would end up with only about $116,000 after paying $40,000 in fees. But you would have lost a lot more than the $40,000 in fees. By paying the fees, you slashed the opportunity to have compounding work on more of your money. Losing that opportunity cost you $125,000. With 2 percent in fees, you would have ended up with about $138,500 after 35 years and missed the opportunity to make another $106,200.

So there you have it. As an investor, you should know that you can't do anything to foresee cycles in the market. A bet on even the best fund can go terribly off course. But you do have control—a lot of it. And it's easy. Just examine two numbers: the expense ratio (or operating expenses) and the load (or sales charge), and you will probably make more money than people who think that finding a phenomenal fund manager will make them rich.

I offer you two warnings, however: First, if you are going to procrastinate about investing unless you go to a financial consultant for some hand-holding, then go, and get the help and pay the fees. If brokers are conscientious, they might offer American funds, a group of relatively attractive funds that charge loads but keep costs fairly low. Just stay in the game by asking your broker about fees. And make sure you understand the conflicts of interest that the broker might have as he makes trade-offs between your need to build a nest egg and his need to boost his pay.

Realize that if the broker or financial consultant depends on commissions, he is probably going to tell you that the funds I discuss in the next chapter, index funds, are no good. It isn't that they're no good for *you*; it's that they're no good for the broker's income. And if you try to talk to a broker about finding investments with low fees and he tells you he offers something better, pick up a recent study done by Harvard economist Sendhil Mullainathan and MIT Sloan School professor Antoinette Schoar. They wanted to find out if brokers would do what was best for clients, so they had 300 actors pretend to be clients. These people went to banks, independent brokerage firms, and investment advisory firms in the Boston area and met with brokers or financial consultants.

When the "clients" showed the brokers their low-cost funds and asked for advice, 85 percent of the time, the brokers advised them to dump the low-cost funds and buy more expensive alternatives. Those alternatives would help the broker make money while zapping the clients' future of thousands of dollars. To help protect yourself, refer to the final chapter of this book so that you get good advice instead of wasting money on high-priced funds.

13

INDEX FUNDS: GET WHAT YOU PAY FOR

You might find this shocking: But when you invest, simplicity works best.

So now that you know the general rules of investing, I am going to make life very easy on you. I am going to lead you to the sweetest deal the mutual fund world offers. It is your foolproof way to amass a fortune. Tuck it into your retirement fund, and you should be more successful than many Wall Street stock pickers with years of experience and elaborate strategies.

I'm talking about what are known as "index funds."

If you have a 401(k) and are overwhelmed with the stock fund choices in it, simply look through the list and try to find the word *index* on one of the funds. It probably will say something like "Standard & Poor's 500 Index" or maybe "total stock market index."

If you spot those words, buy one of those funds. You have found a special kind of mutual fund that has success written all over it. That single fund can be your core investment for life—a no-frills, uncomplicated, cheap mutual fund that invests in 500 of the nation's largest companies, or what is roughly referred to as the stock market. With an index fund, you can be a stock investor the easy way.

You can put money from every paycheck into one of these index funds and turn your back without giving it a second thought. Because you will have 500 or more stocks, you will be well diversified. Because the fees in index funds usually are very low, you are likely to make more money with it than other funds that invest in large companies.

Likewise, if you are starting an IRA and are overwhelmed by the thousands of choices out there, you can go to a mutual fund company known for its low-cost index funds. Then simply plop your money into a total stock market index fund; hold it forever; feed new money into it every week, every month, or every year; and stop worrying about how to discriminate among all the funds with the wacky names.

If you do this, you have to pay attention to just one thing: getting the proportion right in your portfolio. A total stock market index fund invests exclusively in U.S. stocks—no bonds, no foreign stocks. So if you are in your 20s and feel comfortable with the ups and downs of the stock market, you can simply begin your investing years with 100 percent of your money in this fund. If you are somewhat older, the index fund is fine for your stock money, but you need a bond fund too. I'll help you with quantities later in this chapter.

Now, I want you to be aware that index funds come in different varieties. The most common two—the ones most often in 401(k) plans—invest in either the Standard & Poor's 500 or the total stock market. When you see those terms, they mean roughly one thing: the stock market. These are the mutual funds that make sense to buy and hold for life.

If you put your money in either, you will be a stockholder. On the days you turn on the news and hear that the stock market has gone up, you will be able to assume that you made money. On the days you hear that the stock market has gone down, you will assume that you lost money.

If history repeats the way it has for the past 86 years, you will average close to 10 percent annually on your money in that index fund over a lifetime of investing. Remember, I said *average*. Some years you will lose—maybe 20 percent or more. Some years you will win—maybe 20 percent or more. Over the past 86 years, all the wins and losses in the stock market have blended into a decent gain.

If you had money in a Standard & Poor's 500 index fund, you would have lost 22 percent of your money in 2002 and gained 28.5 percent the following year. You would have lost 37 percent in 2008 and gained 26.5 percent in 2009.

After blending together all the gains and losses over the last decade, you would have averaged about a 4.5 percent return annually for each year of the past 10 years ending June 2012.

You might think, "Earning about 4.5 percent a year is not so good. Those index funds didn't even grow at 10 percent, the historical average in the stock market." But the lower return didn't happen because the fund was a dud. It happened because the stock market itself went through some horrible years. And if you had decided to try to outsmart the market by seeking a fund manager who would excel, you would have likely done worse. The average fund with a professional at the helm, who tried to maneuver skillfully through good and bad times, ended up providing you less—a return of only 4 percent a year on average instead of 4.5 percent in the Standard & Poor's 500 index fund.

The simple Standard & Poor's 500 index fund beat 87 percent of all the other funds that hired savvy investing professionals to pick the best large company stocks, according to Morningstar research. In other words, if you had bought an index fund, you would have skipped all the expensive strategies that Wall Street peddles, and you still would have been the winner—a do-it-yourselfer beating the best and the brightest. That's how you become an extraordinary investor without effort.

The past 10 years have not been an aberration. During the last three years, the simple funds crushed 90 percent of the pros, gaining 14.9 percent a year, while the highly paid stock pickers delivered just 12.4 percent. For years, the simple index fund has proven its stuff.

It has triumphed over the majority of stock-pickers who get paid handsomely to try to do better.

What's an Index Fund?

To understand index funds, you have to first know what other mutual funds do. As I explained in previous chapters, most funds in a 401(k), and almost all the funds brokers sell, employ an investing pro to pick stocks for you. He or she gets paid a lot for helping you make money—about $500,000, on average, and often more than $1 million.

The pro's goal is to cherry-pick through the stock market for the very best stocks, the ones that will become valuable and make you money in your mutual fund. When investing professionals or fund managers think they see a winner, they buy it. If the fund managers spot a loser, they avoid it. If the fund managers have already bought a stock that has become a dud, they sell it.

All this sounds attractive to the ordinary person. None of us wants a loser; we all want winners. As I explained in the preceding chapter, the investment industry is built around the concept that investors should be willing to pay a pretty penny for the opportunity to have a pro navigate the stock market for them.

The trouble is selecting stocks is difficult. Even the best investment pros let investors down. All the cherry picking usually leaves investors with less money than they'd have if they simply said they'd be willing to accept all the losers along with the winners in the stock market. They'd simply close their eyes and buy the entire stock market, including its shining stars and warts—great stocks, awful stocks, and mediocre stocks.

This is what index funds do. They don't hire expensive fund managers to navigate through the stock market for you. They just buy everything in the stock market. When you buy a Standard & Poor's 500 index fund, or a total stock market index fund, you are buying the full array of stocks that make up what's known as the stock market. The secret to their success: They don't charge you much—perhaps only 0.17 percent. So you keep more of your money than you would if your fund used a stock picker.

Because this simple, low-cost approach enables investors to repeatedly beat the pros, I think the conclusion is easy: Just invest in the full stock market through an index fund.

A broker might tell you that you can get only mediocre returns that way. They've said to me, "A person doesn't want to be an ordinary student, a mediocre athlete, or an average worker, so why would they want to settle for average as an investor?"

The answer is simple: Mediocre is better than the most highly paid, highly respected fund managers tend to do. People who know a lot more than the novice investor see it this way. Pension funds, which have investment experts at the helm, often use index funds as a core investment in the stock market.

Typically, pension funds use a simple index, like the Standard & Poor's 500 Index, for close to 50 percent of the money they invest in the stock market. These people have a tremendous responsibility: They must amass enough money to pay retirees' pensions in the future. That should tell you something: Byron Wien, who spent years at Morgan Stanley, noted in 2004 that using an index fund once would have been considered heresy in his profession, which makes money by selling investors on the value of stock picking. During the past few years, it has simply been considered smart. Index funds have proven themselves in good times and bad. During the last decade, only 13 percent of the brainy, highly paid professional fund managers have been able to beat the simple Vanguard total stock market index fund.

What's the Stock Market, and What's a Stock Market Index?

We all have a sense of what the stock market is. Each day, TV and radio news tells us, "The stock market was up today" or "The stock market was down today."

What most people don't know is that the stock market isn't just one thing. There are different stock markets—or, more precisely, different pieces of the full stock market. Each has a name you might recognize. Knowing the names is necessary for picking an index fund because there are various index funds—some that make that perfect all-around investment I mentioned, and some that add spice to the core investment you can buy and hold for life.

The Dow

Most people have heard of the Dow Jones Industrial Average. That's usually what TV and radio reports are referring to when they say that the stock market is up or down that day. The Dow is simply an index, a collection of stocks used to easily report on the stock market. It is not really the entire stock market. The full stock market actually includes more than 5,000 stocks; the Dow includes just 30.

Why does the Dow get so much attention every day? Because that index contains an array of 30 powerful companies from every industry. The 30 stocks are looked at as a group—through the Dow index—as a means of taking the economy's temperature or getting a glimpse of how corporate America's health is perceived.

If investors think companies will be delivering strong profits in the near future, they will buy stocks, the prices on the stocks will rise, and the Dow will be up that day. If investors are worried about the health of all or part of the economy, investors will sell stocks, the prices on stocks will fall, and the Dow will be down.

If you invested in a Dow index fund, the fund manager wouldn't try to pick the winners from 30 stocks and avoid the losers. The fund would buy all 30 stocks so that your fund mimicked the Dow index. Consequently, you would own a tiny piece of all 30 industrial giants, everything from ExxonMobil to General Electric. You would have the winning stocks that would become more valuable investments and the losing stocks that might become less valuable—or even ghastly investments. But the individual stocks wouldn't matter to you. You would make money based on the average value of the full array of 30 stocks in the Dow index.

The Standard & Poor's 500

If you buy an index fund in your 401(k), it's likely to be a different index from the Dow, but the concept is the same as I just described. The most common index fund in 401(k)s is what's called a Standard & Poor's 500 index fund.

Instead of containing just 30 stocks, the Standard & Poor's 500 includes 500 stocks from the largest American companies. So a fund manager for a Standard & Poor's 500 index fund would buy all 500 stocks, paying no attention to winners and losers. If you owned a share of a Standard & Poor's 500 index fund, you would own a tiny piece of everything from Exxon and Johnson & Johnson to Wal-Mart and Microsoft. When you heard that the stock market was up one day, you could assume that you made money.

Generally, when you hear Wall Street experts talking about the stock market, they are not talking about the Dow. They are usually referring to the Standard & Poor's 500. When you hear that the stock market has averaged a 9.8 percent return a year over the past 86 years, people are referring to the Standard & Poor's 500. (It is sometimes called the "S&P" for short.) It is Wall Street's favorite shorthand way of taking the temperature of all the stocks bought and sold day in and day out.

Because the stocks in the Standard & Poor's 500 index are so large, the index represents about 70 percent of the value of all stocks that are available. But even though Wall Street repeatedly calls the Standard & Poor's 500 "the stock market," it is not really the full market. It's missing the smaller stocks that make up approximately 30 percent of the stock market.

The Total Stock Market

A handful of other indexes represent roughly the full stock market. One, called the Wilshire 5000, includes more than 5,000 different stocks—large ones such as General Electric and Johnson & Johnson, but also smaller ones such as H&R Block, Expedia, Cheesecake Factory, Hyatt Hotels, Aeropostale, and hundreds of small companies with names you probably wouldn't recognize. The smaller companies and the huge quantity of companies differentiate this index from the Standard & Poor's 500 index.

If your 401(k) plan has a fund that contains words such as *total stock market index,* the fund is about the most diverse one you can find. It is probably designed to mimic the Wilshire 5000 or perhaps a somewhat smaller index known as the MSCI Broad Market Index or the Russell 3000 index.

A total stock market index fund is an easy one-stop pick. If you select it, you will have large stocks and small stocks. You will be a long way toward doing what every investor should do: You will have a diverse mixture of stocks. Your fund will always contain some winners and some losers. Despite the losers, the average annual return for the 15 years ending June 30, 2012, has been about 5 percent. Meanwhile, funds that tried to beat that number by employing savvy stock pickers had less to show for their efforts. They averaged just 4.4 percent a year over the same period. In other word, investors who relied on the savvy fund managers paid more to get less.

Again, the beauty of an index fund and the reason it beats many other funds is that it's cheap. For the privilege of investing in the entire stock market, the investor in the Vanguard Total Stock Market Index (VTSMX) pays only 0.17 percent of his or her assets—a lot less than the 1.4 percent on a fund employing a professional stock picker to find winners and avoid losers.

If you had two funds that had the same return before you were charged fees—a traditional one with a professional stock picker and average fees, plus an index fund—you would end up with a lot more money in the index fund. That's because you give up only 0.17 percent of your money to have the index fund. You give up 1.4 percent to have the stock picker.

The decision is easy: For your core large-cap stock fund, simply buy an index fund full of large company stocks. Two of the lowest-cost funds are the Vanguard Total Stock Market Index and the Fidelity Spartan Total Market Index.

Using Index Funds in a 401(k)

When you have a 401(k), your choices are limited. Your employer gives you only a few mutual fund options. You might not have an index fund among them, but chances are, you do have one. About 60 percent of 401(k) plans offer an index fund, and if you work for a large company, an index fund is probably embedded somewhere in the midst of your fund list.

Usually, the choice would be a Standard & Poor's 500 index fund. If you find this index fund, select it for your exposure to large cap stocks. You won't need any additional large-cap stock funds.

Then, of course, return to your 401(k) list to complete your selections for all the other categories you need. You should sign up for a small-cap stock fund, an international fund, and a bond fund to complete the mixture of investments you need. If you are confused about the right proportions of all of these, go back to Chapter 11, "Do This."

If your 401(k) plan also includes a total stock market index fund, you can make life even easier on yourself. Instead of choosing a large-cap and small-cap fund, you can simply choose that one total stock market index fund. With that one fund, you will invest roughly 75 percent of your money in large company stocks and 25 percent in small ones. This gives you your complete U.S. stock portfolio. It's an all-in-one choice. So if you select it, do not also choose a Standard & Poor's 500 index fund because you'd be doubling up—your total stock market index fund includes virtually the same large stocks as the Standard & Poor's.

If you are debating between the Standard & Poor's index and the total stock market index, the total stock market makes investing easiest for you. After picking it, all you need to do for a simple portfolio is to select an international fund and a bond fund, and you're set.

Your portfolio might look like this if you're about 30:

60 percent in the total stock market index

30 percent in an international stock fund

10 percent in an intermediate-term bond fund

In your late 50s, it might look like this:

40 percent in the total stock market index

20 percent in an international stock fund

40 percent in an intermediate-term bond fund

If your 401(k) gives you the choice of a total stock market index fund or a total bond market index fund, you have hit the busy person's jackpot. Simply divide your money between those two index funds, hold the appropriate proportions throughout your lifetime, and don't worry about sorting through the hodgepodge of other funds.

Let's say that you are in your 40s, and you want 70 percent of your money in stocks and 30 percent in bonds. You would put 70 percent from each paycheck into the total stock market index and 30 percent in the total bond market index. You'd be done.

Over time, your stock index fund would help your money grow, and your bond index fund would insulate you from sharp downturns in the market. You'd be missing just one extra piece, international stocks, which probably isn't the best move. If you are willing to tweak a little more, put about a third of your stock money into a diversified international stock fund that invests throughout the world. You might even be lucky enough to find an index fund that invests in international stocks. It would likely have a name like the total international stock index, and the description would likely say that it mimics either the MSCI EAFE index or the MSCI ACWI Ex U.S. index.

The last index is the broadest way to invest in the full world and to take advantage of fast-growing emerging market countries. AC stands for "all country." It means that you will invest in developed parts of the world such as Europe and Japan, as well as emerging markets such as China, Indonesia, and Argentina. The "Ex U.S." in the name tells you that the fund invests virtually everywhere in the world except the United States. That, of course, makes it a sensible selection because you already get all the U.S. exposure you need from your total stock market index.

Among international selections, the MSCI EAFE has been a tamer index than the "all country" index because EAFE stands for the more established developed countries of the world—everything from Europe to Japan. On the other hand, the emerging markets in the "all country" index give you an opportunity to take part in the fast-growing economies. If you are offered either of these index funds for foreign stocks, you can save yourself money by buying a broad range of stocks cheaply with a single fund.

As with the other index funds, no professional is at the helm trying to buy winning stocks or winning countries. No one is looking to avoid losers. The goal is simple: Just provide stock exposure worldwide.

Now look at how this complete portfolio would look for a person in his or her 30s. This is similar to the previous portfolio for a 30-year-old but includes the names of the indexes. Also notice the ranges for fund quantities. The idea is to adjust portions based on your stomach for risk.

10 to 20 percent in a total bond market index fund (identified as the Barclays Aggregate Bond Index)

25 to 30 percent in a total international stock market index (identified as the MSCI EAFE index the MSCI All Country World Index Ex-U.S.)

55 to 60 percent in the total U.S. stock market index (identified as maybe the Wilshire 5000 or MSCI Broad Market Index or Russell 3000 index)

Some Index Fund Ideas

Here are some fine low-cost index funds: Vanguard 500 (VFINX), Vanguard Total Stock Market Index (VTSMX), Vanguard Total International Index

(VGTSX), Vanguard Total Bond Market Index (VBMFX), Fidelity Spartan 500 Index (FSMKX), Fidelity Spartan Total Market Index (FSTMX), Fidelity Spartan International Index (FSIIX), and T. Rowe Price Equity Index 500 (PREIX). Many low-cost index funds also exist for midsize and small companies. Among them are Vanguard Small Cap Index (NAESX) and Fidelity Extended Market (FSEMX).

Tweak Your Portfolio Once a Year: Rebalance

Just one word of warning: After awhile, the proportions that you are supposed to keep constant in your portfolio—or your recipe for investment success—get skewed without your noticing it.

So remember to revisit your 401(k) or IRA at the end of each year: Look over the portions in each fund and make sure they still fit the model you chose in Chapter 11. You will recall that this year-end process is called rebalancing.

For example, if you are 35 and you want 20 percent of your money in the bond index fund, 25 percent in the international stock fund, and 55 percent in the total stock market fund, your intent should be to keep those proportions roughly intact until you purposefully change them as you age. Yet if international markets have been soaring and the U.S. has languished, you could find 35 percent invested in your international fund and only 45 percent in the United States. This, of course, is not your intent. Your model has been distorted. You would move some money out of the international fund and into the U.S. fund, following the model you preselected. That way, you will be prepared for the next cycle.

Using Index Funds in an IRA

Remember the reason for using index funds: They give you broad exposure to stocks, and they are cheap. Because they are cheap, you tend to get a better return from them than you would with a traditional mutual fund that employs an investing pro.

Index funds are perfect for an IRA as well as a 401(k). With an IRA, you are in the driver's seat because you are not constrained by funds someone else selects for you.

My advice: Make life easy on yourself. Go to a firm such as Vanguard or Fidelity, known for low-cost index funds, and start building your nest egg with the simple funds.

Say you're in your 20s and have $3,000 to invest in your first IRA. You could start the first year by putting your full IRA contribution into the Vanguard Total Stock Market Index. Eventually, you will add some extra funds to your IRA over the years so that you will be exposed to all the investments you need. (If you are confused about this, go back and review asset allocation in Chapter 10, "The Only Way That Works: Asset Allocation.")

But you don't have to move into two or three funds immediately. Just focus on that first index fund for a while. Maybe the second year you contribute to your IRA again. Simply put some more money into the Vanguard Total Stock Market Index. After that, start filling in the slot for another type of investment. If you are young and aren't squeamish about losing money in stocks, you can make your next IRA contribution to the Vanguard Total International Stock Market Index.

As the years go by and you continue to invest in your IRA, you would eventually put some money into a bond market index fund. Let's say that you have reached your mid-30s; your IRA might look approximately like this:

20 percent in the Vanguard Total Bond Market Index (VBMFX), which mimics the Barclays U.S. Bond Index.

26 percent in the Vanguard Total International Market Index (VGTSX), which mimics the MSCI ACWI Ex U.S. Index.

54 percent in the Vanguard Total Stock Market Index (VTSMX), which mimics the MSCI U.S. Broad Market Index.

You can continue to keep investing money in those three index funds throughout your retirement saving years, simply changing the proportions a little year after year to be safer as you approach retirement.

Let's say that you are in your mid-40s. At this point, your portfolio might look about like this:

30 percent in the Vanguard Total Bond Market Index

23 percent in the Vanguard Total International Market Index

47 percent in the Vanguard Total Stock Market Index

When you are close to retirement, it looks more like this:

40 percent in the bond index

20 percent in the international index

40 percent in the total stock market index

Indexes Come in Many Varieties: An Advanced Lesson

You now know the layman's language for the four basic indexes: the Standard & Poor's 500 for large companies, the total stock market index for the full market of large and small companies, the total international index for foreign stocks, and the total bond market index.

Dozens of other indexes exist, so keep your eye on the four basic ones, to simplify your investing decisions. They will serve you well.

On the other hand, if you are an investor who likes to tinker with your investments, a growing array of index funds allows you to do it. New index funds let you fine-tune investments, slicing the market into tiny pieces like microcaps (extremely small companies), emerging markets (developing foreign country stocks), small value stocks, or real estate companies.

Let's say you are interested in fine-tuning your portfolio more than I described with the very broad index funds, and you know that, over decades, small company stocks have provided greater returns than large companies. Let's say you are willing to take on the short-term risk that small companies can crash hard. Let's also say that you want some real estate exposure, besides your home, to diversify your investments. In that case, maybe you would reduce your holdings in the Standard & Poor's 500 somewhat and increase your small company investments.

Here's one mixture that shows you how you could tinker. Notice that, even when you believe in small caps outperforming, you don't use all or nothing; you still keep a diversified portfolio intact.

30 percent in the Barclays Aggregate Total Bond Index (AGG)

20 percent in the Standard & Poor's 500 (IVV)

10 percent in the Standard & Poor's MidCap 400 (IJH)

10 percent in the Standard Poor's SmallCap 600 for growth companies (IJR)

10 percent in the Russell 2000 Value for small value companies (IWN)

15 percent in MSCI EAFE for foreign stocks (EFA)

5 percent in the Dow Jones Diversified Real Estate Index (IYR)

You could do this through a fund company such as Vanguard or Fidelity, matching the names of indexes listed previously to the appropriate index fund. For midcaps, for example, you see that you would choose an index fund that mimics the Standard & Poor's MidCap 400 Index. Knowing the exact name of the fund isn't critical. Knowing the name of the index you want to mimic is the essential piece of information. Just ask for an index fund that mimics the index you want.

Exchange-Traded Funds

Another way to use indexes is go to a broker's office or find a broker on the Internet, such as Scottrade (800-619-7283), TD Ameritrade (800-934-4443), or Charles Schwab (866-232-9890, or use a brokerage part of companies such as Vanguard and Fidelity. Through the brokers, you could buy another form of index funds, called exchange-traded funds, or ETFs, for short.

Don't be concerned about the new vocabulary word I've thrown at you. Many ETFs are just like index funds, except that you buy them in a different way. You go to a broker and buy an ETF as you would a stock instead of just sending your money to a mutual fund company.

How do you decide between going to a firm such as Vanguard or Fidelity for traditional index funds and going to a broker for ETF index funds? Base it on whether you want to make contributions from every paycheck or several times a year. It's often cheaper and more efficient to feed money month after month into a traditional index mutual fund at a company such as Vanguard, Fidelity, or T. Rowe Price than to buy ETFs routinely. You can set up an account so that your money automatically flows into a mutual fund from every paycheck—a smart move.

If instead you want to make only a single $4,000 contribution once a year into one fund in an IRA, the ETF can be a good, simple approach. Look at the portfolio I described on the previous page for the investor who likes to tinker. After each type of investment, I have put letters in parentheses. These letters are the ticker, or "symbol," you use to identify an ETF when you buy it.

In other words, if you want to buy the Standard & Poor's 500 exchange-traded fund instead of a typical index mutual fund, you would visit or call your broker or contact him or her on the Internet. You'd say, "I'd like to buy the IVV exchange-traded fund," or maybe you'd prefer another one called Spiders (SPY). Many different ETFs mimic the same indexes.

You give your broker the money, and he or she buys shares of an ETF for you. With time, you would save money if you bought the ETF over the Internet through the broker's Web site. The broker will tell you how to do it.

When buying ETFs, however, be sure to keep your costs down. If you go to a full-service broker such as Merrill Lynch or Smith Barney, you will probably face higher commissions, compared to those charged at so-called discount brokers such as Scottrade or Charles Schwab. Whether you pay $7 at a discount broker or $30 at a full-service broker, an ETF is the same; there is no reason to pay $30.

Also be aware that firms including Vanguard, Fidelity, Scottrade, Charles Schwab, and TD Ameritrade offer a few basic indexes in ETF form without charging any commission for buying or selling them. That means they keep your expenses down, but it doesn't mean they are completely free. As with mutual funds, you always pay some expenses, and you should always check the expense ratio on ETFs, Make sure you're not overpaying for an index that might be almost identical, but cheaper, under a different company name.

If you are just starting out with ETFs and need some help, consider a discount broker with offices near you—maybe Charles Schwab, Fidelity, or Scottrade. They have offices around the country and brokers who will help you at a lower cost than full-service brokers.

To find ETFs that mimic the mutual funds you have, or to identify ETFs for any piece of your stock and bond mixture, try the screener at www.etfdb.com. You can also get ETF information at www.indexuniverse.com, www.xtf.com, and www.morningstar.com.

Some Exchange-Traded Fund (ETF) Ideas

Vanguard Total Stock Market (VTI), iShares Russell 3000 Index (IWV), iShares S & P 500 Index (IVV), Schwab U.S. Large Cap (SCHX), Vanguard Dividend Appreciation (VIG) Vanguard Value ETF (VTV), Vanguard Growth ETF (VUG), iShares S & P MidCap (IJH), iShares S & P SmallCap 600 Index (IJR), SPDR MSCI ACWI ex-US (CWI), iShares MSCI EAFE Index (EFA) Vanguard MSCI Emerging Markets (VWO), iShares Barclays Aggregate Bond (AGG), iShares Barclays TIPs Bond (TIP), and WisdomTree Emerging Market SmallCap Dividend (DGS).

Tinkering with ETFs: For Advance Investors

Morningstar, which analyzes mutual funds and ETFs, has created what it calls a hands-free portfolio. I show you this shortly. In other words, you can set it up and not feel compelled to change it based on market conditions. Yet despite the hands-free idea, Morningstar also suggests how you can tweak pieces in your mixture of stocks and bonds a little from time to time (maybe just 1 or 2 percent each month) if you want to be attentive to market changes. Through its *ETFInvestor* newsletter each month, you can watch the changes analysts suggest for people motivated to tinker.

Following I show you the Morningstar mixture so you can see how an individual could slice and dice the stock market and bond market with index ETFs into more finely tuned pieces than I described previously. Most of the slices you see are in the broad indexes I already suggested.

But by using smaller pieces of the index, you can fine-tune, if you want. For example, if you look at the bond mixture, you see specific investments in corporate bonds, mortgage bonds, and TIPs (which are U.S. government bonds that help protect you from inflation). The total bond market index I described previously for one-stop bond shopping also includes corporate bonds, government bonds, and mortgage-related bonds, but not TIP government bonds.

With the slicing and dicing you see here, Morningstar decided in early 2012 not to include the U.S. Treasury government bonds that are a significant part of the total bond market index. The reason: At that point in time, interest rates were so low that analysts worried about potential losses if interest rates started to climb. See the section "How to Lose Money in Bonds," in Chapter 8, "Making Sense of Wacky Mutual Fund Names," for the background on how rising rates can cause losses.

Morningstar decided to protect against that possibility by avoiding Treasury bonds, although it retained TIPs, or government bonds that are adjusted to pay more if inflation starts to build. TIPs also can suffer losses, but they can be nice protection if the economy goes through a cycle of rising inflation. Notice that Morningstar also has included in the portfolio a WIP ETF. That's an index that invests in bonds from throughout the world that will be adjusted to help people get through inflationary periods.

Also notice that Morningstar puts a little money into gold through an ETF, another strategy that can protect people from inflation. By slicing and dicing your stock and bond indexes as you see Morningstar do, an investor can increase exposure slightly or decrease it slightly based on market opportunities or concerns on a moment's notice. But do not be alarmed if this seems like too much work. If you don't want to tinker, you can count on your total broad index funds over the many years you will be investing for retirement.

I offer this Morningstar portfolio—roughly 30 percent in bonds and 70 percent in stocks—merely so you can see how you can refine mixtures using ETFs if you are motivated or if control makes you feel better.

Bonds: 30 percent of portfolio

10 percent in iShares iBoxx $ Investment Grade Corporate Bond (LQD)

6 percent in iShares Barclays MBS Bond, which invests in mortgages (MBB)

5 percent in iShares Barclays TIPs Bond (TIP)

4 percent in SPDR DB International Government Inflation Protected Bond (WIP)

5 percent in iShares Gold Trust, which invests in gold (IAU)

Stocks: 70 percent of portfolio

20 percent in Vanguard Mega Cap 300 ETF, which invests in giant companies (MGC)

10 percent in iShares Russell 1000 Value Stocks (IWD)

9 percent in Vanguard Mid Cap ETF (VO)

8 percent in Vanguard Small Cap ETF (VB)

12 percent in iShares MSCI EAFE (EFA)

6 percent in Vanguard Emerging Market Stock (VWO)

5 percent in iShares MSCI EAFE Small Cap Stock (SCZ)

Beginning Investors: Starting an IRA with Pocket Change

Unfortunately, some of the cheapest index funds that mutual fund companies sell directly aren't available to people who don't have much cash. Vanguard, for example, requires that you have $3,000 to deposit immediately up front. Don't let that deter you.

T. Rowe Price is a fine firm and lets you get started in mutual funds or index funds with little money. For example, T. Rowe Price offers the T. Rowe Price Equity Index 500 (PREIX). The price of entry is only $50, as long as you commit to adding another $50 each month. That's a great way to build up retirement money without feeling like you are depriving yourself. If you can provide $50 from every paycheck, or $100 a month, that would be even better.

Another way for people to invest small amounts month after month is to use the zero-commission ETFs that I described earlier. Just make sure that you know which ETFs don't charge commissions and which ones do. You will have to pay commissions to buy most ETFs, and it would be expensive and foolish to pay a $7 or $8 commission every month to invest $50 per month in an ETF. A more reasonable approach would be to automatically put the $50 into a typical mutual fund that doesn't charge a commission.

Warning: Not All Index Funds Are Good

Awhile ago, I was on a radio show and a man named Don called to ask whether I thought he had a good index fund. He told me the fund's name, but like a lot of investors, Don was focused on the wrong thing. The name wasn't important because his index fund was pretty much like any other. Remember, index funds offered by one company or another should be almost identical in content. That's the idea—one Standard & Poor's 500 index should be the same as another because both funds have only one job: to mimic that index. Consequently, the key factor to scrutinize in Don's index fund—or any index fund—is fees. Always keep that in mind. The cheapest one will be the winner.

I looked up Don's fund at www.morningstar.com, and I ached for all the people who had purchased it. Don had bought his index fund from a financial consultant who charged clients commissions. That was costing Don a bundle. The fund had a 1.25 percent load, which, you will recall, is the sales charge you pay a broker or financial planner to sell the fund to you. In addition, the fund was charging Don 1 percent in fees, which is noted as the "expense ratio."

I ran the numbers through the SEC mutual fund cost calculator I mentioned in Chapter 12, "How to Pick Mutual Funds: Bargain Shop," and here's what I found: If Don invested $10,000 in his index fund for 10 years and averaged a 10 percent return, he would end up with about $23,100. If he instead chose a low-cost fund such as Vanguard's, he would pay no load and only 0.18 percent in expenses. The result: He'd have about $25,400 after 10 years and would save himself more than $2,000 on expenses.

Everyone wants to earn $2,000 more over 10 years. That's not the half of it. Look at what the power of compounding did to Don. If he kept averaging a 10 percent return and kept the money invested for 40 years, he'd accumulate only about $299,000 in his expensive index fund. The cheap fund would provide him a whopping $421,000 simply because expenses weren't eating away his return.

Keep in mind that if you go to a broker or any financial adviser who works on commissions, you will likely have to pay excessive costs for index funds. That really doesn't make sense because index funds are the easy funds; most people should be able to select them on their own without an adviser's help. In other words, a broker cannot add value selecting a basic index fund such as the Standard & Poor's 500 or Total Stock Market Index, so why pay him or her to do it?

Instead, if you want to find affordable index funds easily, simply think Vanguard, Fidelity, or T. Rowe Price.

Is Your Fund Good or Bad?

Although you can intentionally select index funds for IRAs, you might not get that choice in a 401(k). Your employer might not give you the opportunity. Also, whether you have an IRA or a 401(k), you might want to venture away from index funds for some funds—perhaps you want a stock-picking pro for small caps and international stocks.

Some research suggests that skilled stock pickers can be worthwhile in the small-cap and international arenas, although other research refutes the finding.

The argument for stick pickers in international and small-cap funds is this: It's silly to use a stock picker for large-cap U.S. stocks because information about the largest companies in the marketplace abounds and many stock pickers are examining that information. Small caps and international stocks, on the other hand, are more difficult to examine because information isn't as plentiful. So a great sleuth might earn his keep.

Still, it's up to you to make sure that spending money on a stock picker is worthwhile. And if you have a mutual fund that's acting like a loser, you will want to know whether you should keep it or dump it and buy another.

To compare funds, you must analyze performance of funds in two ways. First, you must compare only similar funds. Second, you must compare each fund to an appropriate index. For example, if you have a small-cap fund and think it's rotten, compare it only to another small-cap fund, not a large-cap fund, an international fund, a midcap fund, or a bond fund.

Remember, cycles will affect each category differently. So if your small-cap fund is down 5 percent, but the average small-cap fund is down 10 percent, your fund is actually outstanding. If your small-cap fund is down 5 percent, and your large-cap fund is up 10 percent, it doesn't mean your small-cap fund is bad. It probably means that the cycle at that moment is friendly to large caps and not small caps.

Advanced Comparison Lesson

If you are debating between two funds in the same category, that is a valid comparison. Say that you have two large-cap growth funds in your 401(k). How do you know which to pick?

Your employer might offer you a Web site with what's called Morningstar information on it. Morningstar is a company known for its research on mutual funds. That research, available at www.morningstar.com, will make your decisions easier.

To find out whether your fund is a good one, follow this process at the Morningstar site. Type in the name of your fund in the Quote box, and when you come to a report on your fund, look for the word Performance. Then notice whether your fund did better (+) or worse (–) than others like it. The performance information will also tell you whether your fund did better or worse than the index—in other words, whether you would have done better with an index fund.

The easiest thing to do, however, is to focus on % Rank in Category. This shows you how your fund compared to other funds like it. If your fund ranks close to 1, it is outstanding. If it ranks close to 50, it's average, and that's fine. If it's below 50 percent, that's not a good sign. It means that the fund you are considering did worse than half the other funds like it.

Keep in mind, however, that one year is insignificant. You want a fund that consistently is in the top half of funds like it, or one that performs as well as, if not better than, an index fund—but not just for one year. You want to base your decision on several years because one year might have been a fluke during a cycle.

Notice performance for five years and 10 years. Then check to make sure that the same fund manager who was there five years ago is still running the fund. If the fund has been outstanding, but the fund manager recently left, all the performance figures from the past are probably irrelevant (unless a comanager who was working alongside the old manager simply takes over where the old manager left off).

But if the fund has a new manager who hasn't worked with your fund in the past, that person is starting fresh. You really don't know what that new manager will do with your money. He or she might or might not handle your fund like the previous manager did. If this concept seems difficult to understand, think of the teachers you've had over the years. Fifth-grade math is fifth-grade math, but if a new teacher comes into the course midyear, the new teacher might offer a class that differs greatly from the class taught by the teacher you first had.

Then focus on one more piece of information about the fund. You should be able to guess. It's the expense ratio, the one number that tells you more about how you are likely to do with that fund in the future than any other measurement. If your expense ratio is below 1 percent, your fund has consistently been in the top half of its peers, your fund is performing better than an appropriate index, and the manager is still there, you probably have found a keeper.

Remember, what doesn't matter is whether your fund made a lot of money or lost a lot of money. What matters is how it compares to the index. If you have a large-cap fund that's up 13 percent, but the Standard & Poor's 500 is up 15 percent, your 13 percent is stinky. You've been wasting your money on high expenses to do worse than an index. That's foolish—maybe not in just one year, but if it happens year after year, it certainly is.

On the other hand, if the Standard & Poor's is down 5 percent for the year and your fund is down only 1 percent, your fund manager earned his keep. You have an outstanding fund if it keeps outpacing the Standard & Poor's 500 year after year.

The indexes are the key to measuring and evaluating your mutual funds. Savvy investors, such as pension funds, use indexes to tell them whether they have been employing a worthwhile investment manager. The mutual fund industry uses them to determine whether to give a fund manager a juicy bonus.

Here's a simple process for comparing your funds. For any fund that you own or are considering buying, simply see whether its returns measure up to the appropriate index:

For an international stock fund, use the MSCI EAFE or MSCI ACWI Ex U.S.

For a large-cap fund, use the Standard & Poor's 500.

For a large-cap growth fund, use the Russell 1000 Growth.

For a large-cap value fund, use the Russell 1000 Value.

For a small-cap fund, use the Standard & Poor's SmallCap 600.

For a small-cap growth fund, use the Russell 2000 Growth.

For a small-cap value fund, use the Russell 2000 Value.

For midcap funds, use the Standard & Poor's MidCap 400.

For bonds, use the Barclays Aggregate Bond Index.

If your fund performed better than the index for at least three years—and hopefully five or more—you have an outstanding fund if the manager is still there. If it performed much worse, ask yourself why you spent more on fees to get less. Consider dropping your fund and buying an index fund instead.

You can find the indexes and their performance on the Internet. If you simply type in the index names I provided previously, you will find an ETF that mimics that index. If you compare your mutual fund's performance to the ETF that's appropriate, you will be comparing your fund to an index. You will see whether your fund is a laggard or is worth the fees you pay to own it.

How to Analyze a Fund

Let's walk through an example. Say you have been putting money into the Fidelity Contrafund in your 401(k) for years. You want to know whether it's a good fund or a bad fund.

You go to www.morningstar.com, type in "Fidelity Contrafund," and click on FCNTX (the ticker investors use to get information on that fund). After you click on FCNTX, you come to a report on the Contrafund. Immediately, you see close to the top of the page that the fund category is large growth fund. So you know that the matching words you need to focus on are *large growth fund*. In other words, this fund invests in large company stocks, and it would not be meaningful to compare that fund to any other fund except another large-cap growth fund.

You can also see at the upper right that when Morningstar compared the fund to similar large-cap funds, it was a strong performer. See the four stars? That's Morningstar's second-highest rating—four stars on a scale of 1 to 5.

That's a good sign. But you aren't done. Beneath the stars, you see a 0.81 percent expense ratio. That falls within the 1 percent threshold that's acceptable for fees. So expenses are okay if the fund performs well.

Now, you need to examine the fund's performance, or how investors do when they put money into the fund. Under the fund's name, you see "Performance" and a graph that shows how the fund has grown $10,000 over the past few years. Under that, you see performance numbers for several periods. "YTD" is for the current year and is not very meaningful about long-term quality. Look at five-year and 10-year performance instead. In June 2012, you would have seen that, for five years, the fund had given investors an average annual return of 2.1 percent; for 10 years, it was 7.7 percent. But you think, "Is that good or bad?"

The answer comes in the information you see just below those numbers. The Contrafund's return is compared to an index here—the Standard & Poor's 500 (large-cap stock) index—and the results are good.

You see that, in the Contrafund, you earned 8.3 percent a year, on average, for the last 10 years, whereas the index would have paid you just 5.3 percent during the same time period. That's extremely important. It means the investors are ending up with more money in the Contrafund than they would in an index fund, and that's unusual, especially for five years or more. If instead Morningstar had shown that the fund's return was worse than the index, or below 5.3 percent, that would have been a bad sign. It would have suggested that an index fund would be a better deal. Instead, you will see in the information under the performance heading that this fund has been so strong for 10 years that it ranks at number six, almost the top ranking. That's significant.

You need to run one more check before deciding whether the fund is for you. Check on the manager by clicking "Management" in the blue bar at the top. You see that the strong manager is still at the fund and has been there since 1986. Looks like the fund is a keeper!

You can do more research by clicking on all the choices in that blue bar where I had you click on Management. But you have the basics. You found that the fund has continually beat its index, the expenses aren't out of line, and the savvy manager is still there. Doing this analysis took about five minutes.

If analyzing funds still seems like too much work, you can avoid the headache by simply using low-cost index funds—those with an expense ratio of 0.35 percent or less. On the other hand, I have one more shortcut for you, the simplest of anything the mutual fund industry offers.

Now that you understand how to analyze fees and evaluate asset allocation models, you have the background necessary to use this shortcut wisely. It's a couch potato's delight. And you will find it in the next chapter.

14

SIMPLE DOES IT: NO-BRAINER INVESTING WITH TARGET-DATE FUNDS

Now for the easiest choice of all. I mean easy—as easy as putting money into a typical savings account at a bank, only with a much better chance that you will be able to travel and go out to dinner once in a while when you retire.

The mutual fund industry has caught on that people are busy and overwhelmed by the strange words that are thrown at them. So the industry has created a new type of fund that could have been named "mutual funds for dummies" or "mutual funds for couch potatoes" or "mutual funds for nervous Nellies."

The funds actually are called target-date funds, or sometimes life-cycle or retirement-date funds. I know I've just thrown another set of vocabulary words at you. But these are easy to spot and well worth it. If you peruse 401(k) choices and see a number embedded in the name of a mutual fund, you can sigh with relief. Your quest for the simple way out has been solved. Perhaps you'll see a fund with a name like Target Retirement 2045 or

Retirement 2020, or maybe your employer is holding meetings to tell you about these popular additions to 401(k) plans. If you consider retirement investing a hassle, you will never curse the process again.

You can buy one of these "couch potato mutual funds" for your 401(k) and, away from work, you can do the same in your IRA. With these funds, you can put all your retirement savings on autopilot for the rest of your working life.

If you select a target-date fund, you won't have to worry about sorting through mutual fund names and categories such as large caps and small caps. Nor will you have to do any mixing and matching or move money between risky investments and safer investments. The fund itself will do all this for you—and not just for tomorrow, but for your entire working life.

You need to know only one thing: when you'd like to retire. That's it. Simple. Just give the fees a once-over to make sure you aren't paying too much, and you can be done. You won't need any more funds beyond that one.

You might be confused now because I told you previously that you cannot rely on a single fund and you must combine many in your portfolio. However, a target-date fund is the exception because it is designed for one-stop shopping. A single target-date fund gives you large caps, small caps, and international stocks and bonds; then as you age, the fund manager tweaks the proportions so that you have what he deems appropriate for your age.

So if you are procrastinating because you are afraid of making a mistake, fear no more. This is a no-brainer.

Look for a Date

More than half of 401(k) plans now offer these investing shortcuts. If yours does, look for one detail: the number that matches the year you will retire. Let's say you are 39 years old now and plan to retire at 67. That's simple. You will retire in 2040. So you want investments geared to that target, the year 2040. Now all you have to do is find a target-date fund with the date 2040 on it.

Every target-date fund has a year in its name. So if you are looking through a 401(k) list and wonder how to find one, look for a name of a fund with a number somewhere in the 2000s on it. You might see several. Some might have names such as *freedom* or *life path* or *milestone* or *retirement* or *strategy* and an array of different dates on them.

Don't let the variety worry you. The different dates on them are there merely because each person needs to find the fund aimed at his or her particular retirement year. And words such as *life path* and *freedom* are simply supposed to clue you in on the intent: to get your money ready for your retirement date.

If you are 40, you wouldn't pick a fund with *2020* in its title unless you intended to retire early. If you are 40 and are planning to retire at 67, an appropriate fund would be one with 2040 in the name, getting you ready to retire in 2039. The fund dates put you close to but not exactly on your actual retirement date. Most likely, the 2025 fund would be right for someone who is 54. For someone 30, the 2050 fund would be smart, preparing the person for retirement at about age 67, or the year 2050.

If you are 25 and are nervous about investing but have a 401(k) with a fund with *2055* in its title, you can use it and probably relax from that point forward. You can also do the same with an IRA. You simply contact a firm such as Vanguard (800-997-2798), T. Rowe Price (800-638-5660), or Fidelity (800-544-8544); select a target-date fund with the number 2050 in its name; and barely give it a second thought for the rest of your working years. Tell the mutual fund firm to automatically take money out of every paycheck and put it in that one mutual fund over and over again throughout your working life.

At age 67, you should be set, even though you devoted almost no attention to your investments during three decades—that is, of course, if you saved plenty during your working years, too, and didn't simply count on your investments to do all the heavy lifting. No fund is a miracle worker. If you are saving a pittance, a fund manager can do only so much to make it multiply. And you don't want a fund manager to try to make up for your saving shortfalls by taking too many risks in the stock market when you are on the verge of retiring. That could mean you get slammed by a huge loss right when you need your money most.

Tweaking As You Age

Target-date funds are designed for one purpose: to grow your money effectively so you have as much as possible for a set date. You simply clue the fund manager into what he or she needs to do for you by giving the manager your target. You tell the fund manager the date you plan to retire by buying the appropriate fund, the one carrying your retirement date. Then the manager knows what combo of stocks and bonds should fit the stages of life you will go through on the way to retirement. As you age, the manager adapts the mixture each year for the rest of your working years so that it should be appropriate for your age. You will never need to buy another fund.

Your fund manager will be acquainted with academic studies that show how types of stocks and bonds work over time through different cycles. So the fund manager will buy a mixture (with market-cycle shock absorbers built into the mix) and will continually tweak the recipe for your age and the number of years to retirement. When you are young, you will have mostly stocks in your target-date mutual fund, along with maybe somewhat riskier stocks. As you enter middle age, the manager will slowly, year by year, cut back on stocks, adjusting for less risk and keeping more money in bonds and cash.

I don't want you to think that these are magical devices that won't lose money at times. These funds have large doses of stocks, so when the stock market goes down, you should expect to see your fund drop, too. In fact, they can plunge enough to make a person nervous at times. For example, in the 2008 financial crisis, funds intended for people in their mid-20s plunged about 39 percent because they were invested almost completely in stocks. Those for people in their mid-50s lost about 29 percent.

If your fund manager has taken the prospect of horrible market down-turns seriously, you should not suffer a devastating loss when you cannot recover from it. Yet fund managers tend to have an appetite for stocks—sometimes greater than individuals have. The professionals argue that every-one needs significant exposure to stocks, or their money won't grow enough in time for retirement. That argument is valid, but it can go too far for my taste for people relatively close to retirement.

Most funds, geared toward 50-year-olds retiring in 2030, for example, recently divided an individuals' money 80 percent in stocks and 20 percent in bonds. This could mean that a target-date fund might be riskier than a par-ticular person can stomach even though the fund manager considers it best for the individual's age.

People very close to retirement in 2008 were shocked at the risks they were taking with target-date funds. The average fund, designed for people just two years away from retiring then, lost almost 25 percent.

Severe losses sent near-retirees into a panic. Many had assumed that the target-date funds guaranteed they'd have plenty of money for retirement, so they bolted out of fear and locked in sharp losses for life. As a result, they either would face very frugal living in retirement or would have to work for many years longer than expected.

So be aware: Your target-date fund is geared to getting you ready for retirement, but there are no guarantees. Nasty cycles can emerge and play havoc with your money. If you want to make sure your fund manager isn't subjecting you to more risk than you want, look at the mixture of stocks and bonds and compare it to the portfolios I have laid out previously. Check out the portfolios under "A Reality Check for Fear," in Chapter 11, "Do This," to imagine worst-case scenarios and also to understand that a well-conceived mixture of stocks and bonds will recover if you can give it some time.

You don't have to accept a target-date fund that you think is overly risky, especially if you are near retirement. Many different fund companies create these funds, and they vary widely in the risks they take with your money. For example, in 2008, when the market crash came, some target-date funds were careful with money for people planning to retire in two years. The most conservative one had just 3.6 percent invested in stock and left people unscathed amid the market carnage. The riskiest had 41 percent in stocks. People have recovered since then, which should provide some assurance if a market crash happens close to your retirement. Yet angst matters, too. And in 2008, people planning to retire in two years didn't know whether they'd end up with the money they would need.

Realize that much disagreement circulates among professionals about what an ideal portfolio is at certain ages. For example, among 2025 funds geared toward someone around 55, some target date funds had as little as 38 percent invested in stocks in 2012; others had as much as 86 percent.

If you are in your 20s and 30s, and have been convinced that stocks recover over time in cycles, you can go along with the target date fund in your 401(k) that puts almost all your money into the stock market. Little controversy exists about the wisdom of heavy stock exposure for people in their 20s and 30s. But there is significant debate about what's appropriate for people in their 50s and 60s.

Some critics have asked the government to put limits on stock exposure, but the government has left it up to you to know what's in your fund and to decide whether the mixture feels right to you.

Of course, you don't need a target-date fund to get ready for retirement. If you happen to have a 401(k) with a fund that you don't like, you can create your own mixture of individual funds, as I laid out in previous chapters. In fact, if you pick individual funds, and in particular index funds, you will probably keep your fees lower and make more money over time than if you use target-date funds; some target-date funds charge relatively high fees.

But if you are reluctant to give your money the attention I've described in the preceding chapters, a target-date fund is an easy approach that will slide your money slowly but regularly out of stocks and into bonds as your retirement draws nearer.

Say that you are 50 and you buy the Wells Fargo Advantage DJ Target 2030 (WFETX). In that single fund, you have the mixture that's appropriate for a person your age on the way to retirement. In mid-2012, you would have had about 46 percent of your money in U.S. stocks, 21.5 percent in international stocks, 25.8 percent in bonds, and 6 percent in cash. But this is not a static mixture. It's designed only for a 50-year-old who won't panic if the stock market acts up and yet isn't willing to go overboard with stocks. It's called "moderate" for a person who doesn't have a stomach for significant risk but knows it's wise to grow money in stocks. Each year, the fund manager makes changes based on your age, keeping your money safer as time goes on.

A look at another Wells Fargo Advantage Target DJ fund illustrates what happens as the next five years pass. Consider the Wells Fargo Advantage Target DJ 2025, aimed at people around 55 and retiring in about 10 years. A person getting close to retiring can't afford to lose significant amounts of money. So that portfolio is a lot safer than one for a younger person. It would look like this: about 38.2 percent in U.S. stocks, 18 percent in foreign stocks, 37.4 percent in bonds, and 6 percent in cash.

One last comparison will help you understand the shifts. Let's now go to the 29-year-old who would buy the Wells Fargo Advantage Target DJ 2050. That person is trying to grow his or her money as much as possible and can take risks because there is plenty of time to regain ground if the stock market swoons for a while. So here's the portfolio: 59.4 percent in U.S. stocks, 28 percent in foreign stocks, 6.5 percent in bonds, and 6 percent in cash.

If you look up any target-date fund on the internet, you will see a graph of what's called the glide path. It's supposed to show you what happens to your money as you age. The fund manager "glides" you out of stocks on a slow path and into increasing amounts of bonds. So in the case of the Wells Fargo funds, you start with roughly 87 percent of your money in stocks at age 29 or 30 and end up with about 56 percent in stocks as you approach age 60. Wells Fargo is among the most conservative companies. T. Rowe Price, on the other hand, takes the position that when people retire, they still have 30 years of investing ahead of them. So by age 55, T. Rowe Price's retirement-date fund would still have about 78 percent of your money invested in stocks.

That's a lot of stock exposure and fine if you share T. Rowe Price's perspective. It's true that at 55, you are investing for the next 30 or 40 years—leaving time to recover from a stock market crash. But at 55 some people start worrying about what they will have at 65, and they eye their retirement savings anxiously each day to assure themselves they will be okay when they retire. If you are among this group, having 78 percent of your money invested in stocks is probably too risky to stomach.

What to Do When 401(k) Funds Lack Target-Date Funds

If you have a 401(k) and your employer doesn't offer one of these no-brainer funds, get your coworkers together and ask the person in charge of benefits to add one. Encourage the benefits staffer to select low-cost target-date funds such as those offered by Vanguard—but don't be alarmed if you see a target-date fund with a less-well-known name. Plenty of fine firms are designing target-date funds, and some employers offer no-name funds created specifically for their employees. Just make sure they aren't overly expensive, with fees over the average of 0.61 percent. If they are closer to 0.30 percent, that is better.

If you don't have a target-date fund now, you are likely to have one in the near future. They are popular among employers and with individuals who don't want to bother with money decisions. They are also popular with the U.S. government, which has told employers to automatically put their employees into these funds. The government wants to make sure people are getting ready financially for retirement.

Vanguard has estimated that, by 2016, 75 percent of people enrolled in its 401(k)s plans will be in target-date funds. If you don't have target-date funds at work and you can't nudge your employer to use them, don't worry. Target-date funds can help you even if you never invest in one. They can serve as models for asset allocation. You could go to the Internet, look up a target-date retirement fund for your age, and use it as a guide. In other words, if you are 25 and don't know what to do with the small selection of funds an employer has given you in a 401(k) plan, just piece together the puzzle by matching your fund categories to those in a target-date fund such as T. Rowe Price's. You will then have your asset allocation, or percentages of various funds, about right.

Or to decide on the basic mixture of stocks and bonds, consider the averages in target-date funds analyzed by Morningstar in 2011. Here you can see the average portion held in stocks for each retirement date. The remainder typically is mostly in bonds, although some funds have about 5 percent in cash.

Date of Retirement	Stocks
2015	53
2020	61
2025	70
2030	77
2035	84
2040	87
2045	89
2050	90
2055	93

How to Select a Target-Date Fund

If you get your benefits staff to listen, or if you select a target-date fund on your own for an IRA, two major issues need attention: the riskiness of the stock and bond mixtures in each fund, and the fees you have to pay for each fund.

As I explained in the previous section, fund companies don't agree on the risks you should take in stocks and bonds at various ages. So the funds vary greatly.

If you want to know whether the fund you are being offered is excessively aggressive, compare it to the averages I just provided in the previous chart. If the fund for your retirement date in your 401(k) is taking greater risks than you think you should assume at any age, you have a simple solution. Look through your list of target-date funds at work, and pick one for someone older than you.

For example, say that you are in your 20s and would typically pick a 2055 fund. But you see that it puts 93 percent of your money in stocks, and you can't stand the idea of such a large stock market exposure in a horrible market. Instead, you could select the fund with a 2025 date in it, a fund geared toward people in their mid-50s. In that case, only about 70 percent of your money would be in stocks, which would reduce the sting in an awful bear market.

Meanwhile, if you go shopping for a target-date fund for an IRA, you will have a wide range of target-date funds available. Then you will have to decide whether you are more worried about the shorter-term risk of losing money in a bad stock cycle or the longer-term risk of running out of money in retirement because you were too cautious with investments when young.

For a quick peek at your risks in each target-date fund you consider, look up the fund at www.morningstar.com and click on "Portfolio" to see the percentages of stocks and bonds in the funds. Then you can decide whether one feels more comfortable to you than another; perhaps also reread Chapter 9, "Know Your Mutual Fund Manager's Job," and consider the 2008–2009 losses and healing covered in Chapter 11.

As you consider the fees that each target-date fund charges, it might also help to review Chapter 12, "How to Pick Mutual Funds: Bargain Shop." But in a nutshell, the fees you pay for funds can strangle your returns, even if they look like small numbers. And target-date funds can layer on relatively huge expenses that can reduce your nest egg years into the future. So look at what can happen.

Assume that you are going to retire in 2035, and you have $25,000 to invest in a target-date fund. You consider two of them: the relatively expensive Oppenheimer Transition 2030 fund and the low-cost Vanguard Target Retirement 2035. The fees don't look so bad at first glance. Oppenheimer charges 1.25 percent of your assets (or money in the fund), and Vanguard charges 0.19 percent. But assume that the investments in both funds do equally well, climbing an average of 8 percent a year. With the cheap Vanguard fund, you will have about $237,615 after 30 years. With the more expensive Oppenheimer fund, you will have only $162,573. Why? Simply because of fees. In the Vanguard fund, you had a 5.75 percent sales change, or load, upfront and then relatively high fees. They totaled $29,658.

So with life-cycle funds, as with any other type of mutual fund, pay attention to fees in addition to the track record, or returns, over at least the past three years. Morningstar analysts suggest keeping the expense ratio under the 0.86 percent average because there are quality funds within that realm. If you buy one on your own, look to funds that charge no more than Fidelity, at 0.74 percent, or T. Rowe Price, at 0.79 percent. Vanguard is even more attractive, at 0.18 percent.

There is no reason to buy a target-date fund with a load, or a sales charge. As you probably recall from Chapter 12, loads are supposed to compensate brokers for the advice they give you. But target-date funds are no-brainer funds, so you shouldn't need to pay a broker for assistance.

As you evaluate funds offered by the giants in the field (Fidelity, Vanguard, and T. Rowe Price), think of Vanguard as the low-cost stand-out, which takes risks in the stock market fairly close to the average. T. Rowe Price and Fidelity charge higher fees and take greater risks by holding somewhat more stock than the average.

T. Rowe Price is the best choice for investors opening an IRA with very little cash. Most funds won't let you through the door unless you have $1,000 or more, but T. Rowe Price accepts investors with as little as $50. With that sum, however, you must be willing to add $50 a month to the fund.

If this detail makes you nuts about the choices in front of you, don't hesitate. You can't go wrong with any of these funds. All are set up to give you a blend of investments; they ratchet back your risks as you age so you don't have to do the work, and they give you a chance to make a solid return. Procrastinating, however, will do you in. Skipping stock market risks altogether will do you in. Swinging for the fences with a single stock or one hot fund will almost certainly do you in, too.

Getting started is much more important than picking the perfect fund. Just keep in mind that, if you pick a target retirement fund, you don't need any other funds. This might be confusing for you because I told you in previous chapters that you need to diversify and can't rely on a single fund. I'm not contradicting that now, however. A target-date fund is a different animal from a simple large-cap stock fund or a small-cap stock fund. It puts everything you need into one fund, so it's a complete diversified portfolio with an appropriate mixture of stocks and bonds. If you choose a target-date fund and even one more fund in a 401(k), you will throw off the formula, taking on either too much risk or not enough.

The same goes for your IRA. If you pick a target-date fund for it, you are done. You don't need other funds. That's the beauty of it.

Other Similar Choices

The easiest fund of all is the target-date fund. For the person who doesn't want to bother with asset allocation, it would be my choice. But your 401(k) might not offer a fund with a date in the name.

Instead, you might see other so-called "life-cycle" funds. These funds do not manage your money specifically for a certain retirement date, so they aren't quite as simple to use. But the concept is close. They require you to do a little more thinking. They ask you how much risk you are willing to take. And then they decide on a mixture of stocks and bonds based on that.

So you might see funds with names that include "life strategy" or "spectrum" or "asset manager." When you choose one of them, you might have to decide among one that takes the most risks ("aggressive" or "growth"), one that takes fewer but still significant risks ("moderate growth"), and one that is low risk ("conservative").

The beauty of these funds is that they take some of the asset allocation concern off your hands. But unlike target-date funds, they don't remove the entire burden. They all buy a blend of stocks and bonds, but because they base it on risks instead of the time frame to retirement, you can't stick with the same fund for life.

You need to sell one fund and move into another less-risky fund as you age. For example, you might start in your 20s with an aggressive approach, move to moderate growth in middle age, and become conservative during retirement.

Just don't fall asleep at the switch with one of these funds. You'd be making a mistake to have all your money in one aggressive life-cycle fund on the eve of your retirement.

Old-Style Life-Cycle Funds

Your 401(k) might not give you a choice of a target-date or life-cycle fund because these are relatively new. Small employers might simply have a few choices that have been around for years.

But do not fear. You still might have a very easy choice.

Look at the list. If you see the word *balanced*, that fund will also make life easy on you. It won't tweak your mixture of stocks and bonds on the basis of your age, but it will blend stocks and bonds for you at all times— roughly 60 percent in stocks and 40 percent in bonds.

So it might not be as aggressive as you want to be at age 25. But if you find the entire selection process overwhelming and don't know where to start, you won't go wrong with a balanced fund.

You can always start your 401(k) by putting all money into that one fund. It's a classic. Then get comfortable with investing. Learn more, and then maybe get more aggressive a few months later by taking more risks with stock funds. Keep the balanced fund as a core fund, and add a little more stock to your investments with one or two more stock funds later.

15

DO YOU NEED A
FINANCIAL ADVISER?

Want to escape from all of this, turn your money over to an expert, and be done with it?

Go for it, if you really think you need help. But before you do, I have some bad news for you. Finding a reliable financial planner who will be right for you could be harder than following the investing steps I have laid out for you in this book.

Some financial advisers are superb, but a lot of them are not. If you blindly turn over your money to those who are ill trained or unscrupulous, it could cost you dearly.

Over the years, I have seen the remnants of awful advice. As a columnist, I get calls from people when they aren't sure who else to consult. I have had widows call crying because the brokers their husbands turned over their life savings to decimated the nest eggs after their husbands died. The brokers put the money in inappropriate volatile stocks and churned from one investment to another, sometimes out of ignorance, often to wrack up commissions for themselves.

I have had a 22-year-old parking lot attendant ask me to explain the life insurance policy he had just been sold. This was a young man who was scraping by, intent on doing what would be right for his future. He relied on "a great guy" who parked his car at the lot and offered the parking attendant help on his finances. Shame on that life insurance salesman! The young parking attendant had no wife, or kids, or anyone counting on him. He didn't need life insurance. He needed an IRA. But if the insurance salesman had helped him open an IRA and invest it in a low-cost mutual fund that would truly help this young man, the salesman would have foregone his own hefty commissions.

I could go on and on with these stories, including doctors who trusted brokers with hot tips on dubious medical company investments, or people who met financial advisers at church and so concluded that they had to be trustworthy. "The con men can do it because they appear more honest than the honest person," retired Minneapolis financial planner Henry Montgomery once told me, as he urged me to tell people to investigate even highly recommended advisers.

Perhaps some of the wayward advisers never intended to hurt people. They may simply have been foolish rather than unethical. Typically, they are indoctrinated by companies that want them to sell their high-priced annuities, insurance, and mutual funds.

Here's what you need to know before charging into a financial adviser's office, proclaiming your ignorance, and dumping your finances blindly into someone else's lap: The person you are turning to for expertise might be virtually as ignorant as you about financial matters.

This is shocking to people. But anyone can call himself or herself a financial planner. The person needs no education and is not required to take a competency test. In fact, in many states, hair cutters need to jump through more regulatory hoops than financial planners. So if the phrase "buyer beware" ever applied to anything, it applies to financial advisers.

The federal government's approach to regulating the financial services business has been to require the people who serve you to disclose (tell you about) their background and what they plan to do for you. You are then supposed to know how to make an informed decision about them. The trouble is that the disclosures are full of lingo and legalese—more wacky words to understand. Also, some financial advisers think they will seem more valuable if they make investing complicated to you. Even those who have your best interests at heart sometimes forget to speak plain English.

When most people hear disclosures or investment explanations, they aren't sure what they've heard. They have gone to a financial adviser in the first place because they feel insecure about their knowledge and, consequently, don't want to ask what they fear might be "dumb" questions. Also, they are there with one objective: to make life easier on themselves. The last thing they want to do is devote time to checking out the person who will take their money headaches off their hands.

It's ironic when you think about it. If that adviser ultimately is going to be responsible for turning your hard-earned pennies into a retirement fund of $500,000 or more, you'd think you would take a lot of care. We are talking about thousands of dollars, not a few hundred. But people spend more time scrutinizing the fabric in the clothing they buy or reading *Consumer Reports* about an electronic device, appliance, or car, all of which cost a lot less.

Here's what you have to do if you are going to work with financial advisers—whether they call themselves brokers, financial planners, financial specialists, financial consultants, wealth managers, investment managers, investment advisers, "certified" whatever, or something else: Start by interviewing at least three people, perhaps getting recommendations from a trusted lawyer, accountant, or friend. You can also get referrals from three respected financial planning organizations: Contact www.fpanet.org (888-237-6275), www.garrettplanning.com (866-260-8400), or www.napfa.com (847-366-2732).

But don't stop with the recommendation, even if it comes from a person you trust.

As you consider financial planners, be cautious of the titles they attach to their names. This industry has become competitive, and people who aren't well versed in planning have attached flimsy certifications to their titles to make it look as though they are better trained than they are. Look for a certified financial planner. (The common shorthand designation is CFP.)

Unlike people who call themselves financial consultants, the certified financial planner designation actually means something: The person has had training and passed a test.

Even the CFP designation doesn't guarantee skill or ethics, though. You need to dig deeper as you interview three potential financial planners. That first consultation should be free.

Don't work with anyone before checking to see whether that person has been in trouble for ethical violations or even illegal practices. Your state has an office that oversees the securities industry, and you can check there. But nationally, go to www.brokercheck.finra.org to check out any adviser's regulatory background. Then when you interview planners or money managers, ask to see their full ADV forms—you are entitled to see them. Part I explains any legal or regulatory problems the adviser or firm has had. Part II covers fees and strategies. Also consider the following questions.

Does the Financial Adviser Focus on People Like You?

People naturally try to search for a professional who has the reputation of being the "best" in the field. Unfortunately, in the financial advice arena, the very best often aren't focused on people with a few thousand dollars to invest in a 401(k) plan or an IRA.

Most highly respected financial advisers desire clients with $250,000 or more to invest. And that means $250,000 outside a 401(k) plan. Often they make their money by charging the client a percentage of the money they manage. About 1 percent of assets is common. But think about it. If you want advice on your 401(k) plan, you have no money to turn over to the financial adviser. How can the adviser make money?

Here's where the mischief too often begins. The adviser needs to put food on his or her own table. To make money, the adviser needs to sell you investments outside your 401(k) that charge high commissions. Annuities, such as variable annuities and equity indexed annuities, can give you even uglier results, and they are among products financial consultants often push to capture high commissions.

Although there's nothing wrong with this person encouraging you to open an IRA, too often the funds he or she might sell will be mediocre and expensive. Of course, if you read Chapter 12, "How to Pick Mutual Funds: Bargain Shop," you know what that means. Over a lifetime of saving, you could end up with a third less—or possibly even worse—in your retirement nest egg. Remember my $10,000 example, earning $264,000 in a low-cost fund and $116,000 in an expensive one. Variable annuities, a favorite product for advisers seeking high commissions, can give you even uglier results.

It's tricky for people of modest means to find competent advice during their savings years. Often if they go to a well-regarded financial adviser, the top adviser hands off the small account to an underling. If you select a financial planner, ask who will be dealing with your account, check the person's credentials, and make sure you will be valued as much as a client with millions.

Also, if you are getting attention from someone who works with retired millionaires, your needs might be very different as you struggle paycheck to paycheck and raise children. Find out whether the financial adviser works with other clients like you so that you can be assured that the adviser is cued in to the needs of people of your economic background. For example, financial advisers who work with wealthy people typically help them avoid estate taxes. Applying the same approaches to a middle-income family could destroy their opportunity to send their children to college with some financial aid help.

If the adviser is going to do a financial plan for you, ask to see three plans the adviser has done for other clients, including one for a person like you. If all the plans look alike, with similar investments, they are of dubious value.

You should know that many firms that promote themselves as financial planners aren't really focused on planning at all. They are glorified salesmen who turn out mass-produced financial plans from their computers with brilliantly colored pie charts and graphs.

"The dirty little secret in my profession is that most planners don't do financial planning," Laura Tarbox once told me. She's a California financial planner who has taught other financial planners at the University of California–Irvine. Instead, the mass-produced plans, which typically cost you around $500 or less, too often are used as a marketing mechanism, she said. The planners turn out a plan that appears to be customized for an individual, but it becomes the device used to sell high-commission mutual funds, annuities, life insurance, and other products.

A financial plan that is truly designed for you is an elaborate work and often costs about $3,000 or more.

Does the Financial Adviser Have a Conflict of Interest?

Whenever a financial planner gets paid on commissions, the potential for an inherent conflict of interest exists because he or she won't make as much money by selling you less expensive funds—even when they might be better.

The U.S. Securities and Exchange Commission has been concerned about this and has provided warnings for consumers about widespread abuses in brokerage firms. Too often brokers, who may call themselves "financial consultants," work for firms that induce them to sell mediocre expensive mutual funds by offering them bonuses, prizes, or even trips for a lot of sales. Those who don't meet certain quotas can be punished and might lose their jobs.

To protect yourself, refer to the ADV form I mentioned; it explains how the adviser is paid. If the adviser is getting paid by commissions, you must be on guard—realize that the salesman might be trying to generate the highest commission for himself instead of the best results for you.

Also, the Securities and Exchange Commission recommends asking your broker or financial adviser whether he or his employer has a so-called preferred list, or a list of mutual funds from which he chooses. If he does, those funds might not be there because they are top quality. Instead, they might just pay him and his firm top price, and he might consequently neglect to tell you about a better mutual fund that will cost you less.

Ask the adviser the following questions:

- How does a fund get on the preferred list, and how often do you recommend funds that aren't on the list?

- Are you and other brokers in your firm involved in contests or rewards programs for selling certain funds, annuities, or other products? Do you or your firm get any type of payment for selling funds or other products on your preferred list?

- What percent of funds on your preferred list don't make any payments to you or your firm?

- How do you scrutinize the funds you will sell me?

A good answer focuses on keeping your expenses below the 0.80 percent average paid by investors and selecting only funds that consistently perform as well as or better than an index such as the Standard & Poor's 500. Of course, you also should hear that the adviser never ties mutual fund choices to a prescribed recommended list.

If the adviser gets commissions, don't expect a recommendation for a low-priced index fund. You will have loads, which will erode your performance. You have no reason to pay a load on an index fund—it defies the idea of buying a low-priced fund.

Instead of suggesting index funds, an adviser who depends on commissions is likely to tell you that the more expensive fund will be better. Ask to see a Morningstar report on the fund so that you can determine whether that's true. Morningstar studies mutual funds, and you will want to see whether the recommended fund is at least in the top half of similar funds for 5- and 10-year periods and still employs the manager who had excellent performance. If the adviser won't show you this information, or if the fund has been in the bottom half of its fund category for three years or more, I would have doubts about the quality of the advice.

If you are overwhelmed with evaluating fees and commissions, you can also ask your broker to tally all of them and show you in dollars and cents what that will do to your investment over 20 years. Don't expect the broker to be eager to do this. But you deserve the information. Make sure you ask for all "fees, front-end loads, back-end loads, operating costs," and any other fees that make up the "expense ratio" so that nothing is glossed over. You can also use the fee information and calculate it yourself with the calculator I mentioned in Chapter 12. Find one at www.sec.gov and another at www.dinkytown.com.

After you see this information, you might want to reevaluate what you need.

Get Limited Advice

I have always respected the advice of Paula Kennedy, a New York financial planner who no longer works with individuals. She realizes that sometimes people want some hand-holding instead of having to handle their 401(k) and IRAs alone. They need the extra confidence of working with a financial adviser to get the job done.

Instead of procrastinating and putting your future on hold by not getting started, Kennedy suggests going to a certified financial planner once a year for advice. That might mean one or two hours, at a fee of perhaps $150 to $300 an hour, depending on where you live. Clarify the time involved and the fee up front so that fees don't get out of hand later. Then bring your 401(k), IRA, and any other investments to the planner and ask whether you have the right mixture of funds.

With that information, you should have the confidence to go another year, simply feeding new money, paycheck after paycheck, into your 401(k), IRA, or other accounts.

Finding an Adviser

To make sure you get solid advice, work with a certified financial planner who will work for you only on an hourly fee basis, not by charging you commissions. When you assure yourself that there are no commissions, you can be confident that the planner will evaluate your funds on their merits. To find a financial planner, contact www.fpanet.org, www.napfa.com, or www.garrettplanning.com, and specifically request one who will accept an hourly fee.

When you reach the point in life when your decisions are more complex than simply saving and investing money in a 401(k) or IRA, you might want to engage a planner. It's a good idea when you are about 5 to 10 years from retirement or when something unique, such as a major inheritance, falls in your lap.

If you select what's called a certified financial planner, you will assure yourself that the person has training in a broad range of planning disciplines. However, this still does not assure you of the person's ethics, so make the call to FINRA's "broker check" at 800-289-9999. Also, although training prepares a planner to select mutual funds, significantly more education is desirable for selecting individual stocks.

When finding financial advice, be aware that many people are competing for your business by creating titles that sound impressive. Many titles mean nothing. For example, brokers increasingly are calling themselves "financial consultants" but are paid to be salesmen. You will also see many designations that start with the word *certified,* yet they might mean little more than that a person received a few hours of training.

Finally, keep in mind that talented and honorable people in one discipline are not necessarily equipped for another. For example, all doctors are highly trained, but you wouldn't go to a knee surgeon for a hearing problem. The same applies to financial advice. This list will help you select the right person for your needs.

Certified financial planners, or CFPs, are trained in overall financial planning, ranging from asset allocation to taxes and estate planning. They have passed a two-day test and have a college education, although not necessarily a business or finance degree. They are qualified to select an appropriate mixture of mutual funds for you and help you aim at fulfilling financial goals, such as saving enough for retirement. They will be familiar with some tax issues but are not generally trained as well as a certified public accountant in taxes. And they should refer clients to lawyers for help with legal matters like wills and trusts. Their typical training does not equip them to pick stocks.

Chartered financial analysts, or CFAs, are the elite, highly trained stock and bond pickers of the financial professionals. They have had extensive education in analyzing investments (ranging from futures and options to stocks and bonds) and have passed a three-day test that is so rigorous that many fail. Having this background is important for a money manager who will be selecting individual stocks and bonds for you. CFAs also have familiarity with some tax issues, but that's not their primary focus. Nor are they experts on debt management and some financial planning matters, such as picking college savings plans.

Certified public accountants, or CPAs, are experienced and trained with accounting and taxes. They typically have at least a bachelor's degree in accounting, have passed a demanding test in that area of expertise, and are licensed by a state. They are equipped to scrutinize (or audit) corporate financial records and are most skilled at advising individuals about strategies to keep tax bills low. But they might not be well prepared to do financial planning or pick stocks, bonds, or mutual funds. CPAs who have earned the "personal financial specialist" designation are prepared to do financial planning.

Chartered financial consultant (ChFC) and chartered life underwriter (CLU) designations primarily focus on insurance—everything from health insurance to life insurance, but not investing. If you sought investment advice from these consultants, they might be inclined to suggest insurance products such as variable annuities when low-cost mutual funds might be a better choice.

Financial consultants, or stockbrokers, sell stocks, bonds, and mutual funds. They are hired to be salespeople, and most don't have financial planning training. Most also haven't been educated about analyzing stocks. They might have sales quotas to meet.

Credit counselors focus on people with excessive debt. They might have little training, and some firms enhance financial troubles instead of helping clients escape them. To find a reputable firm, call the National Foundation for Consumer Credit (800-388-2227). Avoid firms that advertise.

Advice at Your Workplace

Increasingly, employers are bringing financial advisers into the workplace to help employees handle 401(k)s. I encourage you to go to any one-on-one session you are offered and to listen to any presentations on selecting 401(k) funds. Also call any telephone adviser your employer offers you. This help will be particularly valuable if you feel paralyzed or merely want to double-check your own investment decisions.

Also, once a year, it's important to make sure that the previous year's strongest fund hasn't started to dominate your mixture and throw off your asset allocation plan. An adviser can help you with the process, called rebalancing, or moving a little money from your strongest funds into areas that the latest cycle has not favored.

Still, although I encourage you to avail yourself of the help offered at work, I must provide a warning: Skill levels and ethics vary greatly among the advisers who are providing 401(k) help in workplaces. So take the help offered, but also be cautious. Over the years, I have seen consultants who use 401(k) presentations to build their credibility. Then when an individual seeks their advice, the adviser suggests that they plan a meeting outside the workplace. The adviser then tries to sell expensive high-commission mutual funds, insurance, or annuities that the individual shouldn't have.

To guard against this, evaluate the adviser in your workplace based on the criteria I have outlined in this chapter. The adviser might simply be a glorified salesman. Don't forget to examine fees. And be skeptical if the adviser tries to talk you into taking your money out of the company 401(k) and investing it instead in an IRA or another product outside the workplace fund. I've heard horror stories about this from individuals who had perfectly good 401(k) plans and no need to "roll over" their money into an IRA.

The Bottom Line

Go to the right adviser with the right types of questions. To get the most from the adviser's help, be somewhat well informed yourself.

People do need financial advisers at certain points in their life, especially for a little advice just before retirement. You also might need a financial planner if you are too afraid of making a mistake and, consequently, are procrastinating, squandering the years that will make a difference to your future.

Yet I want you to know that following the step-by-step actions in this book will make you successful. No matter what your age, you will make yourself wealthier than you ever imagined if you start now, open a Roth IRA every year, feed your 401(k) to the max if you have one, and mix and match mutual funds using the easy investing strategies and models in this book.

If you are lucky enough to be in your 20s, just investing $20 to $25 a week will put you on course to being a millionaire. If you are older, you can still accumulate plenty without living like a pauper. If you vow now to correct the investing mistakes that have destroyed your hard-earned savings in the past, your money will be kind to you in the future.

You now have all the tools you need to invest with skill. Just start. Procrastination is your worst enemy. And if you have any questions, you can find me at www.gailmarksjarvis.com.

INDEX

FINANCIAL TIMES

In an increasingly competitive world, it is quality
of thinking that gives an edge—an idea that opens new
doors, a technique that solves a problem, or an insight
that simply helps make sense of it all.

We work with leading authors in the various arenas
of business and finance to bring cutting-edge thinking
and best-learning practices to a global market.

It is our goal to create world-class print publications
and electronic products that give readers
knowledge and understanding that can then be
applied, whether studying or at work.

To find out more about our business
products, you can visit us at www.ftpress.com.